WALL AT WAGAH
India-Pakistan Relations

WALL AT WAGAH
India-Pakistan Relations

KULDIP NAYAR
Member of Parliament, Rajya Sabha

GYAN PUBLISHING HOUSE
NEW DELHI—110 002

WALL AT WAGAH: India-Pakistan Relations
(International Studies, Political Science)

Rs. 540

© Kuldip Nayar

ISBN: 81-212-0829-7

All rights are reserved. No part of this book may be reproduced in any manner without written permission.

Published in 2003 in India by
Gyan Publishing House
5, Ansari Road
New Delhi-110002
Phones - 23282060, 23261060 Fax: (011)23285914
E-mail : gyanbook@vsnl.com
Visit our website at : http://www.gyanbooks.com

Lasertypesetting by: Varsha Graphics, Delhi
Printed by: Print Perfect, Delhi

Contents

Introduction   9

1. **Partion of India and its Impact**   15
   The Partition Scenario • Myths about Partition • Did Jinnah Reject Pakistan? • When Pak Resolution was Passed... • Jinnah Insists that he Alone Represents Muslims • Muslim League Opposed Federation • Britain Sows Seed of Separation • Call to Quit India • The Two-Nation Theory • Parting of the Ways • Reminiscences of Partition Days.

2. **India-Pakistan Dialogue and Foreign Policy**   57
   Talking of Peace • Delegation to Pakistan • Indo-Pak Sour Relationship • A Dialogue with Pakistan • The Blinkers and the Truth • India, Pakistan and Bangladesh • A Country Still at War • Chinese Premier in Pakistan • India, Pakistan and USA • Distrust and Suspicion Remain • Cross Border Terrorism.

3. **Army Rule and its Repercussion in India**   91
   Coming to Terms with the Past • Khaki under Sherwani in Pakistan • Sullen Resignation in Pakistan • Attitude of People in Pakistan • Benazir Bhutto: A New Generation Leadership • Pakistan Diary.

4. **The Problem of Kashmir: Effects on Indo-Pak Relations**   117
   Kashmir, Nehru and Sheikh Abdullah • Political Stand of Hurriyat • Kashmir Committee and Ram Jethmalani • Assassination of Abdul Ghani Lone: A Warning • The National Conference Loses its Charisma • Kashmir and Emergence of Mohammad Mufti Sayeed • Insurgency in Jammu

and Kashmir and Reaction of Vajpayee and Advani • A Long Way to Srinagar • Truth in Lone's Statement • War is Far from Won • The Way to Reconciliation • Kashmir Problem at the Summit: India's Policy • Role of Political Parties-India's Policy • The Talk Must Go On • Hurriyat's Frustration in Kashmir • Kashmir: How to begin? In the Name of Autonomy • A Ray of Hope in Kashmir • Sheikh Abdullah: Demand by Hindu Fundamentalists • Facing the Facts.

5. **Militants and Refugees: Concern of India**   181
What Rajiv and Zia must Answer • Brew of Trouble in Kashmir • The Disinherited People • From Rao to Rao (General Krishna Rao and P.V. Narasimha Rao) • Author's Views.

6. **India and Nawaz Sharif: Efforts for Reconciliation**   197
Pakistan's Third Chamber: The Armed Forces • A Martial Law Culture • Talking to Pakistan Prime Minister • Bus to Lahore • After Lahore Declaration What? LoC becomes International Border • Nawaz Sharif's Ideology.

7. **Farooq Abdullah and His Politics: An Appraisal of India's Stand**   223
Dr. Farooq and Indira Gandhi • Popularity of Farroq • Tactics of Mrs. Gandhi • Farooq Abdullah Critical of Mrs. Gandhi's Policy • Preferences for Mir Qasim • Mrs. Gandhi Attitude • Abdullah's Reception for Mrs. Gandhi • Efforts to Establish Congress (I) • Annoyance of Abdullah • Criticism of Mrs. Gandhi • Principles for Abdullah • Azad's Visit to Srinagar • Abdullah Felt Depressed and Upset • Mr. Qasim's Politics.

8. **Indian Leader's Views: Indo-Pak Relations**   231
Siachin Glacier: Pakistan's Refusal for Joint Survey • Pakistan's Viewpoint • Losses • Kashmir Can Thaw Indo-Pak Ties • Domination

CONTENTS

of Religion • Islamabad under Pressure • A New Formula • Politics of India and Pakistan • Talking to Pakistan Prime Minister • Pervez's Musharraf's Plan • Views of Advani and Hurriyat on Kashmir • Hurriyat on Pakistan • Musharraf, LoC and Yasin Malik.

9. **Rajiv Gandhi and Benazir Bhutto: Hope for a New Phase at SAARC**   249
Benazir Bhutto and Her Ideology • Hope for a New Phase at SAARC • Ten Days in Pakistan • Liberals and Zardari in Pakistan.

10. **Pakistan's Terrorism and Militants' Role: A Serious Concern of India**   263
A No-win Situation • The Religious Virus • Movement for Restoration of Democracy • Policy of Pakistan.

11. **India's Attitude After the Kargil War and Army Coup**   281
The Kargil Fallout • Who Failed Where? • Meaning of the Coup for India • Fallout from the Sharif Trial • Musharraf Sitting Pretty • Cease-fire: Delhi Caught Napping • Pakistan's Winter of Discontent • From Lahore with Hope • Will History Repeat Itself? • The Gods that Failed • Will Musharraf Take the Leap? • An Informal Chat with PM • Where Ignoring is Bliss • What is the Alternative • To Iron Outs the Link • Vajpayee's Predicament • Functioning of the Government in Pakistan • Policy of Pakistan Want Normalcy with India • Vajpayee Favours People-to-People Contact.

Index   359

Introduction

For me, the Partition of India is not an academic subject, something which you can analyse and discuss. For me, it is a series of images. They are etched on my mind. They keep haunting me, even now.

These are some of the images:

Our house of Sialkot, the town in Pakistan where I was born and where my father was a well-known and well-loved medical physician; my father's Muslim friends we used to call *chacha* (uncle); the shops from which we bought chocolates, lozenges and chewing gums; the school where I studied, my teachers; my close friends—many of them Muslims; our affectionate Muslim neighbours; the wonderful food we used to have; the Partition days: the savage riots—burning, looting, killing when men became brutes; how we were forced to decide to leave Sialkot and how I alone among the members of my family got a few inches of space in an old army truck going to India; how I stayed huddled under a rickety couch during the whole journey; how, when we were going past Sambrial, about 20 miles from Sialkot, we saw long lines of haggard refugees trying to trek to India; the old Sikh, with a flowing beard, flecked with grey, who tried to hand over his young and only grandson to me pleading pitifully, "He is all we have. Please, take him to India. At least, he should live", the young woman who tried to thrust her child into the truck imploring, "I shall locate you when we cross over to India and collect my son. Please take him with you"; how it broke my heart when we could not take either of the two children in because there was absolutely no room in the truck; the never-ending waves of refugees with their terror-sculpted faces going to India or coming to Pakistan by the same road . . .

Not only Partition. When people ask me to talk or write about Indo-Pak relations, I'm haunted by the same images.

"Life for me ain't been no crystal stair.

It's had tacks in it,

And splinters,
And boards torn up"

These lines from *Mother to Son* by Laugston Hughes (from Hew Z), the American poet, can aptly sum up the history of Indo-Pak relations.

The course of Indo-Pak relations, like the course of Shakespeare's 'true love', never ran smooth. Right from day one after Pakistan was formed, there were problems: exchange of documents, compensation, Junagarh, infiltration in Kashmir, the 1965 war, the Bangladesh war, Kargil—the list is endless. Not all the perfumes of the Tashkent and Shimla Agreements, nor of the bus yatra to Lahore could sweeten relations between the two countries. And right now, India and Pakistan are again tottering on the brink of war.

Immediately after the formation of Pakistan, Mohammed Ali Jinnah gave this assurance to its citizens: "You may belong to any religion or caste or creed—that has nothing to do with fundamental principle that we are citizens and equal citizens of one State." But this assurance was never translated into action. Maybe because Jinnah died soon thereafter.

The biggest thorn in the flesh of Indo-Pak relations has been Kashmir. Nothing has bedevilled them more than this beautiful mountainous state. Kashmiris say that their state is 'a heaven on earth'. But this 'heaven' has played hell with Indo-Pak relations from the very beginning. For the dispute over it, its ruler, Maharaja Hari Singh, was more to blame than anybody else. If he had decided on Kashmir's accession before August 15, 1947, when Lord Mountbatten, the Crown representative, had the authority to see it through, there would have been no trouble and no Kashmir problem. After gaining independence, both India and Pakistan claimed the state.

Narrow-visioned political leaders and bureaucrats on both sides, instead of bridging the gulf between the two countries, have only widened it. Because they find that the more rigid the line they take against the country across the border, the higher they rise in public esteem.

Foreign powers have also contributed a lot to keeping the two countries apart. Through arms and economic assistance, they have stoked the fires of enmity. They have been following a 'keep-them-divided' policy, either to preserve their 'spheres of influence' and 'areas of interest' or to maintain the so-called 'balance of power' in the region.

Another reason which may have contributed to the worsening of the relations is lack of leaders with stature. Jinnah died shortly after the formation of Pakistan. Mahatma Gandhi was assassinated within a year of India's independence. Pakistan had, after Jinnah, leaders like Liaquat Ali Khan, Ayub Khan, Yahya Khan, Zia-ul-Haq and Bhutto. They did not have the stature of Jinnah. After the death of Pandit Nehru, there were no great leaders to speak of in India. If Gandhi had been alive and Pakistan had a leader of Jinnah's stature, Indo-Pak relations might have improved.

I say, 'might have', because I am not sure. Sometimes I think there is a lot of truth in what Nehru said: "Even if Kashmir were to be handed over to Pakistan on a platter, Pakistan would think of some other way to keep its quarrel with India alive because Kashmir was only a symptom of a disease and that disease was hatred of India."

I too have a feeling that Pakistan tries to keep that hatred alive because it has found its ethos in that.

Sheikh Mujib-ur-Rahman, the Bangladesh leader, once told me in an interview: "All along Pakistan has preached four things: one, Islam is in danger; two, the Hindu is a *kafir;* three, India is the enemy; and, four, Kashmir must be conquered. The Pakistanis have been fed on this propaganda for many years. The hate campaign unleashed in that country is even against the tenets of Islam. Unless there is a change in the mentality of the people of Pakistan, they cannot get out of their make-believe world."

Well, there is no point in arguing about who is responsible for the situation. The point is that the situation must change. As Karl Marx once said: "Philosophers have interpreted the world in various ways. The point, however, is to change it."

But what can bring about this change? Well, many things. The subcontinent can carve out its own destiny according to its own genius if foreign powers let it do so. And if the two nations are allowed to look within, not without. With time, they may be able to forget their quarrel. Jinnah himself once underscored this point: "Some nations have killed millions of each other's and yet, an enemy of today is a friend of tomorrow. This is history."

Normalisation—that is the first thing needed to kick-start a new era in Indo-Pak relations. Economic and cultural relations will develop from there. Normalisation will clear up the doubts and demolish the fears that have taken root in the minds of the two nations. The dialogue, if it comes about, will not only ease tension and mute jingoism. The fall-out from it may even help restore democracy in Pakistan.

The importance of normalisation is also because it will strengthen our secularism. Otherwise, many people in India, harping on the partition sentiments, can turn anti-Pakistan feelings to anti-Muslim feelings.

As for Kashmir, it is not an insoluble problem. It can be solved through mutual cooperation and understanding. Suspicion and mistrust, the two key symptoms of the Kashmir disease, must go first.

Trade and commerce should start between the two countries immediately. Communication and transport facilities should be restored. And people-to-people contacts must be encouraged. If these things happen, all other things will follow. And the Gordian knot of Kashmir will be cut.

An economic common market, involving India, Pakistan and Bangladesh, is another way to ease the tension. Though the idea is good, it may not mature for quite some time to come because India is a developed country compared to these two, but the idea is worth pursuing.

I do believe that the high walls that fear and distrust have raised on the borders will crumble one day. And that the two nations, without giving up their separate identities, will work together for the common good. This is the faith that has sustained me ever since I left Sialkot, my home town in Pakistan, more than fifty years ago. And this is the straw I have grasped in the sea of hatred and hostility that has engulfed the subcontinent.

When I left Pakistan and crossed over to India, I never felt that I had left an enemy country, but a country full of friends whom I would meet again soon. I have visited Pakistan many times after that and interviewed its leaders. Even now I go to the India-Pakistan border at Wagah in Punjab every year on Partition Day and light candles of peace and friendship along with many others.

INTRODUCTION

The other day I was reading a book in which I found this quotation (rubai) from Omar Khayyam, the great Sufi poet of Persia. I will quote it for you. It is the highest ideal I can think of. I wish it was always in my heart. I wish it was always in the hearts of all Indians and Pakistanis:

> So I be written in the Book of Love,
> I do not care about that Book above;
> Erase my name or write it as you will,
> So I be written in the Book of Love.

If you find some portions disjointed, it is understandable. I have put together most of my writings on India and Pakistan. There is bound to be a jolt here and a jolt there. The narration of relations between India and Pakistan is not even otherwise a smooth running. After going through the book, the feeling you have is of better understanding of the two countries and the paths they have covered. Then my job is done. My thanks are to my wife who has my writings bound yearwise.

1

Partition of India and its Impact

The Partition Scenario

It was 1945, two years before the formation of Pakistan, when Quide Azam Mohammad Ali Jinnah came to the Law College in Lahore. I was then its student. After he delivered his speech in support of the subcontinent's division, I asked him, "How Pakistan would react if a third country attacked India?" It was a hypothetical question. Pat came the reply: "The Pakistani soldiers would fight the enemy side by side with India's." He then added: "Blood is thicker than water."

I recalled Jinnah's remark when China attacked India in October 1962. I was then the Press Secretary to Lal Bahadur Shastri who was the Home Minister at that time. He had received from Prime Minister Jawaharlal Nehru a copy of a letter by the Shah of Iran to General Ayub Khan, then the chief martial law administrator of Pakistan. The Shah had pleaded with Ayub to send his troops to India to fight against the Chinese aggression.

Ayub did the opposite. He, in fact, gave China Balisthan and some more territory of Kashmir under Pakistan's occupation. It was an effort to befriend Beijing, which has stood Pakistan in good stead. But Ayub alienated India still further.

Shastri's comment on the Shah's letter was that if the Pakistani troops had split blood along with Indians, the entire climate in the subcontinent would have undergone a change. There would have been such an emotional response in India, Shastri said, that India would have found it difficult to say 'no' if Pakistan had asked for even Kashmir.

I think that Islamabad missed an important turn in the

history of India-Pakistan relations, leaving apart from violating the assurance by Jinnah. The two countries have been going apart since. They are today inveterate enemies, rejoicing the adversity in which the other wallows. Nuclear tests on both sides have made the situation worse. It is a volcano on which the two countries sit. They can continue to be enemies at their peril. And the business of expressing strong feelings is as usual. Some day one of the two countries will have to take initiative to break the vicious circle of hatred.

India has got today an opportunity, which Pakistan lost in 1962. The hawks on our side probably congratulate themselves that they have ruined Pakistan economically and even politically by forcing it to explode the bomb. Its budget shortfall this year will be $ 5 billion. Nobody will lend it money to make up the shortfall. America or the IMF looks like helping Pakistan. But they may exact the price in terms of dignity and honour, which Islamabad cannot afford to pay.

Why should not New Delhi step in to provide Pakistan a leverage against America? At least it will lessen, if not stop, the weight it throws about. India's initiative will disabuse the impression that it enjoys Pakistan's miseries? What I have in mind is an economic assistance to Islamabad. A delegation should go there to assess the needs of the country and try to meet them as far as possible. Steel, cement, coal—all these can be supplied on a long-term credit. This will save Pakistan the much-needed foreign exchange, which it is using to buy the same things.

Such a move will sweep the Pakistanis off their feet. They have been fed with the belief that India has not accepted Pakistan. Once they find us giving them help in their gravest hour, they will feel that they have been under wrong impression. They may hark back the memory of those days when the two communities were in the best of terms. The gesture will evoke a gush of emotions that it will wash away the haystack of ill-will and enmity. The Pakistanis recall fondly Mahatma Gandhi's gesture to force New Delhi, through a fast upto death to pay Rs. 70 crore, Pakistan's share of assets in the wake of partition.

In this context, the controversy over former Defence Minister Mulayam Singh Yadav's statement to provide financial assistance to Pakistan appears motivated and jingoistic. It reflects the thinking of hawks, who stoke the fires of enmity all the time. Left to them, they will do everything to harm Pakistan. What Mulayam Singh Yadav has tried to do is to remove the wool from the eyes of the rulers in New Delhi. It is too bad that the suggestion has not been taken seriously.

The past is too much with both countries. And it is not the recent past. It dates back to the time when the Muslims advanced their claim to national expression on the basis of religion and when the Hindus tried to gloss over their sentiment, however exaggerated, saying that all Indians were the same. And history has been distorted to serve parochial ends.

Wars between kings and overlords have been understood as wars between Hindus and Muslims. Muslims recall the days when they ruled India and Hindus see themselves as the rightful owners of Aryavarta (the land of Aryas), treating others as intruders or plunderers. Both communities miss the dominating and determining force of economic factors in all history.

In fact, history between India and Pakistan is the obverse of hostility between Hindus and Muslims. The two communities continue to think more as Hindus and Muslims than as citizens of the country in which they live. Pakistan has not realised that with partition it snapped its relations with the mainstream of India. India has not learnt how to adjust and live with an intransigent neighbour like Pakistan, often it tends to behave like a big power which has an area of influence and which expects small countries to look up to it. Pakistan genuinely fears that India, a far bigger and more powerful country, will one day gobble it up. It imagines that New Delhi of not reconciled yet to the creation of Pakistan, and cites the statements of Indian leaders on the reunion of the subcontinent.

I do not see the subcontinent being reunited. But I do believe that one day the high walls that fear and destruct have raised on the borders will crumble and the peoples of the subcontinent, without giving up their separate identities, will work together for the common good. This might usher in an era fruitful beyond their dreams.

Political leaders and bureaucrats on both sides have only helped to widen the gulf because they find that the more rigid the line they take against the country across the border, the higher they go in public esteem. Foreign powers have also contributed towards keeping the two nations apart. They have stoked fires of enmity either to preserve their "areas of interest" or to maintain what they consider the "balance of power in the region." They have been following policies aimed at the division of the peoples of the subcontinent.

Islamabad missed a chance in 1962 to come closer to Indians when it sided Beijing instead of standing by New Delhi in the first attack on the subcontinent by a third country. India should not commit the same mistake by not offering Pakistan the economic aid it needs urgently at this time.

Myths about Partition

Partition of the Indian subcontinent is now nearly four decades old but the passage of time has not erased the myths linked with it. Indeed, they have grown. They are created to fit into beliefs with which most people have lived.

Jinnah's Decision. One myth that refuses to die is that Quaide Azam Mohammad Ali Jinnah did not want Pakistan and that he had no choice but to accept when it was presented to him on a platter. This is simply not true. The reason why in June 1946 he agreed to the cabinet mission plan, which gave all subjects except defence, foreign affairs and communications to Muslim-majority provinces, was that the mission stated in clear and unambiguous terms that it could never recommend the division of India and the formation of an independent state.

Role of Mountbatten. When the partition plan was put before Jinnah one year later, June 1947, he readily accepted it. True, he was surprised that the Congress party had come round to agreeing to partition but there was no hesitation on his part in saying "yes". Lord Mountbatten last British Governor-General, whom I met at his mansion, Broadlands, near London, a few years before his death, told me that when he offered Jinnah an independent state of Pakistan and inquired whether he would accept something else or the cabinet mission plan, he said, "Pakistan". Mountbatten said at a reception in London on January 11, 1972, that he had hoped to try and keep a united India but he had met with opposition from Jinnah.

According to Mountbatten, when he tried to argue for a united India, Jinnah replied that even though nothing would have given him greater pleasure than to see such unity, it was the behaviour of the Hindus that had made it impossible for the

Muslims to share it. "Do you regret partition?" I asked Mountbatten. "I do, but I had no choice. Had I gone to India when Viceroy Wavell (Mountbatten's predecessor) did I might have succeeded in keeping the country united," he replied.

Nonetheless, it is true that Jinnah wanted Pakistan to be a secular state. This is clear from the speeches he made soon after the partition scheme was made public. In his speech in the Pakistan Constituent Assembly on August 11, 1947, three days before the birth of Pakistan, he said: "You may belong to any religion or caste or creed that has nothing to do with the business of the state...We are starting in the days when there is no discrimination, no distinction between one community and another, no discrimination between one caste or creed and another...and you will find that in course of time Hindus would cease to be Hindus and Muslims would cease to be Muslims, not in the religious sense, because that is the personal faith of each individual, but in the political sense as citizens of the state..."

Reaction of Gandhiji : About Mahatma Gandhi it is said that he never agreed to partition. True, he had repeatedly said that the division of India would be only over his dead body. But he did go along with the Congress party resolution on partition, accepting it as part of the political reality. There was a strong feeling against the resolution; Gandhiji was asked to intervene. Maulana Abdul Kalam Azad, then the Congress President, says in his book, *India Wins Freedom:* "Neither Pandit Pant's persuasiveness nor Sardar Patel's eloquence had been able to persuade the people to accept this resolution. How could they, when it was in a sense the complete denial of all that Congress had said since its very inception? It therefore became necessary for Gandhiji to intervene in the debate. He appealed to the members to support the Congress Working Committee. He added that he had always opposed partition and no one could deny this fact. He felt, however, that a situation had now been created where there was no alternative".

When the resolution on partition was put to the vote, 29 members voted for it and 15 against. Even Gandhiji's appeal could not persuade more of them to vote for the partition of the country. The resolution was, no doubt, passed but what was the condition of the people's minds?" All hearts were heavy at the idea of partition. Hardly anyone could accept the resolution without mental reservation. Even those who accepted partition had all their feelings against it," the Maulana says.

Another myth is about the demarcation of the boundary between the two Punjabs. The people in Pakistan are convinced that Cyril Radcliffe, who gave the award, changed his original proposal at the instance of Mountbatten to give India "the Muslim majority tehsils of Batala and Gurdaspur to provide a link with the state of Jammu and Kashmir". In his book, *From Jinnah to Zia,* Justice Muhammad Munir, a Muslim League representative on the Punjab Boundary Commission, makes the same point. His contention is that Radcliffe's flight plan, which he could not carry out because of storm at that time, was "identical with the boundary line as regards Gurdaspur and surrounding areas".

Views of Justice Munir : Justice Munir also refers to a cypher telegram received by Evan Jenkins, then the Punjab governor, reading: "Eliminate salient". This, according to Justice Munir, was about the Ferozepur area where the headworks and the entire area on the left of the river in which Ganga canal was located "were left with India".

When I talked to Radcliffe in London some years ago, he denied all this. He told me that he was not aware of "Kashmir thing" at all. "If I had been, it might have been a factor to take into account". Redcliffe was all the time saying that he was rushed. He said: "I had no alternative; the time at my disposal was so short that I could not do a better job. Given the same period I would do the same thing. However, if I had two to three years, I might have improved on what I did".

Statement of Radcliffe : Radcliffe told me that he could not do "justice" to Muslims in Punjab and Hindus in Bengal. "I had no doubt from the beginning that Lahore had to go to Pakistan and Calcutta to India but if I had time I would have done something for Muslims in Punjab and non-Muslims in Bengal". And to my question whether Jinnah had hesitated when Pakistan was conceded, Redcliffe said: "It is very unlikely".

Incidentally, Radcliffe's name was suggested by Jinnah who knew him as Britain's distinguished barrister. Nehru expressed grave misgivings about him because of his close conservative associations. Nehru's recommendation was that the federal court, the Supreme Court of undivided India, should serve as final arbitrator, but Jinnah was adamantly opposed; hence Redcliffe was selected.

However, nothing would be more futile today than the debate about the partition and the boundary drawn between two Punjabs and two Bengals. With the sequence of events stretching back for nearly 40 years, such an exercise can only be an academic distraction. Jinnah himself said after the Redcliff award that: "The division of India is now finally and irrevocably effected... We had agreed to abide by and it is binding upon us. As honourable people, we must abide by it".

For those who still regret the division, I can only say that the British could have probably kept the subcontinent united if they had been willing to ladle out more power in 1942 when Sir Stafford Cripps, then the British cabinet minister, tried to reconcile the aspirations of the people of India with his limited brief. The Congress party could also have done it if it had accepted in 1946 the cabinet mission plan in toto. But the ifs of history are at best hypothetical and at worst subjective.

Purpose of Partition : Has partition served the purpose? I do not know. In Pakistan people avoid the word "partition". On August 14 they celebrate their "deliverance" not so much from British rule as from the fear of Hindu rule. On the other hand, Hindus in India have not forgotten "the vivisection of Bharat Mata" and often express their resentment against the Muslims living in India for what was done in August 1947.

I do not see the subcontinent being reunited. But I do believe that one day high walls that fear and distrust have raised on the borders will crumble and the people of the subcontinent, without giving up their separate identities, will work together for the common good. This might usher in an era fruitful beyond their dreams. This is the faith which I have cherished ever since I left my home town, Sialkot, in Pakistan 39 years ago. And this is the straw I have clug to in the sea of hatred and hostility that has for long engulfed the subcontinent.

Did Jinnah Reject Pakistan ?

One story that props up here and there, even after 44 years of partition, is that Mohammed Ali Jinnah did not want Pakistan. Some of the best Pakistani intellectuals believe this. The argument runs that he fought for Pakistan but when it became a reality, he had to accept it unwillingly because there was no other course open to him.

The most recent book to repeat the story is the *Memoirs* by Hamidul Huq Chowdhury. He was close to Jinnah and he occupied key positions in the Pakistan government before migrating to Bangladesh after its liberation. Chowdhury says: "On June 3, 1947, Mountbatten summoned Jinnah and placed before him the plan of partition. Jinnah was faced with no alternative but to take it or leave it." Chowdhury also believes that the date of partition was changed from June 30, 1948 to August 15, 1947 "to preclude any time for discussion or pre-thinking over the consequences of the plan and the division of India."

When in London as India's High Commissioner, I tried to find out whether Jinnah was forced to accept Pakistan when the partition became a reality. No such hint is available in the papers which Lord Mountbatten, who effected the transfer of power, has left behind. Nor is there any mention of Jinnah's reluctance in the documents which the India Office Library has preserved of that period.

One person who should have known about Jinnah's hesitation, if there was any, is Lord Ronald Brockman, who accompanied Mountbatten as his personal secretary. He is 82 and leads a retired life in London. He reconstructed for me the events leading to the partition. He told me that Mountbatten's "first attempt was to keep the subcontinent together, even in a very limited way, through a federal structure with two or three common subjects at the Centre."

Jinnah was Adamant. "But Jinnah was not agreeable to any such arrangement," said Brockman. He quoted Jinnah as saying: "I want Pakistan and Pakistan alone." The reason for advancing the date for partition, Brockman told me, was: "We could not hold the subcontinent together, although we knew that the partition would spell disaster." Had Mountbatten gone earlier, Brockman said, "We could have kept India together."

In reply to my repeated queries whether Jinnah had second thoughts on Pakistan, when he realised that it was an accomplished fact, Brockman said: "Never." Not even for a second Jinnah hesitated and there was a feeling of triumph on his face when Pakistan was conceded, he said.

Another person, who came to throw light on this, is Campbell-Johnson, who was Mountbatten's Press Attache during those days. When I talked to him in London, where he is living presently, Campbell-Johnson said that none in the team—he included Mountbatten in it—ever doubted, from the first meeting with Jinnah, about his determination to get Pakistan. Campbell-Johnson recalled how on April 7, 1947 Jinnah, during a dinner at the Viceroy's house, was so worried about Pakistan eluding him that he said: "The Congress would accept even Dominion Status to deprive me of Pakistan."

More than 20 years ago, when I met Mountbatten (October 1, 1971) at his mansion, Broadlands, near London, he told me that once the Congress accepted the partition, he took Jinnah to his room and asked him specifically whether he still insisted on Pakistan. Jinnah's reply was: "Only an independent country of Pakistan."

"I tried to argue for a united India," Mountbatten told me. But Jinnah replied that even though nothing would have given him greater pleasure than to see such unity, it was the behaviour of the Hindus that had made it impossible for the Muslims to share it. Subsequently, Mountbatten repeated at a reception in London on January 11, 1972, that he had hoped to keep India united but he had met with opposition from Jinnah.

Radcliffe Award. I even checked with Cyril Radcliffe, who gave the verdict on the dividing lines between the two Punjabs and the two Bengals—the only two states of India that were split after the partition. Our meeting took place in London in 1971. To my question whether Jinnah had hesitated when Pakistan was conceded, he said: "It's very unlikely."

It was not the subcontinent's partition which made Jinnah think for a while; it was the division of Punjab and West Bengal. Mountbatten insisted on partitioning the two provinces on the same principle as had been applied to the subcontinent. Jinnah was for keeping undivided Punjab and undivided Bengal within Pakistan.

"We argued back and forth," Mountbatten has recorded in his papers. "Jinnah's main point being that I must make his Pakistan 'viable'. He quoted the example of the partition of Poland as not having been made on the basis of counting of heads or taking into account the will of the people." Jinnah then argued that the people of Bengal and Punjab were first Bengalis and Punjabis and then Hindus and Muslims. "How could I have accepted that logic? That applied to the whole of India," said Mountbatten.

Whether the border lines drawn by Radcliffe in Punjab and Bengal should have been where they are or not is too late in the day to discuss. Radcliffe told me that if he had two or three years he might have improved "on what he did." There is, however, no doubt that the non-Muslims majority area in Punjab and Bengal did not want to be part of Pakistan; just as the Muslim majority area in Punjab and Bengal wanted to be out of India.

Jinnah and Sikhs. Jinnah tried his best to persuade the Sikh leaders to join Pakistan. But they did not agree to it because they had found from their experience during the pre-partition riots that they were the target of Muslim fundamentalists and zealots. However, the Sikh leaders, as the Transfer of Power papers put it, "do not know what they want but are worried and alarmed."

One leader, Giani Kartar Singh, felt that the Sikhs would be unsafe whether they were in Pakistan or in a unified India. Master Tara Singh favoured a Sikh state, or an autonomous province which, Sardar Baldev Singh said, should include the Ambala, Jalandhar and Lahore divisions of Punjab. But the Sikh leaders ultimately put their weight on the Indian side.

As regards Bengal, Jinnah conceded that if the Bengalis did not want the partition he would have no objection to their having an independent state. He probably visualised that it would be difficult for western Pakistan to hold eastern Pakistan and, therefore, an independent Bengal would serve his purpose better. But after the great killing in Calcutta in 1946, a united Bengal was not possible; the Hindus had seen how the Muslim League ministry in the state was involved in the killing.

Riots. Chowdhury admits in his book that "the initiative for the riots was taken by the Muslims" and that "the unprecedented carnage in Calcutta" came after "the declaration of direct action day on August 16, 1946 by Jinnah." Incidentally when Jinnah was asked whether "direct action" would be violent or non-violent, he said: "I am not going to discuss ethics."

What could have possibly kept together not only the two Punjabs and two Bengals but also the subcontinent is the Cabinet

Mission Plan which, Chowdhury rightly says, was the last attempt to keep India together. The plan envisaged a three-tier structure. At the top was "a Union of India" embracing the entire country, including the princely states, to deal with the three subjects of Foreign Affairs, Defence and Communications. The other two combinations were of provinces having Hindu majority and those having Muslim majority.

The Cabinet Mission. The Cabinet Mission Plan was first accepted both by the Congress and the Muslim League. Later when Nehru raised certain doubts, Jinnah resiled from his earlier position. Mountbatten tried to get the plan revived. "But Jinnah and the League leaders are convinced that Congres has no intention whatsoever of complying with the spirit of the plan," Mountbatten has recorded.

However important these developments, they are part of history. The point to consider is that the partition has not solved the subcontinent's problems, neither communal nor economic. The questions like Kashmir are only a symptom, not the disease. The disease is how to span the distance between the two communities: the Hindus and Muslims. On this also depends the relationship between India and Pakistan. And for this religion has to be separated from politics.

When Pak Resolution was Passed . . .

Deliverance Day. In Pakistan people avoid the word 'partition'. On August 14, they celebrate their 'deliverance' not so much from the British rule as from the Hindu domination.

Partition became Inevitable. Nothing could be more futile than an arguments now about who was responsible for the partition of the subcontinent. With the sequence of events stretching back for several decades, such an exercise can only be an academic distraction. But it is clear that the differences between Hindus and Muslims had become so acute by the beginning of the forties that something like partition had become inevitable.

March 23, 1940, when the Muslim League adopted a resolution to demand the formation of Pakistan, comes to my mind when I think of those days. I was then a student. Lahore, a small city at that time, was agog with excitement that the Muslim League, headed by Mohammad Ali Jinnah, would ask for a separate country. It was a crowded meeting. Squatting on the floor in the front, I could see Jinnah on the dais, flanked by Sikandar Hayat Khan, the Punjab chief minister on one side and Fazul Haq, the Bengal chief minister, on the other. Also present was Liaquat Ali Khan, who later became Pakistan's first prime minister.

Jinnah's Views. In his address, Jinnah said that "the musalmans are a nation by any definition" and that "if the British government are really earnest and sincere to secure the peace and happiness of the people of this subcontinent, the only course open to us all is to allow the major nations separate homelands by dividing India into autonomous national states."

He did not use the work 'Pakistan'. Nor did it figure in the body of resolution, which was hammered into final form at the League's Subjects Committee long after his speech. But Pakistan was by then a popular term, the concept of an independent country for Muslims. Sikandar Hayat was opposed to partition because his Unionist Party, then in power in Punjab, was a platform of Hindu-Muslim-Sikh co-existence. But he was in a minority of one.

The Lahore Resolution. The operative portion of Lahore Resolution or, for that matter, of the Pakistan Resolution was: "That no constitutional plan would be workable in this country or acceptable to Muslims unless it is designed on the following basic principles, namely, that geographically contiguous units are demarcated into regions which should be so constituted, with such territorial readjustments as may be necessary, that the areas in which Muslims are numerically in a majority, as in the North-Western and Eastern zones of India, should be grouped to constitute independent States in which the constituent units shall be autonomous and sovereign."

Jinnah lived to rule the day the words "such territorial readjustment as may be necessary" were used in the resolution. Mountbatten, the last British Viceroy, picked up the words to justify the split of the Muslim-majority Punjab and Bengal when the subcontinent was partitioned. Still catastrophic was the phrase "independent states" because, later the supporters of independent East Bengal (now Bangladesh), argued that the creation of two independent countries, one in 'North-Western' and the other in the 'eastern' zones of India, was conceived in the Pakistan Resolution itself. Jinnah tried to explain this subsequently by saying that it was a typing mistake that made 'state' into 'states'.

Ismail Khan, a non-League leader, said what astounded him was that "Jinnah ruled the word 'states' was a misprint. How can a chairman disregard the phraseology of the written constitution and base his ruling on his own unrecorded memory?"

Views of Bhutto. When I asked Zulfikar Ali Bhutto in Rawalpindi on March 25, 1972 to comment on the 'misprint' story, he laughingly said: "Quite a costly misprint; I must be careful about my stenographer." He said that before the creation of Bangladesh, this point was raised by the Bengali leaders. "But the creation of Pakistan was the result of a total settlement with the British; what the resolution said was not very materials," he added.

It appears that the idea of creating two Muslim states was there when the Pakistan demand was first put forward. In the archives in London, there is a report on the findings of a Muslim League Committee constituted to implement the principle of the Lahore Resolution.

This committee had recommended the formation of the two Muslim states: one in the north-west (Sind, Baluchistan, NWFP and Punjab), together with Delhi after amalgamation with Punjab); the other in north-east (Assam and Bengal excluding the districts of Bankura and Midnapur, together with the district of Purnea from Bihar). Surprisingly, the committee did not say a word on Kashmir, which led India and Pakistan to wars subsequently.

Pakistan Resolution. The Pakistan Resolution did wonders, beyond Jinnah's own expectations. It was an avalanche that swept away all other ideas from the Muslim mind and transformed the League into the Congress of Muslim. Only the Pathans in the NWFP remained unaffected but that was because they had a secular Muslim leader, Abdul Ghaffar Khan—popularly known as the Frontier Gandhi—to guide them.

From then on, Jinnah went on developing, relentlessly and impassively, his two-nation theory and the Pakistan demand. When his opponents talked of matters like the economic non-viability of the state, he envisaged, his reply was: "Then leave us to our fate," When some spoke nostalgically about the composite culture of Hindus and Muslims, he said: "Our sense of values and objectives in life and politics differ so greatly." And when Hindus referred to the Pakistan demand as "vivisection of the motherland," he said that for Muslims it was a struggle for survival.

The Promised Land. For Muslims, Pakistan became "the promised land" and Jinnah a Moses. Rich and poor, politicians and civil servants, farmers and shopkeepers, young and old, men and women, relied behind him. In Pakistan, they saw the realisation of their personal dreams, separation from Hindus, who had more riches and jobs. Still more, they saw in Pakistan the return of the days when Islam was conquering in Spain, Central Asia and elsewhere.

Linlithgow, the British Viceroy at that time, summed up the Muslim attitude in a letter to Amery, then Secretary of State: "No matter what guarantees were given to the Muslim minority, they would always feel like 'a Cindrella with trade union rights and a radio in the kitchen, but still below stair'."

Islam in Danger. The Muslims began to believe more and more the Islam would be in danger in an India with a vast Hindu majority. Little thought was apparently given to what might happen to Muslims living in UP, Bihar, Maharashtra, Karnataka or in the other states which were to remain part of 'Hindu Hindustan' after the Muslims were given their 'homeland' state. And it was strange to find the Muslims of those areas more vocal in support of the demand for Pakistan than those in Punjab, the NWFP and Sind, which were to form parts of the new country.

Jawaharlal Nehru said that the splitting up of India would not solve the problem of 'two nations' for there were Hindus and Muslims all over the place. Maulana Abul Kalam Azad, top Congress leader, warned that the Muslims in UP, Bihar and Madras would "awake and discover overnight that they have become aliens and foreigners. Backward industrially, educationally and economically, they will be left to the mercies of what would then become an unadulterated Hindu Raj."

Reaction of Chagla. When Jinnah was once asked by former Maharashtra chief justice M.C. Chagla what would happen to the Muslims left behind, he said: "They can take care of themselves." And later, he said elsewhere that there would be after all "Hindus in Pakistan just as Muslims in India." It looked as if to solve one minority problem, he was creating two similar problems in India and Pakistan.

How the concept of Pakistan became a reality is a long story which I shall tell in my next eleven articles.

Jinnah Insists that He Alone Represents Muslims

Ideology of Congress and Muslim League. While Congress went from one civil disobedience movement to another, the Muslim League propagated among Muslims that it was "fighting for the supremacy of Hinduism and the submergence of Muslims."

One result of the civil disobedience movement was the two Round Table conferences convened at London—the first in November 1930 and the second a few months later. Both conferences failed because there was no agreement on the number of seats that the minorities should have in various legislatures. The British could claim with some justification that the fault lay with the Muslim League and the Congress Party; with the Hindus and the Muslims; and not with them.

One of the delegates to the round table conference was Mohammad Iqbal, a renowned Urdu poet. He is said to be the author of the idea of partition. He said: "I would like to see the Punjab, the North-West Frontier Province, Sind and Baluchistan amalgamated into a single state...The formation of a consolidated North, North-West India Muslim state appears to me to be the final destiny of the Muslims, at least of North-West India."

View of Rahmat Ali. But it was Chaudhary Rahmat Ali a lawyer in England, who three years later coined the word Pakistan meaning thereby the "land of the pure". In his inaugural address to Bazm-i-Shill, he said: "North of India is Muslim and we will keep it Muslim. Not only that, we will make it a Muslim state. But this we can do only if and when we and our north cease to be Indian. So the sooner we shed Indianism, the better for us all, for Islam."

But Edward Thompson, a British writer, has said that Iqbal had told him that though he advocated Pakistan because of his position as president of one of the Muslim League sessions, he felt sure that it would injurious to India as a whole and to Muslims specially.

Since the question of communal electorates was the rock on which the two round-table conferences foundered, Mahatma

Gandhi and the Congress began to play it down. In the Central Assembly, when the British White Paper was processed to give "more powers" to Indians, the Congress Party stayed neutral on separate electorates. Jinnah, however, supported their continuation "until a substitute is agreed upon by the various communities concerned."

Nationalist Muslims were equivocal in their attitude, even though they knew that the Congress ticket for Muslim candidates would be a dead weight in the elections. Some among them joined together to form the Muslim Unity Board, so as to appeal to the Muslim electorate.

They hoped to cooperate with the Congress after the poll. But this strategy annoyed the Hindus. The moment the Nationalist Muslims looked like giving indirect support to the communal electorates, the Indian press, owned mostly by Hindus, branded them communalists.

League : A Party of Muslims. So far, the League was still a party of the Muslim electorate dominated by the tilted gentry and toadies who went as far as the government allowed them to go. When Jinnah took over its presidentship on March 4, 1934, his first task was to make it representative body by bringing the Muslim leaders of various convictions under one umbrella. For this purpose, he convened a conference at Lucknow. Not all who attended the conference were Muslim Leaguers.

Sikandar Hayat. There was Sikandar Hayat, head of the Punjab's Unionist Party, a body of agriculturists, which included Hindus. Jinnah had won him over by promising to work for full autonomy for his state. There was Fazlul Haq who had won a seat in the Bengal assembly on the Krishak Praja ticket, not on the Muslim League's. They went along with Jinnah because he promised not to interfere in their states' politics.

Even though it was not the usual rigour of party discipline which bound the participants, the fact remained that they agreed to be identified with the League. On that basis, Jinnah claimed to represent the Muslims. Subhas Chandra Bose, then Congress president, provoked Jinnah's wrath when he said that the League was the biggest Muslim body, but not the only one. Jinnah said in reply: "The League is not aware that any other

Muslim political organisation has ever made a claim that it can speak or negotiate on behalf of the Muslims of India."

1937: An Historic Year. There is no doubt that 1937 was a watershed for Hindu-Muslim relationship. For them on the differences which were earlier based on prejudice and social attitudes between the two communities began to be institutionalised. Jinnah took full advantage of the situation and stoked the fires of separation from then onwards.

Uttar Pradesh thus became the cradle of Pakistan. Perhaps, as Maulana Abul Kalam Azad argued later, "if the UP League's offer of cooperation had been accepted, the Muslim League Party would for all practical purposes have merged in the Congress."

Intriguing, nonetheless, is Jinnah's remark to Louis Heren, then the New Delhi correspondent of *The Times,* London, within a few months of the formation of Pakistan that "Nehru was responsible for partition; had he agreed to the Muslim League joining the UP Congress government in 1937, there would have been no Pakistan."

After making this observation during a talk with me in London on October 3, 1971, Heren recapitulated his meeting with Jinnah in a letter to me thus: "I recall that we (Jinnah and Heren) were together one evening, when, while acknowledging the creation of Pakistan and the political necessity for it, I regretted the partition of the Indian subcontinent. I can recall referring to the tragedy—for anybody who knew it in the past—of the division of the Old Indian Army and the ICS. Strangely, he acknowledged all this, and then went on to blame Nehru for partition as I said when we met in London."

Whether Jinnah was trying to shake off responsibility for the division of the subcontinent or merely trying to blame Nehru with whom the invariably clashed is anybody's guess. What Jinnah was referring to was Nehru's refusal to give two seats to the Muslim League in the United Provinces' cabinet. But this was probably an attempt to over-simplify the situation.

But what could Nehru do when a UP League leader, Khaliquzzaman, added to the draft agreement with the Congress a covenant that "the Muslim League Party members in UP will be free to vote in accordance with their conscience in communal matters"? What was meant by communal matters? Where did one draw the line?

Nehru's Explanation. Nehru explained to Khaliduzzaman a few weeks later, on June 27, 1937 : "So far as I am concerned I have carried on in the past and I shall carry on in the future, thinking more of the principles I cherish than of the results that may follow from my actions... I have found life often enough a heavy burden to carry, but I have had some consolation from the fact that I have tried to adhere to some fixed principles."

(In 1959, when Nehru learnt from Azad's book that the latter had blamed him for giving a new lease of life to the Muslim League he explained that as he had been eager to introduce land reforms in UP he had been averse to the idea of the League, which represented "some big landlords," joining the state cabinet.) After rejecting the League's offer, Nehru declared that hence forward only two forces counted, the British Raj and the Congress. But Jinnah countered by saying that there was a third power : the League.

How right he was!

Ideology of Jinnah. "Leave the Muslims alone," warned Mohammad Ali Jinnah, the Muslim League president. His words were directed against Jawaharlal Nehru, president of the Congress party, which had members of all communities, including Jinnah at one time. Nehru's sarcastic reply was: "What does the Muslim League stand for? Does it stand for independence of India?"

And Nehru himself went on to answer the question. "It represents a group of Muslims, no doubt highly estimable persons, for functioning in the higher regions of upper middle classes and having no connection with the Muslim masses and few even within lower middle classes." His last sentence was acerbetic: "May I suggest to Mr Jinnah that I come into greater touch with the Muslim masses than most members of the League."

Jinnah neither forgot the words nor forgave Nehru for having uttered them. Instead, he tried to muster support of the Muslims so that the League would have them all. He approached different Muslim leaders in different provinces. The exclusion of the League from the Congress UP government after the 1937 elections had already reaped Jinnah a big harvest. Influential leaders like Khaliquzzaman, who still worked for amity between Congress and the League, were now firmly on Jinnah's side.

Liaquat Ali. So was Liaquat Ali Khan, who later became Pakistan's first prime minister. The biggest catch was Raja of Mohmudabad, a landlord who earned Rs. 2 lakh a year at that time. He was appointed the League's treasurers and stayed in office till the formation of Pakistan.

Persian Lamb Cap. It was at his house that Jinnah found a black Persian Lamb Cap, which he wore and which came to be known as 'Jinnah cap'. It was distinctively different from the *khadi* 'Gandhi cap'. Anything different, anything that made him convey a separate entity was to Jinnah's liking.

Knowing that UP was already in his bag, he went to Calcutta where the two state Muslim Leagues were vying with each other for supremacy. He was able to get Dacca's United Muslim League party in his League and brought into its ranks such leaders as H.S. Sohrawardhy and Khawaja Nazimuddin. The first became Pakistan's prime minister and the other its governor general. Fazlul Haq, the Bengal premier, and his Krishak Proja Samiti (Peasants and tenants party) were a hard nut to crack. He first joined the League but left it to have a separate entity. When the realised that he would lose the government, he joined the League.

Jinnah could not pull out the same arrangement in Punjab. Sir Sikandar Hyat Khan, prime minister of Punjab, was too powerful and too entrenched to be taken lightly. His unionist party, which had a majority in the Punjab legislature as against two members of the League, had also Hindus and Sikhs as it members. The League, articulating the cause of Muslims, could not admit a party with secular outlook. But Jinnah could not afford to lose Punjab, heart of Pakistan, its core. But Bengal was all right but it was too distant.

Jinnahs' Compromise. Jinnah made a compromise. For Sikandar Hyat Khan's 'Yes' to his leadership. Jinnah gave full autonomy to the unionist party. The League could accommodate within its party a secular party. It was a peculiar arrangement. But if Jinnah wanted the unionist party and, above all, Sikandar Hyat Khan, that was the price he had to pay.

Irked by Congress, he was willing to do so. I was a student at that time. A few of my Muslim friends described how Jinnah sat glum and lonely when the council of the Muslim League passed the resolution for Punjab's 'autonomy' with 'thunderous cheers'. Jinnah's plan was to bring all Muslim leaders on one platform to prove to Congress, more so to Nehru, that the League or, for that matter, he represented the Muslims—and he alone. He want about his business relentlessly and with an evangelist-like zeal. Compromises did not matter.

Once the best ambassador of Hindu-Muslim unity Jinnah was now an inveterate separatist. He said in his pres idential address to the Lucknow meeting in 1937 that the Congress governments "were pursing a policy which is exclusively Hindu" and that "the Musalmans cannot expect any justice or fair play at their hands." He declared: "The present leadership of Congress, especially during the last 10 years, has been responsible for alienating the Musalmans of India more and more, by pursuing a policy which is exclusively Hindu."

An Inquiry Committee. A year later, he appointed an inquiry committee to report on the omissions and commissions of the Congress governments—the Hindu Raj, as he used to say. What came to be known as the Pirpur Report (since the chairman of the probe committee was Raja Sayed Mohammed Mehdi of Pirpur) said that the Congress failed "in spite of its oft-repeated resolution of guaranteeing religious and cultural liberty to the various communities because its actions are not in conformity with its words." A Muslim League committee from Bihar in the Shareef Report was more acerbic and gave an account of "atrocities perpetrated by Hindus at various places in Bihar."

Survival of Hindus. No doubt these reports were exaggerated but they did reflect the mood of the Hindus at that time. After hundreds of years of subjugation, first by Muslims and then by the British, Hindus did feel emancipated even though they were enjoying only limited self-rule. And there were instances to show that chauvinistic trends that had long been dormant were coming to the surface.

Comments of Azad. Maulana Azad, a Congress leader, in his book, *India Wins Freedom,* criticises the Pirpur Report. He says: "Stories of atrocities circulated by the Muslim League were pure invention but two things happened at that time which left a bad impression about the attitude of the Provincial Congress committees. I have to admit with regret that both in Bihar and

Bombay, the Congress did not come out fully successful in its test of nationalism."

The Maulana mentions how Nariman, leader of Congress in Bombay, was denied the state's premiership because he was a Parsi. The position was given to a Hindu, B.G. Khar. Similarly, in Bihar, Dr. Syed Mahmud should have been the state's first Congress chief minister. But he was not appointed because he was a Muslim. Sri Krishna Sinha, a Hindu, was asked to head the government. "Rajendra Prasad played the same role in Bihar as Sardar Patel did in Bombay," says the Maulana.

Jinnah's Politics. Jinnah used the Pirpur and Shareef reports to highlight the differences between the Hindus and the Muslims and made it appear as if the Congress governments had been wreaking vengeance on "the helpless Muslim minority." When they began submitting their resignation from October 28, 1939, to protest against Britain's declaration of war in India's name without consulting them, Jinnah used the opportunity to celebrate it as a "Day of Deliverance and Thanksgiving." To the surprise of the Congress, many non-Muslims, including Hindus, joined in the demonstration.

By this time Jinnah had already joined issue with Mahatma Gandhi and Nehru, and had given ample evidence that he wanted to plough a parochial furrow. When Gandhi wrote to Jinnah to enquire: "Are you still the same Mr. Jinnah... the staunchest of nationalists and the hope of both Hindus and Muslims?" he wrote back: "Nationalism is not the monopoly of any single individual and in these days it is very difficult to define it."

Gandhi and Jinnah. Again, when Gandhi conferred on Jinnah the title of Quaid-e-Azam (the biggest leader) the latter merely said: "What is in a prefix? After all, a rose called by any other name smells just as sweet." In reply to Nehru's letter of April 16, 1938, saying that "the Muslim League is an important communal organisation... but the other organisations, even though they might be younger and smaller, cannot be ignored," Jinnah said: "Your tone and language again display the same arrogance and militant spirit, as if the Congress is the sovereign power... Unless the Congress recognises the Muslim League on a footing of complete equality and it prepared as such to negotiate for a Hindu-Muslim settlement, we shall have to wait and depend upon our inherent strength."

Muslim League Opposed Federation

Formation of a Council. The Council for Defence and National Security, which President Farooq Khan Leghari, has constituted was never in the scheme of things in Pakistan. The council will, no doubt, give legal and explicit role to the military in the country's governance. But it was never envisaged by Mohammad Ali Jinnah, the Pakistan founder.

In what turned out to be his last speech, he said at the Quetta Staff College on June 14, 1948, that "the executive authority flows from the head of the government of Pakistan, who is the governor-general and, therefore, any command or orders that may come to you cannot come without the sanction of the executive head." He praised the armed forces of Pakistan but made the executive head as the final authority.

Decision of Partition. By then the holocaust of partition was over and many people questioned Jinnah whether the division of the subcontinent was a correct decision. "A division had to take place. On both side, in Hindustan and Pakistan, there are sections of people who may not agree with it, who may not like it, but in my judgment there was no other solution and I am sure future history will record its verdict in favour of it. And what is more it will be proved by actual experience as we go on that was the only solution..."

But he said he was convinced that "Any idea of a United India could never have worked and in my judgment it would have led us to terrific disaster." He added, "May be that view is correct; may be it is not, that remains to be seen."

Views of the Viceroy Linlithgow. However, Lord Linlithgow, then the Viceroy, wrote on December 19, 1940 : Once broken into separate and independent entities, India would lapse into a welter of contending powers in which free institutions would be suppressed and in whic no one element would be able to defend itself against external attack."

The viceroy was, no doubt, opposed to the Pakistan demand. But he felt that Muslim support for it would keep on growing unles there was a concrete alternative. And for him, the idea of federation, which the British had envisaged through the Government of India Act, 1935, was the best answer.

Congres was not opposned to the idea of a federal structure but it did not want the scheme to partify British rule and vested interests in India. The Indian State's Peoples Conference, a parallel of Congress in Indian states, demanded that representatives should be elected and not nominated. Linlithgow conveyed through Ghanshyam Das Birla, an industrialist, who used to be Gandhiji's host in Delhi, a warning to Congress that any attempt to change the complexion of the Council of States would encourage a movement for a federation of the North-West comprising the Punjab, Sind, and the North-West Frontier Province and the Punjab states—another form of Pakistan.

He said that "some influential men had openly advocated such a proposal in a private session of a Muslim conference in Lucknow a few weeks earlier. (According to Linlithgow, Birla himself suggested that the best course might be to let the Muslims have their federation of the North-West).

League on Federation. The League also did not reject the federation proposal outright, relying on the promised safeguards and the belief that Britain would be there to help it. But when this expectation did not materialise, Jinnah told Linlithgow that he could not support any scheme which would produce a Hindu majority in a federal India." However, the opposition of the League or Congress was not very material. The Prince of Denmark in this drama was the community of Indian rulers. The British put the scheme in cold storage when the Princes rejected it.

Views of Mountbatten. Lord Mountbatten told me in London in 1971 that if the Princes had not been so 'foolish" as to reject the federal idea, India would never have been partitioned. This is strange because what were these Princes without British support? They were merely marionettes in the hands of London. In fact, when Congress intensified the independence movement in the states, Linlithgow himself wrote to the King of England: "When they are attacked we are bound to give them countenance and, if necessary, protection."

Linlithgow and, for that matter, the viceroys before and after him treated Jinnah on a par with Gandhiji; this impressed dissenting Muslim opinion. Here, not only the British but the Congress also was to blame because both Gandhi and Nehru again and again held talks with Jinnah and wrote to him to find out what the League wanted and what its grievances were.

The more the Congress leaders gave him importance, the taller Jinnah grew in stature, much to the exasperation and deteriment of other Muslim leaders whom Jinnah was denigrating as "showboys" of the Hindus.

Another factor that weighed with the British in giving importance to Jinnah was that they "did not want to see the break-up of the Muslim League" and find themselves "with only on side organised," that is, Congress. In a letter to Amery, secretary of state to India then, Linlithgow said that the Muslims are now a very substantial and well-organised whole, and they have not the least intention of permitting progress to be made on lines that the Congress and the Hindu parties might be prepared to consider."

Letter of Amery. There is a letter of Amery, dated January 25, 1941, in Linlithgow's papers saying: "Jinnah and his Pakistanis are beginning to be almost more of menace (than Congress) and to have lost all sense of realities... If there is to be a Pakistan, Kashmir will obviously have to belong to Hindu India and the Nizam would probably have to clear out bag and baggage. The whole future of his state and dynasty, as in the complementary case of Kashmir, depends on India remaining united and on a basic of compromise between Hindu and Muslim."

After failing in his efforts to get the Congress and League leaders in his advisory committee, Linlithgow tried his best to exploit the differences between the two parties to prevent any devolution of power. However, Churchill, then the British prime minister, was under great pressure from America to associate the Indians with the war effort. He suggested the constitution of an Indian Council of Defence which would represent India at the Peace Conference at the end of the war.

He even wanted to fly to Delhi to disclose it directly to the Indians. But Linlithgow, with the help of Amery, had the project scotched. He did not want his flock, the viceroy's nominated council members, to lose face. This was in February 1942 and it was evident that till then the British government was thinking of an arrangement, however defective in substance, for India to remain as a single entity.

Sir Stafford Cripps. But Whitehall changed its mind very quickly. In about a month (March 29) Stafford Cripps, a cabinet minister, sent by the British government to win over the Indian people's support for the war in exchange for some say in the administration, presented a scheme which looked like sowing the seeds for the partition of India.

While seeking to transfer substantial powers to India, the scheme envisaged that "any province that was not prepared to accept the new constitution" could "retain its existing constitutional position" and that Britain would be willing to accord to "a non-acceding province the same full status as the Indian Union itself" and the right to frame its own constitution.

The Cripps scheme did not mention Pakistan specifically but its essential ingredients were there. Within two days of Cripps's arrival in New Delhi, Amery sent a cable to Linlithgow (March 24) to say: "Jinnah, I should have thought, will be content to realise that he has now got Pakistan in essence: whether as something substantive or as a bargaining point, though no doubt the purely provincial delimitation will went a good deal of adjustment so as to secure what he calls 'Zones'."

In the same cable Amery added: "After all, supposing that Pakistan does come off, there will be possibly two Muslim areas, the whole of the states, Hindu British India (if that does not divide itself up) and finally at least one important primitive hill tribe area..."

Britain Sows Seed of Separation

Views of Jinnah. It was a balmy Monday (March 23, 1942) when Stafford Cripps arrived at New Delhi. Spring was in the air. So was the Muslim League's frenzy because on March 23, two years ago, it had demanded the creation of Pakistan, a separate country for Muslim. Jinnah had reminded people of the anniversary by issuing a statement: "Our blood had become cold, our flesh was not capable of working and the Muslim nation was, for all practical purposes, dead. Today we find that our blood circulation is improving. Our flesh is getting stronger and, above all our mind is getting more clarified."

Cripps' Mission. Cripps' mission was delicate and specific. Delicate because the British government was keen on having the support of Indian people, which by now meant

Congress and Muslim League, in war efforts, without assigning them any decisive role in affairs connected with war. It was specific because for the first time London talked of transfer of power to India. The surrender of 60,000 Indian troops to Japan at Singapore (Feb 15, 1942) — no shot was fired—had shocked even prime minister Winston Churchill, who was opposed to any concession despite President Roosevelt's pressure.

Churchill's Realism. Churchill was realistic enough to see the danger. He declared in the House of Commons (March 11, 1942) that the advance of Japan had forced Britain "to rally all the forces of Indian life to shield their land from the menace of the invader." That was when he announced that Cripps would go to India "to procure the necessary measure of assent not only from the Hindu majority but also from those great minorities amongst which the Muslims are the most important."

The Cripps proposals were only a ruse. What the British government had in mind was clear from a letter that minister-in-charge of Indian Affairs Amery wrote to Viceroy Linlithgow: "If there are sufficient provinces who want to get together and form a dominion, the dissident provinces should be free to stand out and either come in after a period of option or be set up at the end of it as dominions of their own..."

Cripps was aware of Churchill's anti-Congress bias. He also knew that Churchill was in direct touch with Linlithgow on the one hand and Jinnah on the other to ensure that Cripps was on a short leash. Still, Cripps was confident of stretching his brief and convincing his friends among Congress leaders, particularly Abul Kalam Azad, who was then the party president, and Jawarharlal Nehru, that once they assumed office, they would come to enjoy full powers. His real point of worry was Mahatma Gandhi who he had found, during his earlier visit, against Indian participation in the war effort on any count.

Still Cripps recalled how Azad at that time had assured him that if India became free, the whole country would whole heartedly support the war effort. About Gandhi's opposition Azad had explained that while all held him in the greatest esteem and paid the greatest attention to what he said, the majority of Congress and the country were with him (Azad) and Nehru, Indeed, both of them were uncomfortable from the beginning of war because by opposing the allies wittingly, they were supporting the fascists unwittingly.

Azad's 'India Wins Freedom'. In his book, *India Wins Freedom*, Azad gives the gist of an *aidememoire* that Cripps sent him at the end of his earlier visit. He had prepared it after consultation with Gandhi. It said: "The British government would make an immediate declaration that with the cessation of hostilities, India would be declared independent forthwith. The declaration would also include a clause that Indian would be free to decide whether to remain within the British Commonwealth or not. For the duration of the war, the executive council would be reconstituted and the members would have the status of ministers. The position of the Viceroy would be that of a constitutional head. It would thus be a *de facto* transfer of power, but the *de jure* transfer could take place only after the war."

Cripps' proposal was, however, different. It gave India the right to frame its constitution but any province had the right not to accept the new constitution. It could prepare its own constitution and have "the same full status as the Indian Union." The proposal even surprised Jinnah "in the distance it went to meet the Pakistan case," as London's official account records in *Transfer of Power*.

Cripps and Jinnah. Cripps explained to Jinnah at a meeting that the provinces of Bengal and Punjab might pose a problem. But in cases where the vote for accession in a legislative assembly secured less than 60 per cent support, the 40 per cent minority could ask for a plebiscite of the total adult male population of the province. Jinnah welcomed the plebiscite idea but questioned whether 40 per cent was the right figure to apply to a minority.

As a meeting that Cripps held with the members of the Viceroy's executive council, there was a clear-cut division between the Hindu and Muslim members; the latter confined themselves to asking questions on "acceding" and "non-acceding" provinces. Firoze Khan Noon, who later became prime minister of Pakistan, asked whether non-acceding provinces would have their own constitution and whether non-acceding provinces could amalgamate, e.g., the NWFP, Sind and the Punjab. Cripps said that this could be done if they set up their own constituent assemblies.

Gandhi and Cripps. When Gandhi met Cripps he started by asserting that the scheme was an invitation to the Muslims to create a Pakistan. Cripps argued that the question of non-accession would arise only in case the Congress and the Muslims did not agree in the constitution-making body. And, having a dig at Gandhi, Cripps reminded him that the attitude of the Congress had been that once the British government was out of the way, it would be possible for Congress and the Muslims to come to an agreement.

Two days later, Cripps told Nehru that, as he understood the situation, the Congress leaders did not wish to rule out the Pakistan idea and all that his scheme was doing was to leave that as a possibility. According to Cripps' record of his interviews, Nehru, and also Azad said that they thought a scheme by which Muslim provinces could secede after five to 10 years was one that might be acceptable to Congress. The two leaders also accepted the suggestion of a plebiscite in those states where there was a 40 per cent minority for non-accession.

The Cripps proposals conceded Pakistan in principle. They recommended that once the constitution was drawn up any province might opt out from the Indian Union and become a separate dominion. Congress was not willing to accept such a proposition. Azad was particularly against it. Many still argue that Congress should have shared power with the League because that might have settled the communal problem and paved the way to self-rule after the war.

Demand of Sikhs. A Sikh all-parties committee, headed by Baldev Singh who was to be India's first defence minister, gave Cripps a memorandum to complain that the scheme provided "for separation of provinces and the constitution of Pakistan" and that the cause of the Sikh community had been "lamentably betrayed." Master Tara Singh met Cripps privately and said that Punjab would never come into a general Union, nor would the Sikhs tolerate Muslim rule.

But the stage to single out "acceding" or "non-acceding" provinces or the development where the Sikhs could have a grievance was never reached. The Cripps scheme floundered much earlier.

Call to Quit India

Congress and Cripps Mission. In spite of wrong signals, Congress went on believing for a long time that the Cripps mission would not fail. One, he would not himself allow it to happen because of the equation he had with top party leaders like Jawaharlal Nehru and Abul Kalam Azad. Two, President Roosevelt from America and Chiang Kai-shek, China's head, were soo keen on India's participation in the war that they would save the mission from failure. But Congress underestimated Churchill's power of sabotage. He was against transferring real power to India.

Decision of Congress. At on state, the Congress leaders intimated that they were willing to join the government on the understanding that the British Viceroy would preside over the ministers' council. They also accepted the condition that legal powers would be handed over after the war. But Churchill dragged his feet. He did not trust the Congress leaders. Nor did he want Mohammed Ali Jinnah to feel that Britain had preferred Congress to the Muslim League.

Accordingly, he acted. On behalf of war cabinet, Churchill wrote to Cripps: "We feel that in your natural desired to reach a settlement with the Congress you may be drawn into positions far different from any of the cabinet approval before you set fourth... It was certainly agreed that there were not to be negotiations but that you were to try to gain acceptance with possibly minor variations."

Nehru and Azad against Fascism. Nehru and Azad, who were keen to join the war against fascism, had nearly persuaded Mahatma Gandhi to allow them participation in the Viceroy's council on the assurance of full powers once the Allies won. It was a "post-dated cheque on a crashing bank," as Gandhi put it. But he was going along when Cripps was changing and reviving the formula.

Little did he or Gandhi know Churchill's machinations. London's communication ended Cripps mission. He could not even given fresh assurances on the terms he had communicated earlier. Congress had no option except to say no. Jinnah gleefully noted that while rejecting the Cripps scheme, the Congress party resolution conceded that it "cannot think in terms of compelling the people in any territorial unit to remain in the Indian Union against their declared and established will."

Jinnah said that now the scheme was really dead, how "deeply disappointed" all Muslims were to find that the "entity and integrity of the Muslim nation had not been expressly recognised. Any attempt to solve the problem of India by the process of evading the real issues and by over-emphasising the territorial entity of the provinces, which were mere accidents of British policy, and administrative division is fundamentally wrong." Muslim India would not be satisfied unless the right of national self-determination was unequivocally recognised, he said.

Cripps' Scheme Failed. After the Cripps scheme fell through, Congress became more bitter and the British government more repressive. In fact, London's intention to be tough was clear even before the Cripps scheme was made public. Linlithgow in a telegram to Amery said: "I think that here in India we shall have to hold things together with a firm hand."

Nehru's Views. Nehru was not happy. He tried to represent in his speeches as if India was willing to help the British, although Congress had rejected the Cripps offer. Nehru's attitude was a natural result of his understanding of the International situation. He was from the beginning a confirmed anti-fascist. His visit to China and his discussions with Chiang Kai-shek had strengthened his antipathy to fascism. He was so impressed by China's struggle against Japan that he felt that the democracies must be supported at any cost. In fact, he felt genuine grief that India should not be fighting by the side of the democracies.

Jinnah firmed his position. He now wanted parity with Congress on any council of government and open recognition among the Muslims' right to Pakistan in any future settlement. Amery was sure of Jinnah's support. He wrote to Linlithgow. While recalling that Cripps was history, he said that "the Muslim League, I suppose, will still be officially non-cooperative, but probably more cooperative than hitherto in practice in view of the definite concession to the possibility of Pakistan that we have made."

Demand for Pakistan. The demand for Pakistan on the one hand and the Cripps suggestion of grouping Muslim-majority provinces on the other affected some Congressmen, the taller among them was Chakravarti Rajagopalachari (CR). He presided over a meeting of 46 Madras Congress legislators, who urged the All-India Congress party to "acknowledge" the Muslim League's "claim for separation and to consult it to secure support for national government. The Congress party repudiated CR, who resigned from its working committee on April 30, 1942.

Gandhi's Resolution. That was the time when Gandhi sent from Wardha a resolution for the consideration of Congress sitting at Allahabad. The resolution said: "Whereas the British war cabinet's proposals sponsored by Sir Stafford Cripps have shown up British imperialism in its nakedness as never before... The AICC is of the opinion that Britain is incapable of defending India. It is natural that whatever she does is for her own defence. There is an eternal conflict between Indian and British interests... The AICC is, therefore, of opinion that the British should withdraw from India."

While Congress professed India's antipathy to Nazism and fascism as to imperialism, Gandhi said : "I see no difference between the fascist or Nazi powers and the Allies. All are exploiters, all resort to ruthlessness to the extent required to compass their end. America and Britain are very great nations, but their greatness will count as dust before the bar of dumb humanity, whether African or Asiatic..."

When asked what did a free India mean, if, as Jinnah said, Muslims would not accept Hindu rule, Gandhi, said: "I have not asked the British to hand over India to the Congress or to the Hindus. Let them entrust India to god or in modern parlance to anarchy." He also said that the two communities would come together once the British power came to an end. Jinnah immediately responded to his with, "I am glad that at last Mr. Gandhi has openly declared that unity and Hindu-Muslim settlement can only come after the achievement of India's independence and has thereby thrown off the cloak that he had worn for the last 22 years."

Call for Quit India. Congress gave the "Quit India" call and the British planned to use all the forces they could to suppress the movement. Jinnah criticised the proposed movement as "blackmailing the British and coercing them to accede to a system of government and transfer of power to that government which would establish Hindu Raj immediately under the aegis of the British bayonet." Amery assured him that London would not go beyond the Cripps scheme.

The Muslim League no doubt rejected the scheme but had expressed its "gratification that the possibility is recognised by implication of providing for the establishment of two or more independent unions in India." Jinnah nominated a committee of action to organise Muslims all over India to resist the "imposition of an all-India foundation or any other constitution for one united India."

Ideology of Jinnah. Jinnah himself toured the country to plug the same line over and over again: there was nothing common between Hindus and Muslims and the two must part. He said that the only solution of India's constitutional problems was to divide it into Pakistan and Hindustan. And he often added that Pakistan would be "friendly and reciprocal alliance with India."

I recall that when Jinnah came to the Law College, Lahore, where I was studying in 1944, a student asked him if there was any way whereby Hindus and Muslims could live together. With his monocle held daintily between his fingers, Jinnah replied that there was nothing that linked them together. But if they were to separate, they would live happily; there would not be any conflict. "Blood it thicker than water" was his assurance.

The Two-Nation Theory

Gandhi's Comment on Jinnah. In a meeting with Lord Mountbatten, Mahatma Gandhi says: Years ago, Viceroy, Jinnah was the greatest advocate of Hindu and Muslim unity.

Mountbatten : Then what changed him?
Jawaharlal Nahru :-Blind ambition.
Gandhi : No, No. The feeling that Muslims would have no voice :

This is from *Jinnah,* a film which is being shot in Pakistan. There is truth in the Mahatma's observation because before partition, the economic backwardness of Muslims was part of the grist to the Pakistan demand. Jinnah pointed this out to Sir Stafford Cripps during his visit to New Delhi in 1942 and propagated it when he had the field following the arrest of Congress leaders.

The Raj against Quit India. The British response to Gandhiji's slogan, *Quit India* or *Do or Die,* was brutal. Thousands of people were detained without trial. Processions and demonstrations were forcibly suppressed. Tear gas, lathi charge or even straight firing was employed to meet the protest, which reverbated from rostrums throughout India. In the absence of leaders, people reacted wildly, at many places disrupting the railway traffic, industrial activity, government business and whatever went in the name of normalcy. None courted arrest. This was what Gandhiji had advised before his arrest.

Sardar Patel. Sardar Patel had envisaged an underground movement. He approached the communists to carry it out. But with the entry of the Soviet Union, their attitude towards the war had changed. Now it was a people's war, instead of imperialists'. The ban on the party had been removed and the communists carried on a war propaganda. Patel was amazed when they said 'no' to his offer. Not only they, M.N. Roy, a radical humanist, accepted funds from the government and helped war efforts.

Congress leaders of socialist leanings went underground. Jayaprakash Narain escaped from jail; Aruna Asaf Ali evaded arrest by hiding at a top government official's residence and Achyut Patwardhan participated in the activity which the British termed as 'sabotage'.

Many years later when I met Patwardhan to commend his role during the 1942 agitation, he regretted it. He said that the 1942 stir was not necessary because the British would have any way left. This turned out to be a correct assessment.

Failure of Cripps' Mission. But after the failure of Cripps mission, when the Japanese were slicing through British defences in the East like a knife through butter, India's independence looked a matter of faith. There was an atmosphere of despondency. None knew a way out of the thickets of frustration and cynicism. Gandhiji was a ray of hope in the pitch darkness of disappointments.

Nehru and Abul Kalam Azad did not want to embarrass the war efforts which, they knew, were directed towards fighting fascism. The Rajaji group was inactive because it sympathised with the demand for Pakistan without the vivisection of the country. An average countryman, dejected after the failure of Cripps mission, saw in the Quit India call a revival of old days of struggle, which would bring freedom. He did not understand the intricacies of Nehru's interpretation that it was a non-violent revolution, not a non-violent rebellion against the British, the phrase which galled London. But he understood that it was now or never.

The viceroy convinced his superiors that "time has come to stem the flood of seditious and defeatist utterance with which Congress leaders are endeavouring to cover up the failure over Cripps mission." And a reign of terror was unleashed.

According to official figures of that time, at least 340 Indians had been killed by police fire since August 11 and 630 wounded. The Home Department at that time said that the "true total" was considerably higher". Troops were called out in no less than 60 places; some 57 battalions of British army soldiers were used. There is no record of the total number of dead and wounded in Bihar because British aircrafts went on starifing civilians with machine gunfire for days.

Azad's Apprehension. Azad had anticipated that the movement would not remain non-violent. But he had felt that a general upheaval might lead to a deadlock and force the British to come to terms. The manner in which the viceroy rebuffed Mira Ben (Miss Slade), Gandhiji's secretary, by refusing to meet her after the Quit India resolution showed that the British would fight the national struggle like fighting in a war theatre.

Azad to Viceroy. This was clear also from the treatment meted to top Congress leaders. From jail, Azad wrote a letter of complaint to the viceroy that even criminals were allowed to correspond with their near relations or read newspapers but they had been denied these facilities since their detention. Some leeway was made.

In the meanwhile, the Rajaji formula, named after its author, Rajagopalachari, was finalised. He said that he had done it after obtaining Gandhiji's approval in jail. The formula proposed the appointment of a commission to demarcate "contiguous districts in the north-west and east of India, wherein the Muslim population is in a absolute majority" and to hold there a plebiscite on the basis of adult franchise so as to "decide the issue of separation from Hindustan." If the majority favoured "a sovereign state separate from Hindustan," the verdict would be implemented "without prejudice to the right of districts on the border to choose to join either state."

Implications of Rajaji's Formula. The Rajaji formula emphasised that in the event of separation, "mutual agreements shall be entered into for safeguarding defence, commerce, communication and for other essential purposes." Jinnah asked: Who would appoint the commission as mentioned in the formula? Would any border districts have the option to join either state or also "those outside the present boundaries"? And what was meant by safeguarding defence, etc.? Safeguarding against whom?

Gandhiji, who by this time, had been released on ground of ill-health, — he had undertaken a fast in jail — replied: The commission would be appointed by the provisional government. "Safeguarding defence etc. meant a central or joint board of control; and a regards against whom, this would be "against all who may put the common interests in jeopardy."

"There cannot be defence and similar methods of common concern when it is accepted that Pakistan and Hindustan will be two separate independent sovereign states," said Jinnah. But soon the discussion between the meandered into issues like what the differences between Hindus and Muslims were and whether they constituted one or two nations.

Views of Gandhiji. "Let it be a partition as between two brothers," argued Gandhiji. "I proceed on the assumption that India is to be regarded as two or more nations but as one family consisting of many members of whom Muslims living in the north-west zone, that is, Baluchistan, Sind, the North-West Frontier and the part of Punjab where they are in absolute majority over all other elements and in parts of Bengal and Assam where they are in absolute majority, desire to live in separation from the rest of India."

Jinnah said: "If this term were accepted and given effect to, the present boundaries of these provinces would be maimed and mutilated beyond redemption and leave us only with the husk and it is opposed to the Lahore (Pakistan) Resolution."

Gandhi and Jinnah. Both Gandhiji and Jinnah stood poles apart as much in dress as in thoughts. Jinnah was elegantly dressed with a stiff white collar even in hot weather. Gandhiji wore only a doubled-up dhoti. For the one the two-nation theory was a knife to cut the Gordian knot of the subcontinent's independence question for the other the two-nation theory was the perpetuation of the sub-continent's ills. "Vivisect me before you vivisect India," Gandhiji said. Jinnah was "Mr. Jinnah" to the closest of his followers but Gandhi was Gandhiji to even for non-Congressmen.

Parting of the Ways

Mahatma Gandhi and Quide Azam Mohammand Ali Jinnah were now irreconcilably apart. They had corresponded and met but had found no common ground. Gandhiji's argument was that the religion could not be the basis for nationality.

"If tomorrow I embrace Islam do I belong to a different nation overnight?" Gandhiji asked. Jinnah's reply was straight, "The Muslims in the Indian subcontinent are a different nation by the dint of their belief, culture and way of living."

After the breakdown of the talks, Wavell who succeeded Linlithgow as Viceroy in 1944, tried to provided a bridge between Congress and the League. He called on June 25, 1945 a meeting of 21 political leaders, including Gandhi and Jinnah, at Simla. The purpose was to reorganise the Viceroy's executive council to make it more representative and more Indian; the office of Commander-in-Chief which was a bone of contention during the Cripps mission was to stay with the British.

From the very beginning, the Simla conference got snarled over who could represent the Muslims. After Jinnah had taken over the Muslim League in the mid-thirties, his whole endeavour was to get all Muslims under the League's flat. And gradually he had taken the stand that "non-League Muslims are traitors in the enemy camp."

Congress: a Secular Party. Congress, on the other hand, said that it represented all communities, including Muslims. It admitted that it had comparatively few Muslims in its ranks but the ministry in the Muslims-dominated North-West Frontier Province was Congress and stalwarts like Khan Abdul Ghaffar Khan and Khan Sahib (who became chief minister of West Pakistan after partition) were all Congressmen. The Congress president at that time, Abul Kalam Azad, was also a Muslim.

The Congress Party did not mind parity between Muslims and caste Hindus (a phrase coined to describe Hindus other than belonging to the Scheduled Castes). It did not mind parity between itself and the Muslim League. In fact, the list submitted by Congress had only two Hindus. One Christian, one Sikh and one Parsee were the other three. Azad says in his book, *India Wins Freedom*, that "it could have been said that the Hindus, who constituted the majority community of India, would object to such a proposal, but be it said to their credit that the Hindus of India stood solidly behind the Congress."

The point to which it did not agree to was Jinnah's demand that the League alone had the right to nominate the Muslim members. How could a party which was conducting a national struggle for the Indian people as a whole compromise on fundamentals?

Jinnahs' Thesis. At one meeting, when Jinnah was expounding his thesis that Congress represented only Hindus. Khan Sahib, at that time the Congress premier of the NWFP, protested and said: "I am a Muslim." Wavell immediately intervened and said: "I accept that."

Jinnah expanded his demands and argued that since the Sikh and Scheduled Caste members in the executive council would vote with the Congress, nothing should be decided if the majority of the Muslim members were opposed to it. And on the question of nominating the Muslim members, he remained firm- When Wavell told Jinnah quietly that he had better accept a non-Congress Muslim from the Punjab Unionist Part, he said: "No." He wanted that all the Muslim ministers in the Viceroy's executive should be from the League. After Jinnah's rejection of his proposal, Wavell did not consult others and announced the failure of the conference. This further demoralised non-League Muslims, strengthened Jinnah and lessened the chances of a united government. Despite their acute differences Congress and the League did, however, join hands when the Indian National Army men were put on trial in Delhi in 1945.

The INA, primarily a force drawn from among the Indian soldiers captured by the Japanese after the fall of Malaya and Burma in the Second World War, was an anti-colonial movement, led by the former Congress leader, Subhas Chandra Bose, who had quarrelled with Gandhi over non-violence as a method to oust the British.

INA Officers' Trial. The trial of the INA officers—Hindus, Muslims and Sikhs—forged Indian sentiment together and there was a joint countrywide demand for their release. The British government had to comply. This instance indicated that Congress and the League, or for that matter, Hindus and Muslims, could forsake their internecine quarrels and join hand for a national cause.

But never for long, and Whitehall knew it. Though what made it decide to give up the "Jewel of the Empire" was that it had become too difficult to hold India. The Labour Party's victory of June 26, 1945 changed Britain's policy. Holding out the promise of "early realisation of full government for India," London announced fresh elections. Both Congress and the League expressed their disappointment over the wording of the announcement—the former missed any reference to "independence" and the latter to "Pakistan".

But whatever their reservations, they went to the polls to prove their hold over their segments of the electorate. The League likened it as to a referendum for the creation of Pakistan. The Communist Party of India, which otherwise opposed communalism, supported the League because it favoured the emergence of Pakistan. The Hindu Mahasabha fought on the plank of *Akhand Bharat* (undivided India). And the Congress party contested the elections on the basis of *Swaraj* (independence), which promised maximum autonomy to the states.

Congress and League : The results showed that 90 per cent of the Hindus were behind Congress and 90 per cent of the Muslims behind the League. One of the 102 elected seats in the Central Assembly, the Congress won 57 and the League 30. Every Muslim seat in the Central Legislative Assembly went to the League which also won 442 out of the 509 Muslims seats in the provincial assemblies.

Once again the League lost in the NWFP where Congress Muslims won a majority. In Punjab also the pro-agriculturist Unionist Party took away seven Muslim seats from the hands of the League. In the provincial assemblies Congress swept the polls in all Hindus-majority states. The League captured the majority areas except the NWFP where once again the Congress won. Nevertheless, the hiatus between the Hindus and the Muslims was quite apparent.

Within a few days of the election results the British government announced it would send to India a cabinet mission of three ministers: Pathic Lawrence, then secretary of state of India, Stafford Cripps and A.V. Alexander. They arrived on March 24, 1946. The mission's thinking was clear from its observation at its first press conference in Delhi: the British wanted Indians to set up an "acceptable" machinery to realise the full independent status and to make interim arrangements in the meantime. The mission knew where Jinnah stood—that is, for the partition of India. But it did not know how far the Congress Party was willing to go to accommodate him. Therefore, it tackled the Congress first.

An all-party parliamentary delegation, which had visited India a couple of months earlier, had told the mission what Nehru thought, namely that the British government might have to concede Pakistan and that a plebiscite might be necessary in border districts to know the preference of the people of those areas Jinnah had also told the parliamentary delegation that non-Muslim areas like the Ambala division of Punjab could not remain part of Pakistan.

Was Pakistan Inevitable. But were Nehru's views shared by other Congress leaders? Was Pakistan inevitable? Where did Gandhi stand? These question baffled the mission, which first asked Azad, still the Congress president to spell out his party' stand.

Reminiscences of Partition Days

August 14. I can recall that day vividly. Even after 54 years, every detail is etched on my mind. We were living at that time at Sialkot with my parents and two brothers, one older than me and the other younger. We had no intention to leave the town. My father, a doctor, was at the top of the profession. We had a lot of property: many shops and several flats. Where would we go? And why should we? Mohammad Ali Jinnah, founder of Pakistan, had said: You cease to be Hindus and Muslims; not in the religious sense but otherwise. Now you are either Pakistanis or Indians.

Complex Sita. My elder brother was the only one who said that one day we would be forced to leave our home. We laughed at his forebodings. We considered him too pessimistic. How would anyone force us out of our own house? On August 14, servants were still placing food for lunch at the table when we heard the steps of people running on the road below our two-storey house. We ran to the windows. But we could see only the fag end of the crowd.

My father shouted to ask at a passerby what was happening. He said loudly that some people were chasing a sadhu. It shook us. This was the first incident in our town. A few Muslim refugees had spotted a sadhu on the roadside and had followed him. The police rescued him in time.

Horrified, we returned to the lunch table. None spoke. But fear was writ large on every face. Before we could regain our composure, there was rushing of feet on our staircase. Someone flung the door open. Arjan Das, the district jail officer, was there. He was a family friend. "You cannot stay here. This is not safe. I am taking you to my place," he said. None questioned him. He was an official. He knew best.

My mother hurriedly packed a suitcase. We literally sat on one another in the small car which Arjun Das was driving. The jail was on the outskirts. But the road leading to it did not show any untoward activity. It was partly crowded, partly empty, as usual. We felt relieved when we drove into the jail premises.

I told my mother I should return to town to constitute a peace committee. Some of us, Hindus and Muslims, did so whenever there was tension. Arjan Das looked towards me but my father allayed his misgivings by saying: "Don't bother about what the boy is saying." Arjan Das told us that he, as a Hindu Officer, had opted for India. He advised us to leave Pakistan. He had heard from his Muslim colleagues that the Hindus would have to go to the other side. My father and I did not believe him. He got alongwith my elder brother well.

In the security of the jail, behind the thick and high walls, the whole day we heard the sound of firing and explosions at a distance. In the evening all of us came out of the room to see the fires rising above the town: The entire skyline was on the fire and the contours of houses were clearly visible. My mother was standing beside me. She tapped my shoulder and whispered: "The entire town is lit because it is your birthday." Yes, I remembered, August 14 was my birthday. Radio Pakistan was repeating Jinnah's speech: You cease to be Hindus and Muslims. You are either Indians or Pakistanis . . .

One Muslim family come to my father—he was their doctor—the following day and took us all to the cantonment where they lodged us in a bungalow. It was so spacious that it became a mini-refugee camp. Coming to know of our whereabouts, some of our friends and relations joined us. Over the days, the place became a transit camp. People would stay with us until they arranged to go to Jammu, 20 km from Sialkot or to Lahore, about 120 km, for their onward journey to India.

Reaction of the Family. What should we do? It was apparent that we could not stay in the cantonment for long. But, except my elder brother, we were not willing to migrate to India. We believed it was a passing phase. Like other disturbances, this too would subside. We had experienced a few before. Normalcy always returned, Hindus and Muslims going back to their moorings and mutual relationships. This time the uneasy conditions were annoyingly long.

Refugees from India were pouring in with their tale of woes, vitiating the atmosphere still further. Our Muslim friends told us about the anger building up. We decided to go to India for some time and to return once things had settled down. It was nearing to be one month after partition. Things were more disturbing than before and we, in the small town of Sialkot, still were not aware of the destruction and killings that was raging through the two parts of Punjab.

My mother and I rode in a *tonga* (a horse-drawn carriage) from the cantonment to our house to pick up more clothes for stay in India. Everything was intact. The roads were crowded but there was no trouble. My mother had collected a shatoosh shawl when we had hurriedly left with Arjan Das. She changed it for a Kulu one, less expensive. I had brought with me the Modern Library edition of *Jean-Christophe* by Romain Rolland. I put it back in my library. I picked up a soft cover book, *Poverty and People*, which I thought I would throw away on my return. We relocked the house, never realising that it was our last visit. As we descended the stairs, my mother remarked that if anyone wanted to break in, the lock would not deter him.

My father was keen on sending us, his three sons, alongwith an army major on transfer to India. He had come to thank him for having treated his family. His jeep was full. My father persuaded him to accommodate one of us. We, the three, drew lots and I was the unwilling winner. My mother was worried about me. Nawab, a friend with whom I served on peace committees, had come to tell her in my absence to send me away quickly because some people were not happy with my efforts at peace.

Army Major's Help. The major's jeep was piled up with luggage. He, his wife and the orderly, who was driving, sat in the front and the two children and I were put at the back with the luggage. My mother gave me Rs. 150 and asked me to stay at Daryaganj with her sister, married to a head clerk in Delhi. There was no farewell or goodbye because we promised to meet at Delhi around the middle of October, a month later.

Hardly had the jeep covered 20 km and hit the main road when it stopped. There was a sea of humanity. Many rushed towards us. Suffering was writ large on their faces. Weeping, they told their stories—how they had been hounded from their homes and how scores among them had been put to death.

The scene woke me up from my fantasy that there would soon be normalcy and people would return to their homes. I realised that there was no going back. It was the forced migration of population. People going to the other side were Hindus and Sikhs. As the jeep crossed the border, we witnessed the same scene, a stream of people flowing into Pakistan. They were Muslims.

Both sides had seen murder and worse; both had been broken on the wrack of history; both were refugees.

2
India-Pakistan Dialogue and Foreign Policy

Talking of Peace

It was appropriate that the visit of the Foreign Secretary to Pakistan should have taken place after the talks of US vice-president George Bush in Delhi and Islamabad. The estrangement between the two capitals has much to do with Washington; since 1954, when America sucked Pakistan into the Middle-East Defence pact, the Indo-Pakistan relationship has always been affected by the ebb and flow of the US tide. The new wave of fear and suspicion in the subcontinent has been also provided by the fresh supply of sophisticated American arms to Pakistan.

India, of course, has no right to protest against Pakistan modernising it forces when it itself is re-equipping itself with the assistance of the Soviet Union and a few Western countries. But what America has done is to upgrade the weaponry, starting a race between the two countries in acquiring more and more sophisticated armaments.

The American package has "anti-tank guided missiles, light field artillery, an integrated air defence system, radar SAMS, anti-aircraft artillery, self-propelled guns, armed helicopters with anti-tank capability, night vision equipment, sophisticated Cs system, tank and armoured personnel carriers." Even if one is to believe the argument that Pakistan's defence to be bolstered in view of the Soviet presence in Afghanistan, was it necessary to give Islamabad the latest and most sophisticated F-16s?

A lesser version, more defensive in operation—and this was the US State Department's thinking at one time—would have filled the bill. I recall that when I discussed this point with the people in the Pentagon and the State Department nearly three years ago, they appeared to be insensitive to adverse Indian opinion. They were not willing to ask for even a private assurance from Pakistan that the arms supplied would not be used against India.

But perhaps it is futile to discuss what America should or should not have done. As a superpower it has only its own interests in view. And pakistan has a place in its scheme of things, just as India has in the Soviet Union's. What is important is that Islamabad has consistently talked about peace with India. Gen. Zia has no doubt succeeded in making the armed forces, on which he depends to keep himself in power, stronger in the region. At the same time he has made the right noises to satisfy US public that he intends no act of aggression against India.

All of which means that besides trying to match weapons Pakistan is getting all that we can do is to match Gen. Zia on the propaganda front. And it is on this front that our policy makers have faidel dismally. After repeatedly offering a no-war pact to Pakistan, we appeared to be dragging our feet when surprisingly Gen. Zia offered it to us. Some ground was unnecessarily lost before we offered a treaty of peace and friendship instead – and that appeared to most in the rest of the world as more quibbing over words.

Apart from a no-war pact offer, he has suggested a meeting of army commanders of the two countries, proportionate reduction in arms and freezing of defence expenditure. This could, like the earlier offer, be another ploy, but perhaps we could have taken it up if only to call his bluff, if bluff it was.

Comments on India's Attitude. Perhaps Stephen Cohen, an American writer on South Asian Affairs, is correct in assessing the reasons for India's attitude. He has said in an interview in Islamabad that those in New Delhi are "slow in its response" to Pakistan's initiatives because 'they are averse to military governments." In Pakistan itself many people feel that a settlement with Gen. Zia would mean inadvertent support to his military regime.

The Military Rule. But military rule is a fact of life in Pakistan; the country has not seen anything but martial law of one colour or the other except for two short spells. And as the situation is developing in Pakistan-Sind, the NWFP and Baluchistan clamoring for autonomy to offset Punjabi majority rule – the military will always be a political force to reckon with even if Pakistan were to acquire the trappings of democratic rule. Of course we should ensure that any agreement reached with the military rulers does not in any way harm the people of Pakistan. But what we sign is more important than with whom we sign.

And this is the reason why New Delhi's reluctance to accept Gen. Zia's no-war pact offer does not make sense. The draft treaty may not cover every loophole but it could perhaps prepare the ground for a firmer structure to build upon. The entire atmosphere in the subcontinent will change and it will become easier to have a peace and friendship treaty and trade, commerce and information pacts because then the peoples on both sides will be more positive in their approach instead of being fearful and suspicious of each other.

Treaty Draft of Peace and Friendship. New Delhi's draft treaty for peace and friendship may be more comprehensive but the first priority should be to break the ice. The peace and friendship treaty has two main components: one, a guarantee by the two countries that they will not offer bases to any foreign power; two, both countries will not raise or discuss their disputes outside India-Pakistan forums.

My impression is that Pakistan can be brought round to accepting the first. America has reportedly tried to have a base for its Rapid Deployment Force; Saudi Arabia, Pakistan's close ally, supported the move. But Gen. Zia is unlikely to agree to anything like this, at least openly, for fear of giving a much-needed rallying point to: the political parties trying to end the military rule. Public opinion is so anti-American that no regime can get away with giving bases to Washington. Therefore, Pakistan may ultimately give a guarantee on that point, making it still more difficult for Americans to demand it.

But it is unfair to put pressure on Pakistan to agree to the second point. No government, much less a military one, can face public wrath over giving an undertaking that Pakistan will not even mention Kashmir in international forums. After all, only a ritualistic reference is all that Islamabad is left with; let us not ask for more.

The Simla Agreement. Even in the Simla Agreement, which Bhutto discussed when a large chunk of Pakistan territory and 90,000 Pakistani troops were in Indian hands, Pakistan brought in the UN declaration and Principles of International law not to give the impression of capitulation. Mrs. Gandhi said at that time all matters between India and Pakistan should be solved bilaterally without bringing in any third party even indirectly. Bhutto did not go that far.

The subcontinent should refuse to be a pawn in the game of the Big Powers, she said. Bhutto assured her as he told me in an interview later, that he was not "going to run around the chanceries of the world, because 25 years of rushing around the chancerises of the world, has not helped." He said that the reference to the UN was never meant either to involve the international organisation or any third power. India should have left at that.

Aga Shahis' views. Bilateralism, the Pakistanis fear, means that they would not be able to raise any of their problem, current or future, in any international organisation. As Agha Shahi, Pakistan's former foreign minister, told me in February in Islamabad, it would mean future Indo-Pakistan differences could not be resolved except on India's terms." Pakistan, it is clear, is aganist such an undertaking and it will not go through. Already the feeling in Pakistan is that what India means by normalisation is to accord to itself a superior status in the South Asian region.

And one often get the feeling from the pronouncements from Delhi that Mrs. Gandhi has developed a vested interest in raising the Pakistan bogey. She reaps political dividends from it. I do not think that Mrs. Gandhi will go beyond that. She is too shrewd a politician not to realise that even a limited war is unthinkable – the two superpowers could make it a prolonged one. But an average Pakistani lives in the fear of India's attack on his country. Foreign Secretary's visit has not done anything to alley that.

Delegation to Pakistan

India is sending a delegation headed by the defence secretary to Pakistan next month to discuss the Siachen glacier issue.

This follows a specific request by the Pakistan Prime Minister, Mr. Mohammed Khan Junejo, to the Indian Prime Minister, Mr. Rajiv Gandhi, at their meeting in Kathmandu during the summit of the South Asian Association of Regional Cooperation (SAARC) a few days ago. Islamabad followed it up with a communication to New Delhi.

Meeting of two Defence Secretaries. The defence secretary, Mr. S.K. Bhatnagar, has discussed the matter with the Pakistan defence secretary twice, once in Islamabad and the second time in New Delhi. This will be their third meeting.

By the time Mr. Bhatnagar is ready to leave for Islamabad, Mr. K.C. Pant, Defence Minister, would have visited the Siachen glacier. He was to go this week but has postponed the visit.

Pakistan and Siachen. Pakistan is apparently under pressure on the Siachen glacier issue. Recently Miss Benazir Bhutto, the Pakistan People's Party (PPP) chief, alleged that Pakistan had lost a post named after Quaid Azam Mohammed Ali Jinnah. Her other contention was that India had occupied a large track of torritory which belongs to Pakistan.

Checking with the Defence Ministry in Delhi; one finds that Miss Bhutto's claim is not correct. Ministry sources point out that whatever area is under India's occupation has been with it since 1984.

Pakistan has suffered heavy casualties in its attempt to take some posts in the Siachen glacier area. In a recent incursion by Pakistan, it lost many men. Six bodies were returned by India; many had fallen down a cravice and could not be retrieved.

The Pakistan version as reported in their newspapers is: "The military action carried out by the Pakistani forces in September this year near Balafond La to reoccupy vantage positions proved abortive mainly due to the Indian shelling resulting in considerable casualties. In fact, the Indian forces were specially trained and equipped in Antarctic conditions and used long-range mortars and field guns. The Pakistani forces, on the other hand, suffered from debilitating lack of both training and equipment".

At present the weather is so inclement in Siachen that there is no possibility of any major military movement. A strong wind is blowing and the temperature is nearly minus 45 degree. With the help of the research and development (R&D) wing, India has developed a system whereby hot food is provided to soldiers deployed at heights of up to 19,000 feet; drinking water is being processed from snow. Sleeping bags, which were once imported, are being now manufactured in India and they are an improved version, suited to conditions in Siachen.

Clashes or Siachen. The issue has become embarrassing for the Pakistan government because political parties have been telling the public that the Pakistan army has become so "flabby" that it cannot fight the Indian army and that it has lost territory which has been under Pakistan's occupation at one time.

The Siachen glacier is in the north of Ladakh and when after the 1965 war between India and Pakistan the ceasefire line become the line of actural control, this area remained undemarcated. Each side has been trying to interpret this in its own way. In 1984 Pakistan planned to occupy this area but found India sitting on it because New Delhi came to possess prior information about Pakistan's intentions. Many clashes and meeting between the two sides have not resolved the issue.

Indo-Pak Sour Relationship

Pakistan foreign secretary Shahryar Khan is an amiable person, who has grown up in the liberal atmosphere of Nawab of Bhopal's household. Fundamentalists from Pakistan do not like him because of his unbiased approach to the Hindu-Muslim problem. As Islamabad's envoy in London, he got into trouble because he played *tabla* in public and that too in the Indian classical music style, which he loves.

Such a person is an ideal messenger for any goodwill and conciliatory gesture. But he is only civil a servant, carrying out the wishes of the government he serves. The public and the press in India and Pakistan, have unnecessarily given importance to his visit. As he himself said, his was a first formal contact with the Narasimha Rao government. Benazir Bhutto, when she was the Pakistan Prime Minister, also went over the same exercise and pulled out Abdul Sattar, Islamabad's High Commissioner in New Delhi, to call on the V.P. Singh government as her personal envoy.

Sattar could do little because the Pakistan Army, which did not trust Benazir, sent its own man, Sahibzada Yakub Khan, in the wake of Sattar's visist. Yakub Khan emitted fire and the entire effort came to a naught. The Shahryar mission did not suffer from that disadvantage since Pakistan Prime Minister Nawaz Sharif has the backing of the army. And the manner in which General Asif Nawaz Janjua has succeeded General Mirza Aslam Beg as the Pakistan Chief of Army Staff indicates that even the Army is beginning to accept some norms of professionalism.

But the reason why the various conciliation efforts, both by India and Pakistan, have failed is the difference in their perceptions. Islamabad believes that Kashmir is the test-stone of New Delhi's intentions for friendship. New Delhi feels that Kashmir is a symptom, not a disease; and the disease is Pakistan's hate-India policy

True, India has tried to settle Kashmir. Put it has not been able to accommodate Islamabad, where the successive governments have been under pressure to "integrate" Muslims in Kashmir with Muslims in Pakistan. What it does not appreciate is that New Delhi has no option except to hold Kashmir, although it is in ferment, because no country can allow any part of its territory to secede, much less on the ground of religion. Any government in India even discussing something near it cannot last. And even a partial plebiscite would restoke the fires of Hindu-Muslim differences.

Islamabad's compulsions are understandable. But New Delhi too cannot override its compulsions. May be both are hoisted on their own petard. May be both cannot break away from past. May be both are relentlessly drifting towards another round of hostilities.

New Delhi has fought three wars over Kashmir; Islamabad should realise that it cannot take it by force, not as the balance of military power between the two countries exists today. By running to the world chanceries Islamabad may had the satisfaction of defaming India, but the Kashmir question has made no progress.

India's condemnation by the Organisation of Islamic Conference (OIC) is a ritual new; it passes more or less the same resolution every year at the behest of Pakistan. How does that help? It only feeds Hindu chauvinism. The governments, which has not even semblance of democracy in their own countries, can hardly appreciate or preach what the people's rights are. Islamabad should have realised by now that it has drained the last drop of advantage from such forums.

In fact Pakistan has done something worse out of frustration; it has created a frankenstein in the valley. It has trained and armed the Kashmiri youth, which has come to believe that every extortion, kidnapping or killing is justified in the name of Islam. This has made the Indian opinion still more rigid; the exodus of non-Muslims from Kashmir has only heightened the religious divide.

Zulifikar Ali Bhutto at least realised after losing East Pakistan, war over Kashmir made no difference. Nor did the shuttlings of world capitals. He told me then that support to the right of self determination did not mean that "we shall export revolution" and "this position does not exist and it will not exist in the future also." But General Zia-ul-Haq did the opposite and Benazir followed him in "exporting revolution."

At one time, Benazir's father was in favour of "freezing" the Kashmir problem. He told me that it was not incumbent on him or the generation after him to solve it. He argued that it was not possible to seek solutions to all problems in one sweep. His was a step by step approach so as to build confidence and atmosphere to tackle Kashmir ultimately.

Although Bhutto did not sign a no-war pact, he agreed at Simla in 1972 "that the two countries are resolved to settle their differences by peaceful means..." What he or, for that matter, Pakistan admitted was that Kashmir had to be settled by sitting across the table with India.

However, Zia, followed by Benazir, did opposite. Zia initiated war by proxy. Not long ago, a retired Pakistani diplomat, Abdul Washeed, confirmed this in an article in a Pakistani Urdu daily. This is what he wrote; "Zia's policy on Kashmir, through not known to many of us publicly, laid the foundation of the present freedom struggle which hopefully will culminate in the accession of Kashmir to Pakistan. Zia believed that the Kashmir dispute would be solved within the context of an Islamic government in Afghanistan, a struggle in Kashmir and an uprising in Indian Punjab."

The Nawaz Sharif government could have gone back to the principle of peace that Bhutto accepted at Simla. It could have falsified the general belief in India that Pakistan's hatred towards it was not so overwhelming that it would do anything to hurt India. New Delhi sees the training, arming and sheltering of militants from Punjab and Kashmir – Pakistan no longer denies this – in that context. Were Islamabad to accommodate New Delhi on Punjab, New Delhi might in turn accommodate Islamabad on Kashmir. Shahryar should have read this between the lines during his visit to Delhi.

It is wrong to believe that India wants to undo Pakistan or that it seeks to reduce it to the status of Sikkim or Bhutan. Even the most fanatic Hindus do not talk in such terms any more because there is not even a single applause in response. India itself faces a challenge to its integration. To imagine that it would want to disintegrate Pakistan or absorb a population of another hundred million Muslims is to question even the basic intelligence of the Indian people and its rulers.

Pakistan has to learn to live with India, a far bigger and more powerful country. India too has to adjust and live with an instransigent neighbour and it should not behave like big power which has an area of influence and which expects small countries to look up to it.

But the posture of confrontation which the two countries have does not allow normal relationship. Probably the first thing the two countries should do is to sign a no-war pact. Imagine Narasimha Rao first going to Lahore and signing the pact and then Nawaz Sharif coming to New Delhi and doing so. The psychological difference it will make to the pyche of the peoples in the subcontinent may usher in a new chapter of positive thinking.

Not only can they then proportionately decrease the defence budget but also expand trade. A common market is difficult to envisage at this time because India is a developed country compared to Pakistan. But joint ventures and lower tarriffs on the Pakistani goods may offset the advantage that India will reap in having freer access to the Pakistani market. Even now many Indian goods are reaching Pakistan through west Asia or other channels and the people are paying much more than what they doing if they were to import them directly.

Bhutto's step by step approach may prove to be a key to the situation. Since the two countries try to solve too many things at the same time, they set stuck. And the hawks on both sides, in the bureaucracy and politics, are able to play their petty games as they have in the last four decades.

The two countries do not exchange even newspapers or books. There is no contact at the people's level. Every Pakistani is suspect in India and vice versa. The impression that the two countries are enemies has gone down to the lowest tier of administration, particularly police. A free flow of information and visitors should be the first step towards normalcy.

It is understandable that the Kashmir question cannot be frozen. The pressure of public opinion in Pakistan is too compulsive. Here too Bhutto's suggestion may come in handy. He told me: "We can make the cease-fire line a line of peace and let people come and go between two Kashmirs. Then one thing will lead to another."

What India and Pakistan do not realise is that they do not have all the time in the world. Acceptable ideas are dying and the situation is taking a turn which may not be under their control. Another meeting of Foreign Secretaries of the two countries is welcome. But is of no use if it does not fulfil some hopes and remove some fears.

A Dialogue with Pakistan

An India-Pakistan dialogue always evokes nostalgia for some of us who have come from across the border. But every meeting also, underlines the fact how different are our perceptions. We continue to be conscious of history but not geography – we share a border of thousands of kilometres.

Around the table we sat for three days last week in New Delhi. There were some eminent men from Pakistan: Agha Shahi, former Foreign Minister, Lt. Gen. K.M. Arif, retired chief of the army staff, Ajmal Kattak, once in the forefront of our national movement, A. Wardhak, vice-president of the ruling Muslim League, Khurshid Kasuri, secretary-general of the People's Democratic Alliance in the opposition, Niaz Naik, former Foreign Secretary, and editor *Frontier Post* Khalid.

The Indian side was represented among others, by Inder Gujral, former Foreign Minister, Vasant Sathe, former Union Minister, Justice Rajinder Sachar, A.M. Khusro, Mrinal Pande and Girilal Jain, journalists, the two lieutenant generals Vohra and Chibber, two former Foreign Secretaries, C.S. Jha and S.K. Singh, K.R. Malkani vice-president of the Bhartiya Janata Party, and O.P. Shah, who sponsored the dialogue.

The discussions, candid but surprisingly devoid of heat, showed that over the years the irritants between the two sides had lost some rough edges and a sense of mellowness had developed. Kashmir figured in one way or the other all through. Nearly all the Pakistani participants did not budge from the stand that Kashmir should be solved before taking up trade, culture and visa.

But what struck me was that the Pakistani's tacit acceptance of independence status for Kashmir, amalgamating the Indian and Pakistan sides of Kashmir. Significantly, Pakistanis and Indians tended to restrict the dispute to the valley as if both were already prepared for separation of Jammu and Ladakh from the present J & K state. Agra Shahi even proposed that the United Nations should administer the valley and the adjoining Muslim areas till the two sides found a way out.

Almost all Indians were on the defensive. There was hardly any serious voice to point out that Kashmir was an integral part of India. The main argument against the secession of Kashmir by Indians was that it would tell upon secularism; some even talked about the dangers of opening "a pandora's box." But there was none to deny the existence of the dispute and none to advocate that Pakistan had no *locus standi*.

On secularism, I felt let down by some of my countrymen. At the inaugural function, I could tell the Pakistanis that we followed two different systems: one secular and the other religious. But on the second day, when the Vishwa Hindu Parishad and Bajrang Dal hoisted flags on the Babri Masjid-Ram Janmabhoomi structure, despite the High Court order to the UP government to maintain the status quo, I could not look the Pakistanis in their eyes.

None mentioned the incident at the dialogue. But they made a telling point when they said that fundamentalists did not win even half a dozen seats in the Pakistan National Assembly, while they had captured 117 seats in the Lok Sabha in India. In fact, the Pakistanis resented our general assessment that fundamentalists were on top in Pakistan.

Their argument was that anyone who bandied about religion did not carry any conviction in their country. One Indian participant had a point when he said that the "type of Islam" Pakistan had been following was taking shape of some kind of secularism and India, which had been advocating "a particular way" of secularism was developing a fundamentalistic atmosphere in its midst.

I referred to the text books taught in Pakistan, depicting Hindus in an unfavourable light. Kasuri corrected me saying that the books in private schools had been changed. This still did not give the answer to my query that Urdu history books prescribed in schools were far from accurate. The school history books I have read in Lahore played up the wars between Hindus and Muslims, wiht the latter always emerging victorious. Mohammed Bind Qasim and Mahmud Ghaznavi, the first two Muslim invaders of India, are glorified for destroying *kafirs* (infidels).

Although both sides had different viewpoints on security, all participants felt that the two countries were spending on defence far more money, which could be utilised for the betterment of the people. One Indian said that his country should unilaterally freeze the defence expenditure so as to allay the Pakistani fears. Another proposed a proportionate cut in armed forces on both sides. This found favour with the Pakistani. One Pakistani predicted that America, "on which both countries were dependent, "was going to force a cut in their defence expenditure; they might as well begin it on their own instead of being told to do so.

Our perceptions on nuclear weapons were different; they wanted an agreement between India and Pakistan and we were keen on involving China in any accord that we reached. One thing common was that both sides expressed anxiety to have some arrangement to avoid the nuclear holocaust which, many feared, if there was a war. Most Pakistani did not deny the possession of the bomb.

Significantly, there was no denial by the Pakistanis on the training and arming of the militants in Kashmir and Punjab. Some made the point that they were doing what India had done in Bangladesh. One Pakistani was articulate enough to say that unless Kashmir was settled, the interference in Punjab would continue. I argued that if they were to accommodate us in Punjab, we would be able to accommodate them on Kashmir. Some Pakistani welcomed this.

The dialogue revealed that India had gone back on the settlement it had accepted on the Siachin glacier. If this is so, it does not speak well of us. From all accounts, the Siachin glacier is of little military significance; the forces on both sides can be redeployed, as was decided between the defence secretaries of the two countries. This itself will generate goodwill. Pakistan Prime Minister Nawaz Sharif will be off the hook because he needs some evidence to convince his people that although

Kashmir cannot be solved straightaway, there are other problems which are being got out of the way.

Some people may run down unofficial dialogues. But they do have their impact. When governments have failed, others may initiate a process of conciliation. However, I was surprised to find the government-controlled Doordarshan run a series of discussions during the three days of the dialogue on Indo-Pakistan relations to prove that nothing was possible and that the relationship between the two countries was intractable. If this is the accepted stand of New Delhi, it is unfortunate to say the least.

All of us at the dialogue foresaw the subcontinent as a common economic unit on the line of European Economic Community. I do not think that even fundamentalists in our country believe in geographical unity. Therefore, the Pakistanis' fear that India has not accepted partition is not justified. However, many of us believe that one day the high walls that fear and distrust have raised on the borders will crumble and the peoples of the subcontinent, without giving up their separate identities, will work together for the common good.

This would usher in an era fruitful beyond their dreams. The present trade amounting to Rs. 80 crore will expand to thousands of crores, benefiting both sides. The economic prosperity can make the people forget their religious differences and set them to the task of improving their standard of living.

The subcontinent can find its own destiny according to its own genius if left alone and if the peoples are allowed to look within, not without. With time, they may forget their quarrels. As Mohammed Ali Jinnah, founder of Pakistan, had once said: "Some nations have killed millions of each other's and yet an enemy of today is a friend of tomorrow. That is history."

The Blinkers and the Truth

The tragic loss of lives on September 11 last year at the World Trade Centre had another side to it: the humiliation of the strongest nation in the world by a handful of men. Here was America, which represented the unipolar world after emerging victorious in the cold war against the Soviet Union and defeating the ideology of communism. Just one man hiding in a backward country masterminded a plan, which spanned thousands of miles to strike at New York and Washington to avenge the humiliation of helplessness against untrammelled power.

True, almost every nation in the world came to rally behind the US. None dared to stand aside. Countries like India offered even bases for operation against Afghanistan, where arch terrorist Osama-bin-Laden, who orchestrated the strike, without America's asking. Still, all this could not undo the fact that someone had dared to challenge the world's most powerful nation. By defeating the Taliban and the Al-Qaida, America has put another government at the helm in Afghanistan. But it has not eliminated them, much less their ideology of fundamentalism. And the humiliation part still stares the US in the face.

When Washington talks in terms of attacking Iraq and eliminating Saddam Hussain, this humiliation is still at the back of its mind. The downfall of Saddam may establish that America can punish any country in the world. Those who believe that democracy has to be implanted by outsiders where dictatorships have come to stay may also welcome Saddam's exit. Still America's victory will not wash off the blot of humiliation.

The President Bush was justified in declaring a war against terrorism after the September 11 happening has seldom been questioned. He should have done it long before when terrorism was at its peak in our part of the world. America was least bothered about terrorism till the fire reached its shores. But its fight against terrorism, which is far from complete, does not make up for the humiliation.

This is so because Washington's eyes are still fixed at the wrong site. It wants to regain its prestige by acting as the world's policemen not as the one who cares about the humiliation of others. When the American president stands by Israel and justifies its acts of brutality against Yaseer Arafat and the Palestinians, he apparently thinks that the humiliation of the weak does not matter. This is the crux of the problem.

If the world is to be for the survival of the fittest, both respect and humiliation become relative words. They mean different things to different nations. Imposition by the strong does not mean humiliation of the weak. Every nation has its self-respect. When driven to the wall, it will fight back and do anything to project it.

The Taliban and the Al-Qaida were hawking the honour of the Afghans and even the Pakistanis in the name of the religion.

America allowed such fundamentalists to come up and even fed it through arms and other assistance to serve its own purpose. It believed and still does that the people living in the third world deserved to wallow in prejudice and bias and that their genius was not suited to democracy.

In any case if Kabul was considered too far and too weak to challenge the West and Washington. Moscow too had played with Afghanistan's dignity. But none of these powers ever measured the resentment of the Afghans. The world woke up when the terrorists struck at New York. It was too late in the day. By then Washington had allowed the Frankenstein's monster of fundamentalism and violence to take over in many countries.

In India, we are likely to recall December 13 every year as the date when a suicidal attack was made on our parliament, the symbol of our country's democracy. September 11 and December 13 together should have marked the autumn of 2001 as the advent of a new era in international politics. For, terrorism was posing the gravest threat to democracy and to all civil societies which cherished plurality and permitted dissent. India had long been familiar with the menace of terror but the vulnerability of the US came to it as a shock.

True, Islamabad also came to realise the mistake of supporting fundamentalists when they began to kill people in Pakistan. Islamabad was happy as long as the target was India. But those who had tasted blood were bound to sniff for it everywhere. A mild Muslim was not good enough, nor was an aspiring democrat. Fundamentalists wanted to change them. And they killed the defiant.

It is difficult to say whether America's ultimatum to Pakistan for taking sides or the killings by the fundamentalists made President Pervez Musharraf see the reality of the Al-Qaida's cult. But he put his weight behind President Bush and Washington. It is another matter no doubt, regrettable that President Musharraf has a different face for India. His definition of terrorism undergoes a change when it comes to cross-border terrorism.

India's case is pathetic. It announced all the assistance within an hour of the September 11 attack. I wonder if the then Foreign Minister Jaswant Singh, embarrassingly pro-American, had consulted even the prime minister before the announcement. But the tilt of Washington towards Islamabad has not been straightened. Democrat America has all the good adjectives for the military ruler of Pakistan.

After hesitating in the beginning, General Musharraf came all the way. He had no choice. He could not afford to stand alone and become another Saddam Hussain. But India had an alternative. It could have used the opportunity to get the non-aligned nations together to decide on how to fight fundamentalists without America prodding particular countries. Washington would have then realised that it could not take every country for granted.

The manner in which America has gone about curbing terrorism—its proclaimed sole purpose after the attack on WTC—makes one wonder whether the terrorists are sought to be punished or the nations whose views do not tally with Washington's. If America had realised that the sovereignty of every country, big or small, had to be respected, the resentment against Washington would not have been so vocal as it is today. It is a tragedy that the animus of America is now against the Muslims. It is apparent from the way the Islamic countries or the Muslims living in the US are being treated. Sometimes one wonders if after decimating the ideology of communism, America's target is Islam.

Washington should understand that the September 11 action could be repeated. Next time, the target may not be a building but something else. Such an eventuality can be warded off if people do not feel enslaved in their own country. They cannot be an exploited lot all the time. Many in the world are becoming desperate because they are not having enough avenues to overcome poverty, ignorance or ill health. They are helpless. Even the other western countries do not seem to realise this.

Washington cannot overcome its humiliation by humiliating the nations that do not see eye to eye with it on all issues. The international community is beset with contradictions—political, economic and social. It must resolve them peacefully. Instead, the powerful countries are now throwing their weight about in a brazen manner. Such countries will do well if they learn a little humility. It is their refusal to acknowledge this truth that was at the back of the terrorist strikes in the US. If they had understood this basic point, the September 11 disaster could have been avoided.

India, Pakistan and Bangladesh

Bangladesh Prime Minister Khaleda Zia fancies herself playing the role of mediator between Prime Minister Atal Behari Vajpayee and President Pervez Musharraf. She tried to convey the impression that she was "ideally suited for it" when she talked to me at Dhaka a few days before the SAARC summit. Apparently, she did not succeed at Kathmandu although she met both of them there. It is significant that she made no reference to the attack on the Indian Parliament but mentioned the September 11 carnage in her prepared speech at the summit.

Still I found Khaleda less anti-India than in the days when she was Prime Minister earlier. Most of her observations at that time would be laced with her anti-India bias. She assured me a year ago, when she was in the wilderness that she would not indulge in anti-India rhetoric if she returned to power. That probably explains why she did not make India an issue in the last election, which despite rigging, went convincingly in her favour. Khaleda seems to have matured over the years. Her words are now measured and her remarks show that she has thought things out. She remains unruffled even when provocative questions are put to her. Yet she has an imperious flourish in the way she talks or postures herself on domestic issues. Her predecessor Sheikh Hasina continued to retain the common touch during her tenure as Prime Minister even though she became impatient and somewhat authoritarian in the latter half of her office.

"I am not going to allow any nuisance this time," said Khaleda. Her hatred for Hasina still remains implacable. Khaleda had in mind Hasina's announcement that the Awami League, which Hasina heads, would initiate a public agitation to demand fresh polls. Khaleda said "they organised a hartal during the holy month of Ramadan but it was a big flop." She seemed to bring in the word "holy" to underline her religious fervour, which she is trying to revive in a country that has been settling to a secular ethos in the past few years. She has already visited Mecca twice, the first time she delayed even the formation of her cabinet to offer her thanks at the holy shrine.

I was struck by the photos of Sheikh Mujib-ur Rahman still hanging on the wall of the waiting room adjacent to the Prime Minister's office. The credit for this goes to her able Law Minister who reportedly pointed out to her at a cabinet meeting that there was a law, enacted by the Hasina government, to punish those who pulled down Mujib's pictures from government offices or public places. There may be an amendment to the law so that the photos of Mujib and Khaleda's husband, Zia-ur Rahman, can be displayed together. In the meanwhile, she has ordered the removal of Mujib's picture from Bangladesh currency notes.

Khaleda has also stopped official holiday on Mujib's birthday and the day on which he was assassinated. I asked her, why? First she tried to rationalise the order on the grounds that here were too many holidays in her country. But then she was frank enough to justify her action by saying that they (the Hasina government) and cancelled the holiday on September 7. It was the day when her husband took over the charge of Bangladesh after a mutiny by army jawans.

Khaleda had no convincing defence when I asked her about the killing and looting of Hindus in the wake of the Bangladesh Nationalist Party's (BNP) victory. Her explanation was that is happened mostly at the time when the caretaker government was in power. The other argument she advanced was that it was the "doing of the Awami League," which expected the Hindus to vote for it but "pounced upon them" when it found that they had voted for the BNP. "You can ask the Hindus," she said. "I shall give you their names." When she saw that I looked unconvinced, she said that she had ordered a judicial inquiry. She went on in the same vein to put the blame of the Awami League. (The Awami League has already held an inquiry and has found the BNP and its ruling allies, the Jamaat-e-Islami and other extremists, "responsible for the killings and lootings.)" Incidentally, one of the two Jamaat ministers is in charge of the Social Welfare Ministry, which is supposed to look after the Hindu community as well.

Asked how she reconciled herself to the pro-Taliban stand by the extremist parties when Bangladesh was part of the coalition against terrorism, she said the parties were free to have their own policies. "They never brought up the matter at the cabinet meetings nor had they aired any differences at the government level," she said. It was, indeed, comical that the

BNP's extremist partners denounced America day in and day out and yet supported as part of the government Khaleda's pronouncements against Al-Qaida and Osama bin Laden.

While answering questions on relations with India, she was equivocal. But she took care to see that there was no anti-India remark. She said that some irritants remained between the two countries. But she corrected herself and said, "no irritants," only problems. She mentioned the Ganga water treaty, which she said, should be reviewed. But it would create no problem because the treaty is already due for review after finishing the run of five years. The period ended on December 31. I asked her point-blank to specify the problems between Bangladesh and India. "Tension on the border between the police of both countries," was her reply. I purposely mentioned whether she meant the Chittangong Hills Tract, Hasina's commendable effort which the BNP had characterised as a sellout to India. Khaleda said no and made no other comment.

"I have invited Prime Minister Vajpayee to visit Dhaka and he has agreed to it," Khaleda said. Asked if she would be visiting India soon, she said that she had been invited but she has no immediate plans to travel to India. She evaded a straight answer to the question of selling gas to India and allowing transiting its goods to the northeastern state through Bagladesh. I believe that talks on both subjects are in an advanced stage. At one time the BNP was exploiting both points to foment anti-India feelings. It is now the Awami League which is warning the government against selling gas to India. The roles seem to have changed. The BNP does not want to give the Awami League any issue which it may use to mobilise public opinion against the government.

The other ministers, including those in charge of foreign affairs and commerce, I met were positive in their attitude towards India. "We want the best of relations with New Delhi," they said. They wanted close trade relations and unilateral tariff concessions from India. They had their doubts whether it would do so. Khaleda reportedly shares their fears.

A Country Still at War

Every time I go to Bangladesh—and I go regularly—I find the country still in the midst of war. The guns of 1971 stopped long ago but conflicts and tension have not. The society remains divided from top to bottom. The people of Bangladesh can categorised into two groups: pro-liberation and anti-liberation forces.

The first claims to represent the forces which fought against Pakistan to create an independent Bangladesh. It mostly favours Sheikh Hasina, daughter of Sheikh Mujib-ur-Rahman, the founder of Bangladesh. The second group supports Prime Minister Khaleda Zia. Her husband, Ziaur Rahman, headed free Bangladesh through a coup.

After 30 years of independece who did what during the liberation struggle is getting hazier every day, but not the prejudice. Some impressions about people—a few may well be true—remain implacable. The worst part of it is that there is no mood of forgetting and forgiving. The liberation or the anti-liberation lebel has become such a prized possession that the fakes and failures use it to settle scores politically and, worse, violently.

The cleavage, really speaking, is India's caste system, with its prejudices and biases. Appointments, transfers and even allocation of funds are made in Bangladesh on the basis of who was on which side. "All of us are pro-liberation," says the foreign minister. But his remark does not span the distance, which is vawning relentlessly.

True, the country went through hell in the nine months of operations by the Pakistan army. All tiers of government were used to crush defiance and local administrative machinery was wrecked. Freedom fighters were the worst sufferers. Not many people sided with Pakistan at that time. That was three decadea ago. Now the situation is different: 'Who and They.' Some way has to be found to overcome the bitterness which continues to cast a shadow over the nation's homogeneity.

The two leaders, Sheikh Hasina and Khaleda Zia representing two opposite viewpoints could have integrated the society. But their hatred of each other is so deep that when one of them comes to power, the others stokes the fires of revolt. Hasina denounced the elections when she lost. Her party, Awami League, has started a countrywide agitation to throw out Khaleda's government. The latter's response is repression. Khaleda's Bangladesh Nationalist Party (BNP) was agitating till a few months earlier when Hasina was in power.

This political see-saw and the welter of the hatred have not allowed anything common, not even a strain of emotion, to come up. It is a nation which is perpetually tearing itself apart. It is more than cussedness. There are no two opinions that Mujib i the father of the nation. Why should the Khaleda government not give him that recognition? The Sangh parivar has no love for Mahatma Gandhi. Still, the BJP the parivar's member, hails him as the father of the nation and extends him all the honour due to him. In a way it has helped the BJP to hide its Hindutva fangs.

Khaleda has removed even the picture of Mujib from Bangladesh currency notes. She wants to amend the act which prohibits people from pulling down Mujib's picture from public places and government offices. Probably, Khaleda wants to hang the picture of her husband, General Zia, along with Mujib's. Officially it is possible. But how do you put the founder of Bangladesh and an army general on the same pedestal?

Bangladesh continues to suffer from non-issues. I try every time to find an answer to my question from the face in the long queue of people before the immigration authorities at the airport. The scene is reminiscent of what I watched in early 1972. Then passengers were shouting 'Jai Bangla'. They wanted to reach the promised land. They still do. But the queue I see at the airport moves slowly. And the people, mostly young in years, are taking outward flights. Pride is still writ large on their faces but there are signs of strain and sorrow.

It looks as if the zeal exhibited during the days of struggle against West Pakistan has burnt itself out. As happens in every liberation struggle, a better way of life was expected from the time guns fell silent. That did not come true. Most people still live on the periphery of existence. Liberation has brought them sovereigny, not economic betterment. This was the main reason why it broke away from West Pakistan to create a new country. Still poor, the nation has come a long way from the time when every farmer had lost either his bullocks, ploughs or seeds after the withdrawal of the Pakistani forces. The countrywide has repaired itself. It is self-reliant. The 1999 cyclone saw farmers managing the ravages of a big calamity though they had skimpy resources. Hardly anyone has gone to the streets of Dhaka, a practice for years to seek help.

Where I see the nation slipping is in its secular ethos. Muslim fundamentalists went berserk in the wake of the victory of Khaleda. So shocked was liberal press opinion that it brought out special editions to highlight the plight of minorities to shame the Muslim majority. In a special issue titled "A Puja marred," *The Star*, a leading daily, reported how "rape, arson, robbery and forced eviction of Hindu families in some parts of the country, have left the community in shock and fear." Shalier Kabia, author and documentary filmmaker, exposed the naked cruelty against the Hindus. The government imprisoned him for anti-national activities.

When I questioned Khaleda about the incidents, she was defensive. Her explanation was that it had happened mostly at the time when the caretaker government was in power. The other argument she advance was that it was the "doing of the Awami League," which expected the Hindus to vote for it but "pounced upon them" when it found that they had voted for the BNP. "You can ask the Hindus," she said. "I shall give you their names." When she saw that I looked unconvinced, she said that she had ordered a judicial inquiry. She went on in the same vein to blame the Awami League. Incidentally, one of the two Jamaat ministers is in charge of the Social Welfare Ministry, which is supposed to look after the Hindu community as well. Khaleda was equivocal on Bangladesh' relations with India. But there was no anti-India remark from her. She said that there were some kinks. They would have to be ironed out. She was keen on the Ganga water treaty being reviewed. I asked her point-blank to specify the problems between Bangladesh and India. "Tension on the border between the police of both countries," was her reply. Reported infiltration of religious fundamentalists into India may aggravate the problem.

The reason why there are lengthy queues at Dhaka airport is the failure of successive governments to provide opportunities. Even the reservoir of gas, which could have been utilised to keep the wheel of industry in the country moving, has remained untouched. The ruling BNP did not allow the sale of gas when it was in the wilderness. Now the Awami League is deadly opposed to it.

My assessment over the years is that both parties, indeed, both ladies, have done little to solve most of the country's trouble.

All that people could do was to ensure that the military stayed in the barrack. They have restored democracy. But what they have failed to do is to put pressure on the two ladies to change. They join them during the agitations. What will happen next? "Much will depend on the groundswell of opinion in our favour," a tall Awami League leader told me when I asked him about the prospects of an agitation to throw out Khaleda.

Chinese Premier in Pakistan

Chinese Prime Minister Zhao Ziayang's visit to Pakistan is seen here as part of an exercise by Beijing to further strengthen its stand on the border dispute with India.

Mr. Zhao, during the five-day stay in Pakistan last week, is reported to have received full support from Islamabad on China's "offer" to India on the border. And Beijing has been praised for "persistent offers of a peaceful solution" in the face of "hostile acts by India".

The Karakoram highway was referred to as a symbol of friendship between Pakistan and China. Significantly, part of that road passes through an area which New Delhi regards as disputed.

Mr. Zhao said more than once that the Chinese would be Pakistan's "trustworthy friends". This is meant to meet the criticism voiced in Pakistan that China did not come to its help during the Bangladesh war in 1971.

China, departing from its past practice, has given an interest free loan of 27 million dollars, apart from contracting to buy some things from Pakistan. This attitude of China is not surprising because during my recent talks with the Chinese leaders in Beijing, I found them having a soft corner for Pakistan. One foreign diplomat told me that Pakistan had the same status in China as India had in the Soviet Union, and "it is good that you do not throw your weight about in the Soviet Union nor does Pakistan in China".

Indo-Pak Relations. On India-Pakistan relations, China makes no secret of its bias. The argument runs like this: you are trying to suppress Pakistan, and China is only helping the weak. However, the official line is that "China's policy is to have good relations with all countries, including India" and that it "judges every problem on its merit".

When it was pointed out to one leader that during the 1965 war between India and Pakistan, Beijing had issued an ultimatum to New Delhi, he first denied it and then said: "India was then trying to annex Pakistan."

China does not think that the US military assistance is in any way a threat to India. "You really think that Pakistan can beat you?" is the question asked. It is stated that India is too strong and should not bother about Pakistan.

"You are also getting arms from America," a high military officer told me in Beijing. "They are giving them to you because they do not want you to be completely dependent on the Soviet Union," he added.

"Why do you not solve your problems with your neighbours?" This was the question posed to me by the top leaders in the government and the communist party whom I met in Beijing. Another observation of men made was that out of 16 countries in its neighbourhood, China has solved its problems with all except two, India and the Soviet Union.

Beijing and Afghanistan. Beijing makes no bones about India's policy on Afghanistan, and the impression is that India does not want to annoy the Soviet Union. "You should have told Russia to get out of Afghanistan; your own security is involved," said a high-up.

Even on Vietnam, there was a tendency to blame India. It was argued that if New Delhi had put enough pressure on Moscow not to give help to Vietnam, the latter would not having its troops in Cambodia—the Chinese refuse to call it Kampuchea.

India, Pakistan and USA

I. Pak and USA. Assuming there is no war or a large-scale retaliation against Pakistan because of America's pressure and other considerations, what would India do if there were yet another incident like the one near Jammu? The limit, if there was any room, was reached after the Indian Parliament was attacked more than five months ago. The outcry at that time was no less than what it is today.

Understandably, no government can sit quiet when its capability, if not legitimacy, is questioned. But has it any long-term strategy? After every attack by the terrorists, it is given out that the diplomatic activity would be widened and the border vigilance increased. But what has happened so far?

As for diplomacy, no country in Europe is willing to buy our line that General Pervez Musharraf is not sincere in suppressing terrorism against India. Winning back opinion in our favour is the real test of diplomacy, not the false claims by the Ministry of External Affairs. Regarding the vigilance on the border, terrorists from across continue to strike at will despite the wall of soldiers.

It seems the hardliners are determined to sabotage everything, including the coming state elections. Abdul Ghani Lone, who was shot dead, was a moderate. That slogans like Pakistan *zindabad* were raised at the meeting where Lone killed is significant. Pakistan is wrong to infer that India does not want to solve the problem of Kashmir. In all Indo-Pakistan agreements from Tashkent to Lahore, New Delhi has mentioned Kashmir. But is cross-border terrorism the solution to the problem?

New Delhi's credibility is doubted since the government has not issued any White Paper to give concrete evidence on how the number of terrorists trained, armed and sheltered across the border is increasing, not decreasing as the State Department says. When it comes to reaction, New Delhi is fierce but rhetorical, threatening but tentative. It lacks a policy. Pakistan is an intransigent neighbour and, good or bad, we have to live with it.

Civil society in Pakistan is our best constituency. We have practically no contact with it. Whatever little link there was, we snapped it by stopping the train, the bus and the plane operating between the two countries. Unwittingly, we have made people in Pakistan pay for the follies of the military government, knowing well that the public does not count in the governance of that country. It is as much fed up with the regime as we are. The demand by political parties that a caretaker government should replace the military junta spells out popular feelings.

Our policy after the takeover by General Ayub Khan in 1958 should have been to help the Pakistanis to get back democracy. India's first Prime Minister Jawaharlal Nehru was correct to bemoan in Parliament the military takeover in Pakistan. But then the "doctrine of necessity," the reason which the Pakistan Supreme Court used to ratify the coup by Musharraf has guided New Delhi as well. Without demur, it has accepted the military rule in Pakistan as if it is inevitable.

Instead of getting absorbed in sterile Track-I or Track-II talks between people selected by the two governments—it was Washington's idea—India should have worked for the restoration of democracy in Pakistan. It is true that it is up to any nation to have the government it likes. But do the Pakistanis have any choice? Military rulers have come whenever they have wanted to and withdrawn they found the people's ire against them.

Without interfering in Pakistan's internal affairs or adopting a holier-than-thou attitude, our endeavour should be to enable the people in Pakistan to rule themselves. We should openly and persistently knock at the door of countries all over the world to point out how the military in Pakistan pushes out the elected governments at will.

It would be ideal if the West, particularly, America, were to join in this effort. A country that swears by the charter of freedom cannot and should not be on the side of military dictators. But then Washington has a penchant for autocrats. It believes that the ideal of democracy is dispensable if there are compensating considerations.

By pointing out to Washington that it has gone back on its promise to fight terrorism wherever it existed, we will not reach anywhere. It would not have woken up to menace of terrorism in the first place if the happenings in New York and Washington had not taken place. So it is futile to expect anything from it except sermons on restraint.

One does feel sad that Indo-US relationship that was on the up has been adversely affected. Both the Prime Minister and the Home Minister returned from Washington last year with the assurance that the tilt, if any, would be towards India.

No doubt, America has not spared words in condemning the acts of terrorism in India but it has never mentioned any country by name. It is difficult to believe that Washington does not know the name. With all its intelligence agencies working in Pakistan and India, in fact all over the region, and the satellites hovering in the sky, America has a full and clear picture. But it prefers to keep quiet.

Obviously, it wants Pakistan's support in dealing with the Taliban and Al-Qaida who are spread all over Pakistan. They have the support of religious elements from within. That may explain why Islamabad has said 'no' to America's action in

Waziristan on the Pakistan-Afghanistan border, where thousands of Taliban and Al-Qaida militants are living after leaving Afghanistan.

It is obvious that America does not want to take a stand, which is not to the liking of Musharraf. It does not seem to realise that he has two yardsticks for measuring terrorism one for Washington and another for India. He believes that when it comes to India he does not have to comply with the promise he made in his January 11 speech to suppress the jehadis and religious zealots. In fact, he has released most of the fundamentalists he had arrested. Seventy training camps of terrorists have come up already.

Washington realises that Musharraf is under pressure from within and should not be driven to the wall. New Delhi does not believe this because it is well known the Taliban and the Al-Qaida are the creation of Islamabad. It is not beyond the military regime to chastise them or their supporters in Pakistan. When it could contain them during America's action in Afghanistan, why not now?

Musharraf had to divert attention from the dubious referendum he held to install himself President for five years. He could not get the legitimacy that he wanted to earn because most people stayed away from the polling booths. He considers confrontation with India the best way to end the debate on his election.

There is little likelihood of terrorism coming down because Musharraf believes he can thus focus international opinion on Kashmir. From the Kargil war to the incident in Jammu, his entire effort has been directed towards it. America can influence Musharraf, not through sweet talk but by withdrawing the economic munificence it continues to shower on Pakistan.

Islamabad must realise that for any attempt to solve the Kashmir dispute, there has to be an atmosphere of peace where India and Pakistan could sit across the table and also involve the Kashmiris at an appropriate time.

The problem with the two countries is that the grey area between the two has shrunk so much that what is visible is either white or black. It is sad that no serious effort has been made even by eminent people on both sides to discuss Kashmir to find some mutually acceptable solution.

Both were well timed: the arrival of US Defence Secretary Donald Rumsfeld in New Delhi and the lifting on Pakistan flights overflying our airspace and the withdrawal of naval ships. It looks as if Washington had arranged everything behind the scenes: President Pervez Musharraf's assurance to stop infiltration in India and Foreign Minister has not said anything beyond what he had stated in his address to the nation on January 12.

What both sides should realise is that war is never an option. It should never be, not in the land of Mahatma Gandhi. In the case of India and Pakistan, war is too dangerous to contemplate because it can go nuclear.

"If you drive us to the wall, we will use the bomb," Dr A.Q. Khan, father of the Pakistan bomb, warned me after disclosing for the first time that they had the bomb. When I pressed him to elucidate his observation, he said he had in mind India's role in the secession war of East Pakistan.

That was more than three decades ago. Khan's words come to my mind often these days. If there is a reverse to any side, Islamabad may use the bomb. Such a possibility is very much there because India is superior to Pakistan in conventional warfare.

Islamabad's UN ambassador Munir Akram has already made it clear that since they do not have the capacity to match India in the conventional force, it will depend on the bomb. President General Pervez Musharraf's horror over the thought of nuclear holocaust only deepens doubts. His UN ambassador could not have mentioned the use of the bomb without clearance from Islamabad. I would not be surprised if Munir was asked to say a piece to draw the world's attention.

It is no more a secret that Pakistan establishment had considered the use of the bomb at the time of Kargil war before Prime Minister Nawaz Sharif flew to Washington to have President Bill Clinton's intervention to rescue Pakistan. It is not beyond the realm of possibility that Musharraf may use the bomb if and when he realizes he cannot cope with India's advance in Pakistan. Whatever he says now, he will also be under pressure from within Pakistan to perform. At one time, Sharif did not want to explode the bomb because of the interference which America offered but the pressure of public opinion on him was too strong to resist.

I do not want to spell out the devastation that the nuclear war would cause. Millions will die on both sides when the bomb is thrown and many millions later because of the after-effects. The devastation is unimaginable. Afghanistan President Hamid Karzai told the leaders of both India and Pakistan a few days ago to visit his country to see the destruction that the war caused and then decide their course of action. He was talking about limited conventional war.

Gauhar Ayub was the foreign minister when I visited Pakistan after it had exploded the bomb. He kept impressing upon me that the bomb would cause more damage to India than Pakistan. "Your country has its population concentrated in cities, while ours is spread out." I was so horrified over the vein of his argument that I said: "Sir, we are talking about human beings."

If all that was required was America's association, why it could not have been done earlier. After all, India was to offer everything to America after the terrorists attack on New York and Washington. Probably, Washington was not willing to go that far.

When entire international community is saying that Pakistan must stop infiltration and assuring us that proof would be coming forth, we should not be giving the impression as if we are at the stage of positioning our last man before embarking upon action against Pakistan. Home Minister L.K. Advani's statement that we should have spent more on defence than education is only rhetoric. His statement is no reply to the Nobel prize winner Amritaya Sen who said that education would have helped solve India's problems. Indeed, he is right. Had we concentrated on education—40 per cent of the country's population is illiterate—we would have solved many of our problems.

Sports Minister Uma Bharti is another hawk who has no control over the language she uses. Her poem to castigate Pakistan was an hideous as the picture of her riding the shoulders of Human Resource Development Minister Murli Manohar Joshi at the time of Babri Masjid's demotion. The hardliners on our side are as much bent upon jeopardising peace as are the jehaids and fundamentalists on the other side.

Prime Minister Atal Behari Vajpayee's suggestion on joint patrolling by India and Pakistan may turn out to be a step towards de-escalation. Earlier, Pakistan's former Home Minister Dr Ijaz Ahsan, had made a similar proposal. He said: "Pakistan should offer joint patrolling of the LoC by Indian and Pakistani soldiers. If such a scheme is implemented, it will be clear to everyone that no border crossings are taking place."

Rumsfeld's proposal to association America and Britain with the supervision of the LoC is worth considering. No doubt, it will bring back UN observers whom we stopped recognising after the 1971 war. That was the time when the ceasefire line became the line of control. But we can specify their role and indicate a time limit which we can extend if need be.

War cannot possibly lead to a solution of any problem, because war has become much too terrible and destructive. If the solution we aim at cannot be brought about by large-scale war, will small-scale war help? Surely, it will—not partly because that itself may lead to a big-scale war and partly because it produces an atmosphere of conflict and of disruption.

It is absurd to imagine that out of the conflict, the right type of forces, which are opposed to terrorism and fundamentalism, will emerge. In Germany, both the Communist Party and the Social Democratic Party were swept away by Hitler. This may happen in our part of the world.

Distrust and Suspicion Remain

Pakistan is uneasy even after the return of Mr. Abdul Sattar, the Pakistan foreign secretary, from New Delhi, though the fear of immediate hostilities has receded to a large extent.

Distrust and suspicion of India remains high and many families from the border areas, particularly Norowhal in west Pakistan, across Jammu, and in Khokharpar in Sind, have moved elsewhere.

The TV network in Pakistan has shown General K.M. Arif, deputy chief of the army staff, visiting the troops in the Wazirabad area, nearly 65 kms from Amritsar and advising them to realise that "their hard work today would prove beneficial for them in the hour of trial tomorrow". The official media has done many other things to ally the concern of the people and boost up their morale.

Although the people have felt relieved after the agreement in Delhi reached between the two foreign secretaries, they increasingly believe that the governments on both sides overreacted to the situation. Many say that there was never a question of war and that 'political compulsions' of leaders on either side made them to station troops on the border.

Bad Atmosphere. The atmosphere was pretty bad, verging on nervousness when I reached here 10 days ago and travelled to Islamabad, Rawalpindi and Karachi. Almost everyone I met—politicians, lawyers, journalists, academics and government servants—asked me one question: why are the Indian amassed on such a large scale on the border?

Very few people believe that Pakistan may have to blame as well for the situation. Their argument is that what it has done in terms of moving troops to the forward areas is part of self-defence. However, a few knowledgeable persons do concede that Pakistan moved "some other troops" from the interior so as not to be caught napping as it happened in 1965 and 1971.

One thing that came out in every discussion was the realisation that Pakistan was "too small and too weak" against India's "mighty military strength and size". This is in sharp contrast to the talk of bravado which I used to listen to before the 1965 and 1971 wars. At that time every Pakistani soldier was considered equal to four Indian soldiers.

There are several interpretrations given to India's military exercises. One is that India wants to pressurise Pakistan so that it comes to a settlement with the Soviet Union on Afghanistan on the basis of Moscow's latest offer. Another interpretation is that India, pressed in Punjab, is trying to make Pakistan as a "scape goat". Still another is that India is set against Pakistan making the bomb and hence the threat of war to "force us to abandon the project".

Reaction of Press. Newspapers are full of stories about the movement of Indian troops and their copy suggests that the Indian jawans have taken position in trenches. There is a lot of emphasis on the fact that the exercises conducted by the Indian troops is with live ammunition. Whatever BBC says about Indian troops—and it is talking in terms of their threatening postures—is reproduced fully. Compared to English newspapers, Urdu papers, which constitute the bulk of Pakistan press, are giving prominent display to the situation on the border; their comments are vociferous, and they openly say that India cannot be trusted.

It appears that even after Mr. Sattar's return the Pakistan government is not doing much to lessen the tension as if it has some vested interest in sustaining it. However, the people are more relaxed and even talk of hostilities in lighter vein.

Cross Border Terrorism

It looks as if Prime Minister Atal Behari Vajpayee has called General Pervez Musharraf's bluff. Otherwise, the Pakistan President would have immediately reacted favourably to Vajapyee's offer for a dialogue. After all Musharraf had been repeatedly saying that he was ready for talks at any place, any time. Why did he not himself welcome the offer?

The official statement reacting from Islamabad to the offer has been rather disappointing. Pakistan is reportedly trying to appoint a representative for the talks. This is a step in the right direction. But what about Prime Minister Vajpayee's suggestions that cross-border terrorism should stop and the training camps should be demolished? These are no "pre-conditions" as the Pakistan government has made out. All countries follow such norms. They do not allow their soil to be used for terrorism in neighbouring countries or elsewhere. To consider stoppage of terrorism equivalent to setting preconditions is to admit your own guilt.

Why doesn't General Musharraf make his promise good? He told America that he would have the infiltration stopped and the training camps demolished. Washington passed on this information to us. But there is no let-up in cross-border terrorism. In fact, a US Congress team has said in its report that the infiltration went up last year and will increase still further this year. To make matters worse, Pakistan Foreign Minister Kasuri wants to drag six or seven European nations to supervise the border and see whether there is infiltration. Since what Kasuri says contradicts what Musharraf told the US, suspicions are bound to arise. Is Musharraf playing a double game?

I do not know if the resignation of Mr Robert Blackwell, America's ambassador to New Delhi, has anything to do with

Washington's failure to rein in Pakistan. His statement that "the fight against international terrorism will not be won until terrorism against India ends permanently" gives us a clue. It is apparent that he wanted more pressure to be applied on President Musharraf to stop cross-border terrorism. President Musharraf may ultimately agree to what the American representatives visiting the region next month will dictate.

The wave of jubilation, which has spread all over Pakistan and India, indicates that people on both sides want peace and conciliation. Bringing in other things at this time is to introduce extraneous considerations. It is obvious that the military in Pakistan has developed a vested interest in not sorting out problems with India. The more hostile Pakistan's relations with India are, the greater would be the need for the military's presence at Islamabad. It may be thinking along these lines. Pakistan's Prime Minister Jamali has himself said that General Musharraf is his boss and not parliament.

I have no doubt that the dialogue between India and Pakistan will take place sooner or later. America is relentlessly applying pressure on both countries to have a dialogue. The question is how to make the dialogue meaningful. There is a point in former Jammu and Kashmir chief minister Farooq Abdullah's statement that the ground should be prepared. A solution between India and Pakistan has to be evolved. It cannot be an overnight happening. Probably that is the reason why the Lahore bus trip did not come to much and why the Agra summit was not successful.

In any case, for the atmosphere to become conducive to a dialogue there has to be peace. Prime Minsiter Vajpayee's initiative should be grasped by Pakistan with both hands. I hope the Lshkar-e-Toiba's vow to carry on jehad in Kashmir is not with the blessing of Islamabad. Things can go out of hand. Now that New Delhi is willing to have talks with Islamabad there is no reason why Musharraf should be dragging his feet.

I wish that if and when the proposal to have a dialogue between India and Pakistan is finalised, some top bureaucrat is not chosen to take over Vajpayee's initiative. All these matters are political. And they require finesse and a sense of accommodation which bureaucrats do not have, particularly retired ones.

3

Army Rule and its Repercussion in India

Coming to Terms with the Past

Come September, the 1965 conflict between India and Pakistan returns to notice. It conjures up certain incidents—legends—which the passage of time not been able obscure. This is one of those wars which both countries claim to have won.

Scores of books have been published in India to prove how New Delhi accomplished its task of destroying the Pakistan war machine. Equally vast is the literature in Pakistan to assert that Islamabad repulsed waves after waves of attack by large Indian forces and did not allow them to enter either Lahore or Sialkot city. The debate will not probably and even in 1965 when all papers relating to the operation are supposed to be handed over after 30 years to the archives for public gaze.

In the meanwhile, one more book, *Ayub Khan-Pakistan's First Military Ruler,* has appeared in Pakistan. This is a 540-page study by Altaf Gauhar, who was General Ayub Khan's top civil servant. He has mentioned the abortive attempt to revive the Kashmir question through infiltration in 1965. At that time the Kashmiris themselves handed over infiltrators to the Indian Army.

The failure buried the Kashmir question for nearly a quarter of a century, as a Pakistani commentator put it. However, infiltration has re-surrected the question, and it has assumed far more serious proportion than ever before. Even 400 Islamic militants, according to the *New York Times,* have joined what is described as *jehad.*

I am afraid the situation may go out of hand. Foreign powers, already on prowl, may complicate the question to the extent where both India and Pakistan may find it difficult to settle on their own. Statements and stories emanating from capitals like Washington and London suggest that they want to have a say.

Although Indian Foreign Secretary Dixit has ruled out America's intervention, his observation that it could "help in the process" indicates that New Delhi is under pressure. His announcement that India will hold talks with Pakistan after the elected government takes over at Islamabad is a welcome statement. But had this sentiment been conveyed to Islamabad before Dixit met U.S. officials in Washington, it would have been interpreted as a good-will gesture. Now the impression in Pakistan may be that New Delhi has done it at America's bidding. Islamabad may also pat itself on the back that its effort to raise the question at every forum abroad has yielded results.

Islamabad should, however, ponder over the consequences of internationalising the Afghanistan, where America interjected too many weapons and whetted too many tribal ambitions. That country may explode into a civil war.

Now that Pakistan Foreign Secretary Sheryar has also announced in Washington that Islamabad would welcome talks under the Simla Agreement, the ground has been prepared for a dialogue some time in November or early December. This is an opportunity which the two sides should not spoil by hurling accusations or counter accusations. Both New Delhi and Islamabad agreed at Simla in 1972 to seek "a final settlement on Jammu & Kashmir".

The atmosphere can further improve if the Inter Services Intelligence (ISI) stops the flow of arms into India. New Delhi has already noticed "a considerably decrease" in it. Washington and London have also informed New Delhi about the lessening of inflow after hearing from Islamabad. But the use of arms should also stop. The cult of gun is taking over and the subcontinent looks like sitting on a powder keg.

Talks with Kashmir militant outfits, particularly the Jammu & Kashmir Liberation Front (JKLF) and Hizbul Mujahdeen, are as necessary as is the dialogue with Islamabad. There was a time when New Delhi and Islamabad could have settled the question themselves. Now the Kashmiris will have to be associated. But touching all the three points—Delhi, Islamabad and Srinagar—at the same time may not be productive or politic. Any two points at one time will make more sense.

Ayub Khan, at the helm of affairs in 1965, never liked the idea of infiltration. When I asked him about it in 1972—he was then living in retirement at his house in Islamabad —he said: "Ask Bhutto, it was his doing". Subsequently, I checked with Zulfikar Ali Bhutto, then the Pakistan President. He made no secret of infiltration and defended it. His logic was that the various ordnance factories, which New Delhi had established but had not yet gone in full production, would make India too strong to be beaten; therefore, Pakistan had to act soon.

He said: "... There was a time when militarily, in terms of armour, we were superior to India because of the military assistance we were getting and that was the position up to 1965. Now, the Kashmir dispute was not being resolved. ... So it would, as a patriotic, be better to say, all right, let us finish this problem and come to terms, and come to a settlement. It has been an unfortunate thing, so that is why up to 1965, I thought that with this edge that we had we could have morally justified it."

Little did Bhutto realise at that time that the infiltration strategy would work 28 years later. There has been infiltration in reverse in the sense that many Kashmiri youths have gone to Pakistan to get training and arms. True, Pakistan's assistance has helped them but so has India's denial of basic domocratic rule and economic development in the State.

Not on the political aspect but on the military assessment of the 1965 conflict, a book, *Behind the Scene,* by retired Maj. Gen. Jogindar Singh has appeared in India. I do not know why he had to run down Lt. Gen. Harbaksh Singh, then commanding the Punjab front, while analysing the pluses and minuses of the conflict. When personal reminiscences try to lower the Jogindar Singh has converted facts into fiction.

He has controverted Harbaksh Singh's main strategy of making the Ichhogil canal, outside Lahore, as India's basic defence line. His idea, as Harbaksh Singh says in his book, *War Despatches,* was to convert the canal built by Pakistan as an impediment to his use to save troops. "I had no reserve in Punjab", he says. The course of war has proved his strategy right.

Still worse is Jogindar Singh's assertion that General J.N. Chaudhari, then Chief of Army Staff, did not suggest the withdrawal of Indian forces behind the River Beas. Harbaksh Singh recalls a meeting with Gen. Chaudhari at Ambala on September 10 in the wake of early reverses in the Khemkaran sector. According to Harbaksh Singh, Chaudhari told him to withdraw behind the Beas as the security of entire army was endangered. Harbaksh Singh said he refused to do so and wanted orders in writing. The matter ended there and then. He never got any orders. After 28 years, Jogindar Singh says that the withdrawal story is "baseless".

Jogindar Singh has quoted Maj. Gen. Narinjan Prasad as his main source of information. But Prasad has had the distinction of being dismissed from the front twice, once in 1962 during the India-China War and then during the India-Pakistan conflict in 1965. "Jogindar Singh is a biased account," says Harbaksh Singh.

There is still controversy who in the army initiated the move to cross international Punjab border. This was meant to relieve pressure in the Akhnoor sector in the J&K where India was at disadvantage because of U.N. restrictions. Harbaksh Singh says that he requested Gen. Chaudhari to seek the government permission.

Once I asked Lal Bahadur Shastri, then Prime Minister, who gave the actual orders to cross the international boundary. "I did," he said. Chaudhari and others were taken aback when I asked them to march into Pakistan." Harbaksh Singh tells me that the Army can never forget "this tallest decision by the shortest man" (Shastri was about five feet tall).

Khaki under Sherwani in Pakistan

Though martial law has been lifted in Pakistan, no one has been left in any doubt that martial rule is far from being ended. And if the military has its way, it will never be. It is evident that many senior officers were not pleased at the prospect when the countdown for the lifting of martial law began after the return of General Zia-ul-Haq from New Delhi.

When at a meeting of martial law administrators and state governors he convened on December 20, General Zia hinted at the removal of governors, mostly army commanders, Lt. Gen. Fazil-ul-Haq, then governor of the North Western Frontier Province (NWFP), who had said some time back that "all of us came together and would go out together", was visibly disturbed. He asked General Zia where he had failed him and why he was being asked to quit the governorship. Lt. Gen. K.M. Arif, Deputy Chief of Staff, General Zia's Man Friday, had to raise his voice to quieten Lt. Gen. Fazil-ul-Haq.

It is also interesting to note that at least some of the President's men are aware that the people have become cynical of official announcements. The order declaring lifting of martial law was to be made on December 29, and it was to be operative the next day. However, Brigadier Mohammed Siddiqi Salik, General Zia's speech writer and conscience keeper, told him that newpapers had carried too many times that martial law would "soon" be lifted; so the declaration should be that it had been lifted. The date for the delaration was then changed to Demember 30.

Brig. Salik did not, however, get any reply when he asked Gen. Zia what he should say about the future arrangements for the post of Chief of the Army Staff, a hat which Gen. Zia has been wearing with that of presidentship. His reported reply was: "Don't say anything". And there hangs the tale of Gen. Zia's intentions; he wants to rule, wearing the khaki beneath the sherwani. In fact, the amended Pakistan constitution makes an exception in his case; the president cannot hold any office of profit but Gen. Zia can continue as Chief of the Army Staff.

The lifting of martial law does restore the fundamental rights of the people regarding personal liberty and freedom of movement. Technically, the press and the judiciary are free. But what has been given with one hand has been taken away with the other. Many martial law orders and decrees made under martial law remain effective even after the withdrawal of martial law rule because they have been either incorporated in the constitution or endorsed by the National Assembly, Pakistan's lower house, and the Senate, the upper house.

The press ordinance, not withdrawn yet, authorises the government to cancel a paper's declaration of printing or to demand fresh deposit. Papers like *Musawat, Hilal-e-Pakistan* and other pro-Bhutto publications continue to be in the hands of the authorities, not with the rightful owners.

As regards the judiciary, the President can "modify the appointment of judges" of the superior courts at any time. He can also transfer a judge to any other assignment or ask him to "perform such other function as the president may deem fit". The present crop of judge, who have sworn and resworn to avow allegiance to Gen. Zia's fiats do not dare to go against the regime.

Political prisoners, numbering 1500, are still under detention and those who were sentenced by military courts for their "anti-government activity" continue to languish in prison; the judiciary has been denied jurisdiction to review their cases. The detention order on leftist leader like Rasool Bux Paleejo and Jam Saqi have been pre-dated because after the lifting of martial law the authorities forgot to revalidate the detention orders under civil rule.

As president, Gen. Zia, who got himself elected through a managed referendum last year, enjoys the right to dissolve the National Assembly. He appoints the governor in consultation with (not advice of) the Prime Minister and they in turn, nominate the provincial chief ministers. On top of it all, he makes no secret of the fact that civilian rule is only a "continuation" of martial law rule.

These are the main reasons why the people in Pakistan are cynical about the end of martial law, Gen. Zia who epitomises martial rule and its excesses, will continue in office up to 1990, and this alone is enough to make them suspect that the change is an eyewash.

They also feel that the members elected to the National Assembly, the Senate and the provincial assemblies are not their real representatives. The legislators were returned when political parties were banned and candidates unacceptable to the military junta were not eligible to contest. Their credibility got further damaged when they added unanimously Indeminity Law (eighth amendment) to the Pakistan constitution, giving retrospective validity to the fiats of the military regime, including the orders of the military courts and tribunals.

If free elections were to be held today, not even 10 per cent of them would be returned. And they are aware of it. Indeed, the governments has taken full advantage of this – the threat of a mid-term poll has worked to discipline even the few fiery independents and the threat will continue to be used in the future.

The challenge to "civilian rule" will be posed by non-establishment politicians. The tallest among them is Benazir Bhutto, who is expected to return to Pakistan from abroad next month. It is certain that she will not be allowed free movement because, as one top diplomat in Islamabad puts it, if she were to travel by train from Karachi to Peshawar, she would either be eliminated or force the government resign by the time she reached the destination. Her Pakistan People's Party (PPP) remains the most popular and if and when there are free elections in Pakistan, Benazir Bhutto will sweep the polls in Punjab and Sind and get a majority even in Baluchistan and the NWFP.

Air Marshal Asghar Khan, the Tehrik-e-Istiqbal Chief, and Ghous Bukhsh Bizenjo, President of National Awami Party (NAP), told that they would be able to bring the people into the streets force fresh elections and restore the 1973 constitution without the amendments effected during the martial law rule. The people are indeed interested in reviving democracy but it is unlikely that they will listen to the call of anyone except Benazir. The old politicians, particularly those who connived at the hanging of Bhutto, are not acceptable to them.

A large number of people have been depoliticised. The confrontation between the orthodox, including the mullahs and Jammiat-e-Islami, and the radical, including liberal parties and the communists, made the people suffer the such an extent – the Bangladesh secession was its fallout – that many have to come to fear politics of the old kind. The economic boom, through jobs in the Gulf and aid from America and Saudi Arabia, has made them complacent; they; particularly the Punjabis, who wary of anything that might risk their economic wellbeing.

"Let us wait and watch" is a comment attributed to Gen. Zia. Prime Minister Mohammad Khan Junejo and his cabinet members were reportedly in favour of declaring an emergency after the lifting of martial law. But Gen. Zia. made it plain that he would say in public that it was the Junejo government that imposed the emergency, not he. Realising that he would lose face, Junejo did not insist. Gen. Zia's calculation is said to be that in the absence of the emergency, political leaders and parties would array themselves against one another, disturbing the peace which prevailed at present. The old rivalries of Sind, Baluchistan and the NWFP to dilute the domination of Punjab in the services, business, industry and agriculture would also come to the fore. And this might not only exasperate the people but also pave the way for another martial law regime, the fourth in the series. That explains why Gen. Zia is still Chief of the Army Staff.

But what Gen. Zia forgets is that just as he had to lift martial law, he may be forced to quit. The Pakistanis are the same people who had made Bhutto leave after he had rigged the second term.

General Zia-ul-Haq may lift martial law in form but not in effect; he wants to legalise power that he has usurped, without any intention of giving it up.

This is what Air Marshal Asghar Khan said in an interview with me. After six years of detention or house arrest, he remains undaunted and the Tehriq-e-Isteqlal, the party he leads, is getting ready to launch a movement to restore democracy in Pakistan.

Air Marshal Asghar Khan said that General Zia might abolish military courts and even change the army personnel here and there but the courts would be replaced by something he could dictate and in place of army personnel he would have such bureaucrats who would be cent per cent loyal to him. He might even allow political activity but only in "a controlled way".

Talking about the recent elections in Pakistan, Mr. Asghar Khan said that the people voted in a "positive manner" and defeated those who were close to Gen. Zia, particularly candidates belonging to religious parties. "They trounced Gen. Zia, who claims to be the biggest moulvi in Pakistan, in a referendum."

"Now it depends on the climate outside; if we are able to build up pressure and agitate, some of the assembly members will be pushed to say something. I do not say that something will happen in Pakistan in the next few weeks, but it will happen because the people have shown in the elections that they want a change," Mr. Asghar Khan said.

Asked if the presence of Mrs. Nusarat Bhutto and Ms. Benazir Bhutto would have made the difference, Mr. Asghar Khan said that they should come to Pakistan. "We have been saying that the same results cannot be achieved from outside. You cannot do the Khomeini way all the time; it is a great pity that they are still outside."

Air Marshal Asghar Khan said that Prime Minister Mohmmad Junejo was a "front man", in fact, the National Assembly was that of "loyalists"; it was no real opposition and the candidates who contested campaigned in a particular style. The basic issue was accepting the military a permanent feature in the life of Pakistan. "We, in the MRD (Movement for the Restoration of Democracy), did not participate in the polls because we refused to accept the army as a senior partner. We are not aganist Gen. Zia as a person, but is in the institution of the armed forces which we oppose; it is a question of principle."

Asked whether the affluence of Punjabis came in the way of their participation in the MRD movement two years ago, Mr. Asghar Khan said that it was not true. "The people in Punjab were as poor as in Sind or elsewhere. Two things had helped Gen. Zia: one, the Soviet intervention in Afghanistan and two Gen. Zia's propaganda on Islamisation. The first thing continued but as far as the Islamisation was concerned, the effect was wearing cut. The people were now seeing through it. Personally speaking, the state should not interfere in the religion and it would be dangerous to combine religion with the states, Mr. Asghar Khan said.

Air Marshal Asghar Khan said that he could not understand why India was spending so much money on weapons. There were no domestic compulsions and the society was free. In Pakistan, he said, all avenues to ventilate public opinion were suppressed and therefore no protest against huge military expenditure could be voiced. "Pakistan must adjust foreign policy in such a way that we stop" stop spending money on non-productive things. Our army, even the double of its side cannot afford to attack India unless it runs amuck."

Pakistan has permitted Karachi to be a rest and recreation (R&R) centre for soldiers as Bangkok was during the Vietnam war. This facility will come in handy to the US Central Command (Rapid Deployment Force) for operations in the Gulf region. In fact, Pakistan now has a crucial support role to play.

General Zia-ul-Haq, Pakistan's President, has denied that he has given bases to the Americans but Islamabad is developing a comprehensive military infrastructure in the coastal region of Makran which overlooks the Gulf. A 500-mile highway will run down the Makran coast from Karachi to the Iranian border and, with US aid, 23 new airports are being constructed in Baluchistan. These are obviously for use by the Americans if and when needed.

The opposition movement for the restoration of democracy (MRD) has accused the government of handing over to the US the port of Gwadar, long used by fishermen, which is now a Pakistani naval base. MRD sources also point out that US aircraft have been landing frequently at Pakistan Air Force bases near Karachi. They say that Gwadar has become a major US electronic listening base.

The MRD allegations are widely believe in Pakistan and anti-US feeling in the country is at a high pitch. Open admission of US facilities on Pakistan's soil may trigger off riots against the US and so it is likely that secrecy will be maintained over the arrangements that have been made between Pakistan's military leaders and the Pentagon.

The increasing American presence is evident in that every three weeks the Pakistan customs clears one car duty free for the use of US personnel. A large number of US officers in Islamabad are said to be from the CIA and they are said to be working under cover in the US embassy, USAID officers, the American Centre, etc.

The CIA has stepped up its operation in Afghanistan and this is one reason why more of its men are being posted. Pakistan intelligence agencies are closely associated with the operation.

One of President Reagan's first steps within days of his re-election was the announcement that US aid to the Afghan guerillas would be nearly tripled to $ 285 million a year from $ 100 million. This aid is disbursed by the CIA and, according to a recent article in *The Washington Post,* is given directly to the Pakistan government, which then distributes it to guerillas based in Pakistan.

At the same time Islamabad is jittery because of Moscow's "stiff attitude" on Afghanistan. Gen. Zia is believed to have been told by President Gorbachev when they met during Chernenko's funeral that if Pakistan did not stop "interfering" in Afghanistan, the Soviet Union might be forced to retaliate.

Both President Zia and Prime Minister Junejo in their speeches before the National Assembly admitted that the Soviet Union has "threatened" Pakistan but went on record as saying that they would not close doors to Afghan refugees in the interest of Islamic brotherhood.

Meanwhile, many in Pakistan have veered round to the view that they should hold direct talks with Mr. Babrak Karmal, the Afghanistan President. The government is not prepared for direct talks, though it now makes no secret of the fact that a political solution is the only way out.

Pakistan has communicated to India that General Zia's observation regarding Gilgit, Hunza and Skardu did not in any way change the position prevailing before partition.

Their status is the "same" as it obtained "before", Pakistan has informed. The fact that observers from the three territories have been attending the Majilis-e-Shoura (a nominated Parliament-like body) did not mean that the status of these places was sought to be altered.

In this farewell interview, Mr Abdus Sattar, Pakistan's ambassador in New Delhi, reportedly told India's foreign office that Pakistan honoured the status of Gilgit, Skardu prevailing before partition.

India's foreign office confirms that it has received Pakistan's clarification. The Pakistan sources also confirm having communicated to India's foreign office that there was no change in the status of Gilgit, Hunza and Skardu and the position was the same as it existed before the sub-continent was partitioned.

In a press interview Gen. Zia said in April that Gilgit, Hunza and Skardu were "not the disputed area" and that they used to be part of Kashmir but did not now "form part of the disputed area between India and Pakistan on the Kashmir issue. The ceasefire line is on the far side; Gilgit, Hunza and Skardu are parts of the northern areas of Pakistan. They are not a disputed territory".

This statement created a furore in India and New Delhi lodged a formal protest. The transcription of Gen. Zia's press interview was obtained from Islamabad and it confirmed India's fears. However, Pakistan has now made amends.

Meanwhile, India is making preparations for the resumption of talks with Pakistan on the no-war pact proposal which broke off after Pakistan compared Kashmir to Palestine in Geneva at Human Rights Conference. Mr. M.K. Rasgotra, Foreign Secretary, who is going to Islamabad on August 9 will stay back after participating in the meeting of the foreign secretaries of Pakistan, Bangladesh, Nepal, Bhutan and Sri Lanka, to discuss regional problems. He is expected to pick up the thread from where Mr. R.D. Sathe, former Foreign Secretary, had left.

Mr. Paracha, the Pakistan ambassador-designate to India, will reach New Delhi on July 19. But he will return to Islamabad after presenting his credentials so as to be able to participate in the talks between India nd Pakistan.

Sullen Resignation in Pakistan

I went back to Pakistan a few days ago to attend a seminar on South Asia Cooperation, barely a month after my last visit to to the country, and found an increased feeling of resignation with which the people accepted martial law rule ever more marked. Not that the resentment against Gen. Zia has ended, but there is sullen acceptance that he is there to stay and that as long as the dominant Punjabis stay aloof the rest of the people cannot oust him through agitation.

To some extent, the suspension of the Movement for Restoration of Democracy (MRD) is responsible for the present mood. The organisers could not but suspend it as brutal repression had blunted it and even village-level leaders in Sind, where the MRD was most active, had been arrested. And some *vedharas* (landlords), earlier in the forefront, were afraid that the *haris* (tenants) were getting radicalised. For example, the hold of left-oriented Sind Awami Tehrik (SAT) has spread considerably.

And the distant aloofness of Punjabis, otherwise sympathetic to the MRD, did not wear off during the agitation. The Punjabis did not participate even when Nusarat, Bhutto' wife, appealed to them from abroad to rise against the Zia regime. With the majority of Pakistan's population remaining cold – the Punjabis are 67 per cent – the MRD could not hope to succeed.

Adding to the people's dejection was that Benazir Bhutto chose to go abroad. Although they do not trust the government-planted rumour that she "bought" her release, there can be no doubting that a standard of revolt raised from aboard is less credible than one kept flying even if in confinement in one's own country. The military junta clearly feels relieved that she has left the country. I got the impression that Gen. Zia might try to stage some sort of elections in her absence. However, the legend of Bhutto stalks the land and that harrasses the military rulers: his PPP (Pakistan's People Party) still commands the largest following.

Abbotabad, and Ghulam Mustafa Gen. Zia's men have met Air Marshal Asghar Khan, confined to his house in Jatoi, in jail outside Karachi. Perhaps he is trying to win their support to his plan for elections to have a stamp of legitimacy. But they have reportedly demanded the release of all political prisoners and permission to resume political activity before committing themselves to any plan of action. Some MRD leaders I meet added that there would be no compromise until a commission has been set up to inquire into the atrocities committed by the military in the first few months of MRD agitation.

This is a demand that is unlikely to be accepted. One military commander told me in Islamabad that he was surprised that anyone could blame the government for violation of human rights. "The streets in Pakistan are safe to walk in any time of day or night," he said: It is true that in the towns I visited, Lahore, Rawalpindi and Islamabad there were no troops out with guns at the ready, nor were there other visible signs of a country under martial law. But the military government does not need to make its presence felt in the streets because the government keeps the population under very close surveillance; Big Brother is watching, and no one doubts it.

It is estimated that 15,000 people are still in jail. Most of them were arrested during the MRD movement and have been in detention without trial for six months or more. For those who have been tried punishment has been heavy. There are others; for instance, three lecturers of an Islamabad college were dismissed, fined Rs. 50,000 and five lashes each for being found in possession of a petition asking for restoration of democracy in Pakistan. Some of the senior-most staff of *Pakistan Times* were fired because they signed such a petition. When a journalist drew Gen. Zia's attention to these dismissals, he said they should thank their stars that they were not shot dead. A few days ago, 11 women lecturers in Lahore were dismissed without assigning any reason.

This is a measure of the contempt Gen. Zia has for civilians. In marked contrast is his attitude to his fellow generals; "though several of them are superannuated and have been for years, they are all still in service, some as governors and some in other positions. Once Gen. Zia proposed the retirement of two generals he did not like but the rest got together and told him: "we came together and we shall go out together." Next month he will again face the problem of re-extending the superannuated topbrass, brigadiers and officers below them are stuck; already there are as many as 126 major generals and above.

Gen. Zia apparently feels that what danger he has to face will not be from the people. And so military rule seems unending. But would be a mistake to think that the people are defeated.

They openly say that though the first round of the MRD movement is over, the second will begin if Gen. Zia refuses to see the writing on the wall. At least in Sind the feelings are so strong that some talk in terms of seeking India's aid for their liberation.

During the MRD movement, the slogan of "India zindabad" was at many places and in some even India's flag hoisted. The MRD converted itself into a Sind movement and though this limited its effect, it has led most people in Pakistan, especially in Punjab which enjoys supremacy in the country's affairs to realise that the time has come to hammer out an agreement among the four constituent, Punjab, Sind, the North West Frontier Province and Baluchistan to prevent the danger of disintegration.

There is no doubting that the demand for a democratic system has taken hold; Gen. Zia's alternative of an Islamic system of government has very few supporters. Even Jamiat-e-Islami members say that the parliamentary system of government is not anti-Islamic in character. It is strange how Gen. Zia's propaganda has only strengthened opposition to a religious polity.

Suppression has silenced the people and strict press censorship has kept out most criticism from newspapers. But there is growing resentment among the people; the armour is beginning to show chinks. A few weeks ago a plan to assassinate Gen. Zia was nipped in the bud. Some 30 officers, majors, colonels and squadron leaders were arrested; the highest rank officer among them was a brigadier who, when challenged at a house in Lahore, reportedly killed two military men before surrendering.

Nobody knows what will make the people explode and when. They are full up to their throats and say so. Whenever any incident takes place, as it happened in Lahore a few days when students clashed with bus drivers, many begin to see in it the much-needed spark. But Gen. Zia has proved to be more shrewd than Gen. Ayub Khan, who had allowed in March 1969 the killing of a student outside Rawalpindi to develop into an uprising that swept him out of power. Gen. Zia settles disputes quickly and generously; a few years ago when the Shias surrounded the secretariat in Islamabad to protest against the imposition of *zakot* (a fixed portion of income which Muslims have to contribute compulsorily for charity purposes), Gen. Zia readily conceded the demand; Shias like non-Muslims do not pay *zakat*. In fact, his reputation is that of a non-vindicative autocrat; he wears velvet over a mailed fist.

But what has helped him in recent days more than his tacticts in New Delhi's domineering attitude and the talk of possible war between India and Paklistan. Mrs. Gandhi's support for the MRD hurt the cause; now her statement about "war clouds on the border" or "Pakistan's preparations" has scared the people to an extent where they feel that their sovereignty is in danger and that their first priority should be the defence of their country.

The fallout is to Gen. Zia's advantage. He feeds himself on the people's fear that Mrs. Gandhi may engage them in a limited war over the "Azad Kashmir" to improve her chances in the forthcoming elections. Rajiv Gandhi's recent speech that Pakistan might attack India is seen as the ruling party's attempt to create a war psychosis in India; in fact, every such statement on our side is discussed and rediscussed for days and the conclusion often drawn is that Mrs. Gandhi is looking for an excuse to attack Pakistan.

A silver lining to these fears is the realisation, though yet limited, that a strong opinion has developed in India against war with Pakistan. It is conceded that both public and press forced the Indian government to accept Pakistan's no-war pact offer after New Delhi had rejected it; it is also conceded that the people on both sides are ahead of their governments in their desire to normlise the relationship between two countries. But what stops the Pakistanis from going further is their belief that Mrs. Gandhi does not look kindly towards them. And they wishfully recall the Janta government's period which they believe was the golden period in the history on Indo-Pakistan relations.

Attitude of People in Pakistan

If India and Pakistan were to sign a no-war pact, history might well find it a most curious document. For it will not bring a no-war state of mind in either country. Both will continue to prepars for war; one has just signed an agreement with France for the delivery of the Mirage 2000 in 1984 and the other has started receiving the F-16, from America.

They have had three wars, in 1948, in 1965 and in 1971. And they know that a fourth will be disastrous for both but seem to think it inevitable. Ironically each has been more wary every time the other has talked of a pact forbidding war.

When General Zia-ul-Haq, Pakistan's President, first said in October 1981 that his country would like to enter into a no-war pact with India, Mrs. Indira Gandhi, India's Prime Minister, said it was a trap. But finding that her comment roused strong criticism in her own country and abroad, she changed her stand and said that India was ready to reciprocate Pakistan's gesture, if it was bona fide.

Suspicion, perhaps was natural. For only 19 months earlier Gen. Zia and rejected the suggestion of a no-war pact. In a press interview he told me at Islamabad at that time that there was no use having a no-war pact because the Shimla Agreement between the two countries was as good as such a pact. (The Shimla Agreement says: "... The two sides are resolved to settle the differences by peaceful means....").

I asked him in March 1982 why have had changed his mind. He said: "It was because of the two revealations. I was told that India fears that Pakistan will attack. I asked (Indian Foreign Minister) Narasimha Rao this and he said, "We fear that you are going to attack"... "When I learnt this I said, all right, if this is the case then here is my reply: in all sincerity Pakistan offers the hand of friendship. I also wanted to see how sincere India was in offering the original no-war pact. That is why I offered a no-war pact. This is the reality."

Yet the progress made so far is limited. New Delhi suspects Gen. Zia's motives; it fears he wants to gain time till he has received all the military weapons from America, trained his men to use them as well as acquired the bomb. And hence the battle of drafts.

Pakistan has sent India a draft of the no-war pact, enunciating the principle not to resort to arms to resolve any problem. India in turn has sent two drafts: one for the constitution of an Indo-Pakistan commission and the other for a friendship and peace treaty which seeks to bind Pakistan not to rasie any bilateral dispute in international forums.

The three drafts are yet to be discussed. Normally officials prepare the ground; but Gen. Zia wants to quicken the pace by meeting Mrs. Gandhi. There are many reasons for his doing so.

Behind the scenes, while discussing the armaments deal with Pakistan, the Americans may have put pressure on Islamabad not to turn militant. A warring subcontinent, with the presence of Russian troops in next-door Afghanistan, might be an open invitation for Soviet intervention. And whatever its grievances against New Delhi—fewer after Mrs. Gandhi's recent visit to America – Washington perhaps realises that it is not in its interest to weaken India or to provoke a war which may suck the Soviet Union with which India has a 20 year "friendship" treaty.

Probably it is the Soviet intervention in Afghanistan that queered the pitch for a no-war pact. By taking an equivocal stand on the issue India lost the opportunity of winning over Pakistan which wanted a clear condemnation of Soviet aggression. Had India at that time initiated a move to formulate a regional defence strategy, Islamabad, which suspects collusion between New Delhi and Moscow, might have been reassured of New Delh. But Mrs.Gandhi tended to lean towards Russia and by the time she decided to suggest withdrawal of Russian troop, Pakistan had joined hands with America and its allies in the Middle East. When I asked Mr. Agha Shahi, then Pakistan Foreign Minister, in New Delhi why Pakistan did not think of a regional approach to the Soviet occuption of Afghanistan he said: "You had already taken a pro-Soviet position which left us with no option expect to look elsewhere."

However, some believe that Pakistan's calculations have undergone a change after the stationing of 100,000 Russian soldiers in Afghanistan and has come to the conclusion that it should befriend India so as to insulate one border. "It is simple: we trust you more than the Russians," said a top Pakistani editor in Lahore when I sought reasons for this.

For Gen. Zia there could be yet another reason: to get recognition from democratic India. When Ayub Khan took over Pakistan on October 7, 1958, Nehru termed it "a naked military dictatorship." But a little more than two years later he went to Pakistan to sign the Indus water treaty with Ayub Khan. Gen. Zia came to power in 1977 and it has taken him five years to be acceptable enough to be invited to Rashtrapati Bhavan and have lunch with Mrs. Gandhi. This will pay him dividends in his own country where he is considered only a dictator shunned by demorcratic New Delhi.

But all this does not mean easy solution. The two sides have a long way to go because the perceptions of the two countries are different. For Islamabad a no-war pact is an end in itself, to insulate its eastern border or ward off the possibility of preemptive strike by India against its nuclear installations to prevent the manufacture of the "Islamic bomb".

For New Delhi, a no-war pact is the means to an end; it will help it to have closer relations with Pakistan which is allowing itself to be sucked into the American strategical arenas. That is the reason why India during the talks so far has insisted on an assurance that Pakistan will not give bases to the US. The seven-point memorandum, which New Delhi sent last year to Islamabad and thereafter, made it clear that the principles of "co-existence" and "non-alignment" that India wanted Pakistan to accept envisaged denial of bases to any foreign power.

Where India and Pakistan differ most is on "bilateralism". India wants problems between the two countries to be solved without any third party's involvement; it also means that Pakistan should not to raise the Kashmir question in any world forum. In a way, it would be freezing the Kashmir issue. The people in Pakistan may not react favourably to this proposal even if Gen. Zia were to agree to it. In fact, India's initiatives in the past did not materialise because Kashmir came to occupy the centre of the stage, sometimes the entire stage. When Jawaharlal Nehru offered a no-war decleration to Pakistan in 1949, the reply of Liaquat Ali Khan was that the causes of war should be removed first, and he listed Kashmir and Indus waters among them.

Nehru then said that such declaration itself would produce an atmosphere that would facilitate settlement of major disputes. Liaquat suggested a time-table for negotiation, after which "all points" of disagreement would be referred for arbitration. Nehru's reaction to this approach was hostile: "To think *ab initio* of a third party.. will also be confession of continued dependence on others". Subsequently, an agreement on the division of the Indus waters was reached but not on Kashmir.

The reaction of Mohammad Ali, Pakistan's Prime Minister in 1953, to a joint no-war declaration was even more unhelpful than Liaquat's. He had once addressed Nehru as *Bada Bhai* (elder brother), but later blamed him for blocking a plebiscite in Kashmir and for leaving "no scope" for settlement. He said: "The case, therefore, must revert to the UN" (where it is still pending).

And as days went by this very proposal for a no-war pact became suspect in the eyes of Pakistan; it came to mean "subservience", even "surrender," to India and acceptance of what is considered Indian annexation of Kashmir. So much so that when India and Pakistan were discussing a peace agreement in Tashkent in January 1966, following the war in 1965 and Lal Bahadur Shastri took up with Gen. Ayub Mohammad, then Pakistan's President, the question of renunciation of force, he did not agree to it. After many days of deadlock, Ayub brought a four-line draft which was only a general statement on the efficacy of finding a solution to Indo-Pakistan problem through peaceful means. Shastri was not satisfied and suggested an amendment which Ayub accepted – in his own hand, the Pakistan President added to the draft the phrase: "Without resort to arms."

But when India asked for an official confirmation of the amended draft, Pakistan said that there never was any draft. Zulfikar Ali Bhutto, then Pakistan's Foreign MInister, apparently had threatened to go back to Pakistan straightaway and "take the nation into confidence", making Ayub knuckle down. The general could not take chances; he had emerged weaker from the 1965 conflict.

When Bhutto was at the helm of affairs in Pakistan after losing East Pakistan (now independent Bangladesh) in 1971, he did not favour a no-war pact. Mrs. Gandhi in 1972 specifically requested Bhutto in Simla to agree to a formal no-war pact, he said it would look like surrender and he could not sell it to his people after losing the war against India.

Now Gen. Zia has picked up the thread. He is conscious that the people in Pakistan do not want another war with a country which is bigger and more powerful. "The people of Pakistan do not want war; their military rulers have realised this, "Mr. Narasimha Rao told me. And he believe it. In India the climate is the same. For the first time there is no consensus on a war with Pakistan. And that explains why both India and Pakistan have not differed on the main two points – "non-aggression" and "peaceful settlement of disputes" – which figure in the aide-memoire they exchanged before the talks and which the Foreign Minister and secretaries on both sides have emphasised.

It has to be concerned that Gen. Zia, a miliatry hic in politics, has proved to be an astute tactician. The other day he went to the extent of saying at a press conference in Karachi that India could send its observers to assess the size of Pakistan's army. He added: "We have already given up (claims to) equality". Agreed, he is trying to score one more propaganda point but why does India lag behind? Why does it not ask Pakistan to make the statement good? Instead India is lost in its own jargon; is effort is to find a "conceptual framework". What does it really mean? Why does not New Delhi came straight to the point? If in its scheme of things, conciliation with Pakistan is important, there is no purpose in delaying a no-war pact, even though there is more than meets the eye in Gen. Zia's moves. New Delhi should accept what Islamabad offers and then build upon them.

In fact, Gen. Zia has gone still further to propose a proportionate reduction in arms. India is bound to argue that since it has to defend longer borders and vast coastline, it needs much more arms than Pakistan. Pursuing Gen. Zia's proposal for reduction of arms and a no-war pact does not mean that India approves of what he does in his own country—his rule is repressive, with no human rights and liberties allowed to his people. But New Delhi has to recognise the facts in Islamabad, however much it dislikes the military junta. The talks held so far between the two countries does suggest that New Delhi does realise this. And there is also the resolution, much is to be gained from peace, for example, the fall out of trade from peace. The two can come nearer through trade, not through a common market—an idea disliked in Pakistan because India is in comparison is a developed country. Bhutto once said: "We will have to see whether we can mutually benefit but in principle I think, as far as a common market is concerned, we are not ready for such an agreement." One estimate is that if India and Pakistan were to have even normal trade, the turnover would be around Rs. 2,000 crore a year.

But both countries, despite the talk of a no-war pact, do not trust each other. And the summit meeting between the Gandhi and Gen. Zia can do little if there is no faith and trust. It will be a tragedy if they continue to be neighbours, mere pawns of the super powers.

Benazir Bhutto: A New Generation Leadership

Talking to Miss Benazir Bhutto in Pakistan last week, I found her friendly to India, with a positive outlook, unlike her father, Z.A. Bhutto who often talked in terms of thousand-year-war against India.

The acting chairperson of the Pakistan People's Party (PPP) said that Pakistan and India must bury the hatchet; "we have had enough of it. Let's start a new chapter".

Miss Bhutto said: "India has a new generation leadership. And I hope that Pakistan will also have a new generation leadership. I hope that these new generation leaderships will be to settle problems, dealing with each other without any of the bitterness of the past and without any of the prejudices of the past."

At public meetings Miss Bhutto speaks in chaste Urdu, Pakistan's official language, which she was not fluent in even two years ago. She has worked hard to learn the language; she has also worked hard to gather facts and figures with which to condemn the military regime in Pakistan.

The interview she gave me was in English and she was very critical of the role of the military and General Zia-ul Haq, the Pakistan President. But of her observation were moderate and she gave the impression that she does not want to stir up the people's anger.

Miss Bhutto is many things to is people. She is their catharsis whereby they purge their sense of guilt for not having protested against the execuse of her father, now a legend in Pakistan: "Bhutto ham sharminda hain, tere katal zinda hain" (Bhutto, we are ashamed because your killers are alive, one of the slogans the people chant, while beating their chests, at the massive gatherings she is attracting even at wayside places.

The following are questions and answers referring to India:

You once mentioned that Pakistan should not play the Sikh card. Do you have firm evidence of Pakistan's complicity?

You see, there are times when I have information on certain matters, but I do not believe in ever speaking about them because it is not fair to somebody. And I being a Pakistani, it is not fair for me to speak in a manner that could further embarrass my country whether I agree or do not agree with the regime. Let me say that as far as PPP is concerned we do not believe in creating tensions; we believe in reducing the tensions. It is a matter of pride for the party that during the period of PPP that democratic India and democratic Pakistan were able to arrive at the Simla Agreement which has provided the longest basis for good relations in the subcontinent . . .

Did you follow the Shah Bano case in India?

I did hear something about how it created a rumpus. I personally believe that I there should be a personal law and civil law. And let the individual decide on the basis of personal law or on the basis of civil law. I do not believe that the government should interfere too much in the privacy of individual's life. But at the same time I do not believe in the cruel, barbaric punishments and laws which this regime (Zia's) has tried to bring about. We believe in equality of man and woman and dignity of each and every individual . . .

Have you any plans to meet Prime Minister Rajiv Gandhi?

At present, as you can see, I am very involved with my aims and objectives for securing elections. But the Prime Minister of India has taken up many challenges and I wish him well in the task he is facing. No doubt, India is facing many problems. But I am sure that he has the energy and capacity to deal with them because he has a good team to help him.

Pakistan Diary

A book in Urdu, *Will Pakistan Break Up ?,* has an interesting passage which suggests that Islamabad had a hand in the 1993 bomb blasts in Mumbai. The author, Munir Ahmed, a journalist, quotes Pakistan's former President Ishaq Khan as having said that one top officer was indulging in such dangerous activities as were harmful and disconcerting for Pakistan. "I had to tell the prime minister that the particular officer wanted to push us into a war with our neighbouring country," said Ishaq Khan.

The pertinent passage reads thus: Former President said that on March 23 the situation became so serious that foreign secretary Shariyar came to him in a disturbed state of mind and said that the leadership with India following the bomb blasts had deteriorated so much that it had threatened to go to war . . . "I told the prime minister to get in touch with New Delhi to stop further deterioration in our relations. He said he (the prime minister) would do it. But he only talked to the Pakistan High Commissioner in New Delhi . . ."

Once in a while a books come out in Pakistan to tell something startling but frank. For example, Altaf Gauhar's book on Ayub Khan, Pakistan's Martial Law Administrator, tells a blow by blow account of Islamabad's involvement in starting the 1965 war. A day before Operation Gibraltar, the code used for 1965 infiltration, was approved by Bhutto, who had been reappointed as foreign minister. He wrote a letter to Ayub in which he advised him that India was "at present in no position to risk a general war of unlimited duration for the annihilation of Pakistan." According to him, "Pakistan enjoyed relative superiority . . . in terms of quality and equipment."

Ayub, although a reluctant participant to what Bhutto did, said "to expect quick results in this struggle, when India has much larger forces than us, would be unrealistic. Therefore, our action should be such that can be sustained over a long period. As a general rule Hindu morale would not stand more than a couple of hard blows at the right time and place. Such opportunities should, therefore, be sought and exploited."

Fundamentalists in Pakistan do not forget and forgive. They have killed Lahore High Court judge Bhatti for having released two years ago a Christian boy, who was wrongly indicated for having cast aspersions on Islam. The boy is living safely in Germany, where he had sought refuge. The judge has, however, paid the price for giving the verdict which the fundamentalists did not like.

People in Lahore recall the judge's assassination with regret. This incident and some other instances of browbeating has made the liberals afraid of fundamentalists. There is fear in the air, although people generally feel that the type of Islam the fundamentalists represent has hamstrung their way of living. But they are too timid to speak out.

When it comes to relations with India, the fundamentalists are intractable. Even a tinge of indication of thaw between the two countries is damned as a surrender to Hindus. That is the reason why the relationship is struck where it was 50 years ago. That also explains the absence of Pakistanis on the Wagh border on the August 14-15 night from the celebrations of the 50th year of the subcontinent's Independence.

While in Lahore, I complained to many who had promised to come to the border but did not. They said Jamait-e-Islami threatened to kill anybody who would go to the border. Threats were followed by telephone calls to prominent persons and leaders of several organisations. The propaganda unleashed was that the celebrations were an attempt to undo partition. Still more than 10,000 people would have reached the Wagah border. But then the Punjab government at Lahore stepped in and issued an order under Section 144 to ban the assembly of more than five people and also sealed the roads leading to the border.

The fundamentalists seem to have frightened Prime Minister Nawaz Sharif as well. He has issued an order that women appearing on television should cover their head and that boys and girls should not sit side by side in public. There is also an unofficial word that records of Indian songs should not be played in public. However, a recent study done in Pakistan indicates that shops from Karachi to Peshawar stocked 92 per cent of records and video cassettes from India.

Government, more so the establishment, puts all the time spokes in the path of relations with India. However, it is amazing to find the warmth a Pakistani has towards an Indian. He goes out of the way to shower his affection and hospitality. One hears them talking about their friends living across the border and wishing further relaxation in the visa system. There were complaints from some that their applications for visas were rejected without any rhyme or reason. But the delay was mentioned by many.

Surprisingly, when it comes to political hold, the fundamentalists have very little to show. It seems that the Pakistanis do not vote in the name of Islam. In fact, candidates with such plank are roundly defeated. The Pakistan National Assembly does not have even five members of fundamentalists. Pakistanis do have a swipe at us by pointing out that the BJP appealing in the name of Hindutva has 30 per cent of seats in the Lok Sabha.

The old Dingha Singh building at the Mall in Lahore is due to be demolished. After partition, scores of people occupied the building and became owners over the years. Their demands for ownership were so many that the court could not reconcile them. It ordered that the building be auctioned and the money collected from it be distributed among the claimants.

While talking of migrants, the Mujahir Qwami Movement (MQM) is quiet. When I was in Karachi some time in 1996, they almost dictated terms. The city was tense and there was flight of capital. This has almost changed. Now there is no fear even when you walk through the MQM congested areas. There is normalcy. However, hundreds of MQM leaders and followers have been physically eliminated. In some cases, it has been a cold-blood murder. But then the argument is "how do you deal with violent movements?" It is the same question which is posed in India at disturbed places. I still believe that the law protectors cannot take the law into their own hands. There is something called human rights and they should be protected.

It is an interesting interview by Quaid-i-Azam Mohammad Ali Jinnah that a Pakistani newspaper has published. It is from the days when the division of the subcontinent was two months old. This is significant in the present context when the two countries are trying to develop good relations. Jinnah said he would not accept the proposal of forming a Union of the two sovereign countries of Pakistan and India under a common Centre. Dilating upon the two-nation theory, he said that the theory was not only an ideal but a concrete reality. He said India had been divided on the basis of this historical truth. Horrible incidents that occurred during the last two months and the scheme of evacuating Hindus from Pakistan by the Indian Union had established the truth of the two-nation theory.

Jinnah characterised the communal riots as a deep-rooted conspiracy, the main purpose of which was to shake the foundation of the new state of Pakistan. The remedy to this agonising situation, Jinnah asserted, was that India should crush the demon of communal riots with an iron hand and break the web of conspiracies woven in this regard. He regretted the mischievous propaganda that the Muslim League had betrayed the Muslim minority in India, where it would continue to suffer in the future and that Pakistan would not be able to take care of them.

4

The Problem of Kashmir: Effects on Indo-Pak Relations

Kashmir, Nehru and Sheikh Abdullah
This is not the first time that Srinagar and New Delhi will be talking over the quantum of accession. Some 40 years ago the same exercise was done. Sheikh Mohammad Abdullah had been released after a decade of internment. Prime Minister Jawaharlal Nehru had realised the mistake of having detained him after his statements conveying that Kashmir was not a bonded slave of India.

Nehru's interlocutor was Lal Bahadur Shastri. The Sheikh's associate was Mirza Afzal Beg, a Kashmiri with vast legal and constitutional background. The talking point was the fallout from the instrument of accession which the Maharaja of Jammu and Kashmir had signed to integrate the state with the Indian Union after the British had left. This instrument had given New Delhi only three subjects: Defence, Foreign Affairs and Communications.

After the detention of the Sheikh in 1953, the whole concept of autonomy underwent a change. New Delhi got pushed beyond the three subjects. Many laws were "enacted" by the pliable state assemblies. The Sheikh questioned the basis of all such laws and wanted them withdrawn.

Shastri, the Sheikh and Beg would talk almost every day on this subject. I was then Shastri's information officer. The press briefings were dull because there was no real information to communicate except that the three had met. After a few days, the newspapers stopped carrying even that bit.

I would often inquire from Shastri what they were discussing. He would reply, "Practically nothing." They went over again and again which laws were enacted in the state or extended to it when the Sheikh was under detention. To verify whether they were outside the three subjects—defence, foreign affairs and communications—the Sheikh's repeated question was how New Delhi had come to extend certain central laws to Jammu and Kashmir when it had no authority to do so. Shastri was on the defensive.

"What is in the mind of the Sheikh?" I once asked Shastri privately. First, he hesitated a bit, then said that the Skeikh was for independence. Reports in the fifties were that the concept of independence was someting which Adlai Stevenson, who once contested the US presidential election, had told to the Sheikh at Srinagar when the two met.

The talks between Shastri and the Sheikh were suspended when the latter visited Pakistan. Nahru's idea was to associate Pakistan with a final solution. Sheikh did not talk about independence to General Ayub Khan, then martial law administrator, as the records say. But the Sheikh reportedly proposed a condominium or confederation. Ayub Khan rejected both the proposals. Nehru died suddenly in 1964 and Shastri in 1966. This ended the Sheikh's dream.

Prime Minister Indira Gandhi picked up the thread in the beginning of the seventies. GP Parthasarathy, a senior bureaucrat whom she used often for important talks, was the interlocutor. By then East Pakistan had seceded from Pakistan to become independent Bangladesh.

During his dicsussions with Parthasarthy, the Sheikh was in a chastened mood. He dropped the title of Prime Minister for the chief minister of Jammu and Kashmir. He accepted many laws which the centre had extended to the state "with its permission." They went beyond the three subjects—defence, foreign affairs and communications. What is known as the Indira . Sheikh accord was reached and Kashmir could review central laws extended to the state. Its was not the autonomy of the 1953 status but it gave Jammu and Kashmir a visible identity. The Sheikh did realise that he did not have the pull which he had once at the centre. The matter was left at that.

Chief Minister Farooq Abdullah and his son Omar Abdullah, the National Conference president, are legally correct in their contention that the state acceded to India, only in three subjects. But when the Sheikh, the person who was mainly responsible for accession to India, himself agreed to rules and regulation beyond the three subjects, how can his successors reopen the whole thing and reject the changes the Sheikh had concurred with?

The threat by Omar Abdullah that New Delhi should either accept the 1953 status or face thee Hurriyat's independence does not create any ripples. If he can reconcile himself to his presence in the BJP-led government even after the Gujarat carnage, he can also water down his demand. He should learn from his father that riding two horses at the same time is politically possible, if not morally.

The 1953 autonomy is certainly a possibility. But it can't happen until the rest of India is convinced that after the 1953 autonomy status there will be brought round—may be America and the UK can do so.

My fear is that the RSS, whose parivar includes the BJP has already made up its mind. It has proposed the trifurcation of the state because it has come to believe that the 1953 status will not be the final solution, acceptable either to the Muslim-majority valley of Kashmir or Pakistan. It is a communal approach. But the RSS is not associated with anything else. It thinks that the Hindu-majority Jammu and the Buddhist—majority Ladakh must be "saved."

Unfortunately Kashmiriyat, a secular pull, has weakened in the state over the years. Terrorists have played havoc with it. They have communalised the movement, which was once for a democratic, secular state. Their planned killing of Hindus and Sikhs has contaminated Kashmir. Whether it was Qasim Nagar a few days earlier or Kala Chat two months ago, their target was one religious community. Jammu is a Hindu majority region which has largely stayed away from the movement in the valley. Its problems with Srinagar are many but it has been part and pacel of secular democratic structure. The exit of Kashmiri pandits gave the state a jolt but it was able to hold together. The climate is changing now. The killing by the terrorists and the propaganda for trifurcation are too much for Kashmiriyat. On top of it some in the Hurriyat do not believe in the concept of pluralism. And the Pakistan establishment has seldom it shirked from playing a communal card.

Islamabad may have reached infltration but the damage it has done to itself and India in supporting religious and jehadi elements is irreparable. A new mood has come to prevail, that of fundamentalism. It is a Frankenstein's monster and it is now eating up Pakistan. It also has an adverse effect on India's pluralistic society. Muslims are bearing the brunt. This suits the Hindutva forces. They can spread their hate-Muslim policy more effectively.

The Muslim community is not getting its due either politically, economically or socially. Less than three per cent of Muslims have employment in government. The representation in state assemblies and Parliament is also low, not proportional to the 15 per cent population. And when a carnage like the one in Gujarat gets pushed into the background without the guilty being punished the secular character of India becomes a bigger question mark.

Even then a Muslim has been elected as the President of India. Two Muslims made the country proud when India beat England in the Natwest Trophy cricket final at Lord's. Another Muslim produced a film, *Lagaan*, which reached the highest slot by getting nominated for an Oscar. Such instances sustain hopes that despite the efforts to Hinduise the society, the minority community is not disheartened and is with the majority in wanting to take India to the pinnacle of glory.

Certain problems get more tangled with the passage of time. Both Kashmir and Nagaland would have been easier to sort out if they had not been allowed to accumulate the dust of convenience and callousness.

India could have won the plebiscite it promised to the people of Jammu and Kashmir until 1952 when Sheikh Abdullah, who had helped integrate the state with the Indian Union, was detained without trial. Phizo in Nagaland was more tractable in 1950 after the Shillong accord that promised autonomy to the Nagas. Both the Sheikh and Phizo felt betrayed when New Delhi tried to sell the illusion of power.

India has been impaled on the horns of a dilemma for a long time. It cannot let Kashmir go even though the links are more legal than emotional. After repeatedly saying that the state is part of motherland, it has to reckon with public repercussions. Nagaland's case is still more curious. It was never part of India during the British period. Having declared it as a state in the Union, how can New Delhi allow it to break away or justify even something closer?

Generations after generation, boys and girls have grown up in India with the belief that Kashmir and Nagaland are integral parts of the country. No government at the centre has ever conveyed any other impression. Nor has any political party has had the conviction or courage to say anything different. People are convinced that all the territory—from Kashmir to Kohima—is India's and anyone raising a doubt about it is a "traitor".

Consequently, the attempts to solve the two problems have been limited to certain parameters: how to reconcile the demands of sovereignty by certain sections with a status within the Union. The demand for secession or independence has been derided, never put on the agenda.

Over the years, national sentiments on both Kashmir and Nagaland have got so hardened and so entrenched that any concession suggesting a status beyond India is sure to be considered a 'betrayal All' governments and political parties know that. True, there is a consensus not to disturb the status quo, if nothing else is possible.

The stationing of the armed forces in the two states—Kashmir and Nagaland—have strengthened the feeling that those challenging the integration have to be crushed forcibly. Any eruption is looked upon as the violation of India's security. Different army commanders posted in the two states have said that the solution to the situation is political, not military.

New Delhi tends to agree with that. But what does it offer to the militants in Kashmir or Nagaland, which satisfies them without impinging on the country's unity? No out of—the—way solution, much less radical, seems possible because the nation has never been presented with the alternatives. Nor is it prepared for them.

India's first Prime Minister, Jawaharlal Nehru, who did probably realise the problems the country would face in Kashmir, sent Sheikh Abdullah to Pakistan to meet General Ayub Khan. It was a bit late because by then the Indian opinion had hardened, particularly when Nehru had himself said that Kashmir was part of "our motherland."

It is difficult to believe what Ayub's close aide, Altaf Gauhar, has written about the meeting between the Sheikh and Ayub .Gauhar has said in his book, *Ayub Khan*, what the Sheikh told

Ayub: "The future of Kashmir lies with Pakistan." There was nothing in the Sheikh's activities after his return from Islamabad in 1964 to indicate that he could have said so. In fact, after sweeping the polls in Kashmir in 1977, he said that the vote in his favour was "for accession to India."

The Nagaland problem too saw some activity. The then Assam Chief Minister, Chaliha, headed a team to talk the Nagas. An official ceasefire was announced and a white flag was flown over a place to underline that the two sides would begin talks in an atmosphere of peace. But nothing concrete took shape.

As days went by, Nehru transferred to the Home Minister the charge of Nagaland, which was looked after by the ministry of External Affairs. This ended the semblance of belief that Nagaland was not a domestic problem. Phizo, desperate and disillusioned went to London, sensing that New Delhi was not yet prepared for political negotiations.

The nation could not suspect anything. The Nagas participated in elections for parliament and the state assembly the voting was always above 50 per cent. The violence in the area was considered part of hazards a country faced on its frontiers.

Kashmir at least showed its resentment over the status quo through the boycott of polls. Since the major part of military was from across the border, the Kashmir movement, at one time mostly indigenous, lost its elan and sympathisers in India. Human rights activists did point out the excesses committed by the security forces. But the rightists pounced upon them as if what they were doing was anti—national.

Fortunately, the government has again begun probing to find out if there is a possibility to move further in Kashmir and Nagaland. It has sounded influential segments within the Nagas to know whether a settlement of sorts is possible. But New Delhi's predicament is that it is no sure what it can ladle out to meet the expectations, which are high both within Kashmir and Nagaland.

The Hurriyat in Kashmir appears once again determined to boycott the election. Its argument is that its participation would harm its cause of independence because as candidates, they would have to affirm their loyalty to India's unity and integrity. The Hurriyat leaders are unnecessarily stretching the point. If they could give a similar affirmation while applying for their passports, why not do so while contesting elections? Ayub rejected the idea of condominium or confederation between India, Pakistan and Kashmir when the Sheikh mentioned it to him. Ayub believed that federations came to be dominated by the major parties.

New Delhi can sit back and wait for the contradictions to appear within the Hurriyat and the Nagas. It can even encourage them but it will be a shoddy spectacle, which may tangle the problem still more. Perhaps one way can be to hold and free elections in both the states in the presence of human rights activists from within India. Some groups in Kashmir and Nagaland may boycott but New Delhi's declaration that it would discuss the future with the elected representatives will go a long way to persuade many.

As far as Nagaland is concerned, a close associate of Phizo, Khodao-Yanthan, told me in London in 1990, when I was India's High Commissioner there, that Phizo had wanted to settle the Nagaland question with the Indian leaders and he wanted to advise his friends to give up violence and seek solution within the framework of India. I passed on the information to New Delhi. Why this point is not on the agenda of talks with the Nagas is something I really do not understand. Why has it not been included?

Still it looks as if it may be possible to bring round political parties to give Kashmir—as well as Nagaland—a special status. They will have complete autonomy except in the areas of defence, foreign affairs and communications, as was the Kashmir Maharaja's original instrument of accession. But this can be the final solution, not the starting point. The nation is in no mood to accept anything else. Against the backdrop of the resurgence of Hindu fundamentalism, it may be tough going for the Muslim—majority Kashmir and the Christian—majority Nagaland.

Even after India completing 55 years of independence, Kashmir remains a problem. And New Delhi has messed it up again. This time it is doing of the BJP-led government. Heavens would not have fallen if the state election had been deferred. Surely, the purpose is not to go over the exercise but to involve people. When Prime Minister Atal Behari Vajpayee repeatedly says that election will be free and fair, it amounts to an assurance that there will be such an atmosphere where every voter can participate.

When there is not even a semblance of effort to create such conditions, there is bound to be suspicion and doubt over the government's intentions. It is apparent that the main political parties were expecting New Delhi to have talks with them through its various interlocutors before the announcement of election. Naturally, the reaction could not be favourable.

The Hurriyat is categorical in its 'no'. Shabir Shah, the mildest among "the separatists" says he has no option except to boycott. He indeed wanted to participate in the election and was looking for some gesture to justify his participation. Even the Mufti Party's Mehbooba, who challenged New Delhi's arrogance, but not its authority, had expected that the government would do something, at least impose governor's rule, to make her cooperation feasible. She is far from happy. The Congress, the main opposition, is yet to assess the sincerity of the Vajpayee government holding free and fair election. What has been said or done in the state does not appear credible enough to the party.

New Delhi should have neen concerned over the way the main political formations are behaving. It cannot afford to have a situation where the ruling National Democratic Alliance is the only player. How will it serve New Delhi's purpose in its endeavour to put Jammu and Kashmir on the track of representative governance? New Delhi should realise that the coming election in the state is crucial to establish its credibility not only in India but the world over. The very solution of the Kashmir problem is linked with the polls. The Vajpayee government cannot go in the cavalier manner it has done so far.

The international community, waiting anxiously for the election, will also be looking for the turnout. One need not take its reaction seriously even though Secretary of State Collin Powell has said that Kashmir is on the "international stage" . Still the boycott by the major parties may raise eyebrows and lessen the credibility of the polls. And what does New Delhi prove if the ruling National Conference (NC) makes it alone? The manner in which the party withheld the pressure of terrorists is commendable. It stands courageously in the field despite the murder of hundreds of its activists. But had it given the reins of administration to the state governor after the announcement of election, its stock would have gone still higher. But then even Omar Abdullah, chairman of the NC, has not resigned from the central cabinet.

Yet it is not too late to retrieve lost ground. Let New Delhi say it loud and clear that the government will hold talks with the elected representatives on the future of the state within the Indian Union. The proposal by the Hurriyat's Sajjat Lone that the election can be part of a dialogue with them (the separatists) is worth pursuing. He has given New Delhi an opening as his father had done before his assassination.

New Delhi should not be unnecessarily chary of suspicious of the new crop of elected representatives. They would have affirmed loyalty to India's integrity before their contest. The Hurriyat's objection to such a requirement is only for record. Their leaders have submitted a similar affirmation whenever they have gone abroad on an Indian passport.

Still the government cannot run away from the fact that the state has a special status under the constitution (Article 70). This is because the state joined the Indian Union on certain conditions, giving New Delhi only defence, foreign affairs and communications. It is for the state to expand the three subjects, not for the Union to do so. In fact, Kashmir's first chief minister (then called Wazir-e-Aazam) conceded quite a lot of power beyond the three subjects.

The real problem is that New Delhi has always fallen short of expectations of the people of Kashmir, first by encroaching on their exclusive constitutional territory and then suppressing their legitimate demands by force. Today the same situation exists in a different way—Kashmir asserting its right to maintain its identity and the government of India using all methods to water down even the reduced powers given to the state. However, both chief minister Farooq Abdullah and the Hurriyat have gone about the wrong way to restore the state's identity, the former by avowing all loyalty to New Delhi; the latter by introducing violence with the assistance of Pakistan. In the process, the people of Kashmir have got alienated.

The BJP-led central government has aggravated the situation: it has taken up its Hindutva agenda in right earnest in the state itself. This will further distance Muslims in the valley where the Gilanis in the Hurriyat have already destroyed the

Kashmiriyat, a plural concept. The proposal to bifurcate the state into the Buddhist Ladakh, the Hindu Jammu and the Muslim valley is meant to divide it on communal lines, with a bigger agenda in the rest of the country.

The BJP has said that it is opposed to bifurcation. Nobody takes it seriously because the proposal has come from its parent body, the RSS. The latter has already constituted the Jammu State Morcha to contest the election. Its appeal to the BJP to jointly fight the election to avoid a split in the parivar vote is to span the seemingly opposite positions. Strange, NC continues to be part of the ruling National Democratic Alliance at the centre.

The fresh bout of violence—the government has failed to protect the Amarnath yatris despite all assurances is meant to scare away voters. This can further lessen the turnout. By allowing international observers, New Delhi will be helping them to put thing in a proper perspective. If it does not like "white—skinned observers," let it invite NGOs from the SAARC countries. They will go down well with the Indian activists.

Political Stand of Hurriyat

With due deference to the Kashmir Committee, the exercise it going over has been gone over many a time before. There is little use in repeating it. The Hurriyat stand is well known and so is that of Shabir Shah and others. I have not seen anything which suggests that they have resiled from their position. By covering the same ground, the committee has unnecessarily evoked hope which has no basis.

The problem is with New Delhi. At one time it said that the sky was the limit. On another occasion it gave the impression as if it would consider a status within India which need not be within the constitution. Then there was the talk of going back to the status, which the state enjoyed before Sheikh Abdullah arrest. Now the word is "decolution" of power. This is applicable to the rest of India where, after the Sarkaria Commission's report on centre-state relations, power should have been decentralised from the centre to the states and from the states to the districts and villages. But the BJP has always favoured a strong centre.

Therefore, it is not possible for the states to get more powers till the Vajpayee government is at the centre. The case of Kashmir is, however, different. The appropriate word is autonomy. It joined the Union on the understanding that its integration to

India was confined to three subjects—defence, external affairs and communications. Article 370 of the constitution recognises the fact. What more subjects the state should transfer to the Union are the prerogative of Jammu and Kashmir. Its assembly is the authority. After his release, Sheikh Abdullah conceded some more territory to New Delhi. The rest is encroachment.

During the last session of Parliament, the deputy prime minister, L.K. Advani, said there was no going back to the original status. That is not for the Union to decide. It will be reneging on its promise to the state at the time of integration if the state's autonomy is chipped away without its consent. In fact, New Delhi is mainly responsible for today's state of things, first having its own nominees at Srinagar and encroaching on the state's rights to choose the government and then not creating the democratic climate which the other states in the country enjoy.

The threat by Omar Abdullah that New Delhi should either accept the 1953 status or face the Hurriyat's independence demand does not create any ripples. If he can reconcile himself to his presence in the BJP-led govenment even after the Gujrat carnage, he can also water down his demands. He should learn from his father that riding two horses at the same time is politically possible, but not morally.

The 1953 autonomy is certainly a possibility. But it cannot happen unit the rest of India is convince that after the 1953 autonomy status there will be no problem called Kashmir. Both the Hurriyat and Pakistan have to understand this. They have to be brought round—may be the United States and the United Kingdom can do so.

My fear is that the RSS, whose parivar includes the BJP, has already made up its mind. It has proposed the trifurcation of the state because it has come to believe that the 1953 status will not be the final solution, acceptable either to the Muslim-majority valley of Kashmir Pakistan. It is a communal approach. But the RSS is not associated with anything else. It thinks that the Hindu-majority Jammu and the Buddhist-majority Ladakh must be "saved".

Unfortunately Kashmiriyat, a secular pull, has weakened in the state over the years. Terrorists have played havoc with it. They have communalised the movement which once stood for a democratic, secular state. Their planned killing of Hindus and Sikhs has contaminated Kashmir. Whether it was Qasim Nagar a few days earlier or Kaluchak two months ago, their target was one religious community. Jammu is a Hindu majority region which has largely stayed away from the movements in the valley. Its problems with Srinagar are many but it has been part and parcel of the secular democratic structure. The exit of Kashmir Pandits gave the state a jolt but it was able to hold together.

The climate is changing now. The killings by the terrorists and the propaganda for trifurcation are too much for Kashmiriyat. On top of it, some in the Hurriyat do not believe in the concept of pluralism. And the Pakistan establishment has seldom shirked from playing a communal card.

Islamabad may have lessened infiltration but the damage it has done to itself and India in supporting religious and jehadi elements is irreparable. A new mood has come to prevail, that of fundamentalism. It is a Frankenstein's monster and it is now eating up Pakistan. It also has an adverse effect on India's pluralistic society. Muslims are bearing the brunt. This suits the Hindutva forces. They can spread their "hate Muslim" policy more effectively.

Kashmir was never easy to solve. But the hardliners in the Hurriyat have made it still more difficult. True, they have their own interests to serve to keep the question burning. Still they could have let Kashmir settle down to even a modicum of peace, which it badly wants. The Hurriyat seems hoisted with its own petard. It has to sustain violence to keep the spotlight on Kashmir's "unrest".

Dictating terms to the Prime Minister, who said he was willing to meet the Hurriyat, is neither public nor realistic. He is the one it has to deal with and no amount of bravado can work. It looks that after the assassination of Abdul Ghani Lone, there is so much of fear that even the moderates prefer to keep quiet. I believe Maulvi Omar Farooq wanted to meet the Prime Minister during his Srinagar visit. But the hardliners reportedly came in the way. The presence of Yasim Malik, in jail at present, may have made the difference. But New Delhi does not know how to deal with him.

The Hurriyat is fractured combination that may not last in its present form when there is a let-up in the current phase of confrontation between India and Pakistan. The hardliners for associating Pakistan with the talk is understandable but it is putting the cart before the horse. It goes without saying that Islamabad will be brought into the picture before any agreement. New Delhi has itself conceded this in the Shimla Agreement that representatives of the two sides will meet "for the final settlement on Jammu and Kashmir."

Dictated by Abdul Ghani Bhatt and Syed Ali Shah, the Hurriyat is spoiling its case by openly siding wih Pakistan. The frequency with which the two are in and out of the Pakistan High Commission at Delhi has already raised doubts about their credentials. In fact, the entire Hurriyat has come under suspicion because of people like them. What is not realised is that the terrorists are only creating anti—Kashmiri feeling in India. Ultimately, its Parliament will endorse if the settlement goes beyond the limits of the constitution. How does the present role of the Hurriyat help? As an adversary, it has annoyed even those parts of the country which used to shrug their shoulders whenever the name of Kashmir was mentioned. And the Hurriyat stand on the Kashmiri pandits makes little sense when its chief Bhatt says that their return to the valley would depend on the solution of Kashmir. Had it their support, the problem would have assumed to more acceptable complexion.

Even otherwise, the Hurriyat has allowed itself to be hijacked by the fundamentalists. They have given religious colouring to a movement which began a revolt against rigged state elections in 1987. Still worse is the Hurriyat's entire focus on the preponderant Muslim-populated valley. This has alienated two other parts of the state—Jammu with its Hindu majority and Ladakh with its Buddhist majority. Influential official circles in Pakistan do not hide the fact that they want only the valley—is the unfinished agenda of partition. General Pervez Musharrf's reiteration that "Kashmir resides in the hearts of Pakistanis" only whips up the sentiment; if does not solve the problem.

There is little thinking on the harm the division of the state on communal lines would do to whatever secularism is left in India after the Gujarat carnage. Islamabad is riding the horse of fanaticism and sponsoring terrorists with instructions to select Hindus for their bullets for repercussions in the rest of India. If Islamabad wants a solution of Kashmir—so do members of the international community—the communal divide has to be ruled out. Unfortunately, Pakistan and its cat's paw, the Hurriyat, have nothing else on their mind.

There is no doubt that leaders like Malik have failed to influence the thinking of the hardliners in the Hurriyat. But he can take the credit for changing people in the valley from their tilt towards Pakistan to independence. Is such a solution possible? Islamabad may be encouraging it because it believes that the independent valley will ultimately join Pakistan. No such proposition is saleable to any political party in India, much less to the ruling BJP which wants to scrap even Article 370 that gives a special status to Kashmir. Even the demand for autonomy whereby four or five subjects are administered by the centre and the rest by Jammu and Kashmir has been rejected by the BJP-led central government despite the state assembly passing a resolution to that effect.

The Prime Minister, in his Kerala musings last year, said that he did not want to traverse the beaten path. Surely, after 50 years there has to be something tangible. Even the military, which has now become part of Kashmir's landscape, says that the solution has to be political. The reason why the problem has been hanging fire for so long is probably the absence of a policy on Kashmir.

A fair, free election is the means, not the end. Where do we go from there? It cannot be one set of rulers going out and another set coming in. Secession in any is ruled out but has any exercise been made to find out what else I acceptable to the valley? Economic package is all right but this alone cannot meet the aspirations of Kashmiris.

New Delhi should realise that it is also to blame for the mess in the state. People were never allowed to rule themselves as was the case in other parts of the country. Election after election was rigged to install the government the rulers at New Delhi found convenient. The administration was repressive and unaccountable. There were innumerable human rights violations. Every protest or dissenter was suppressed because New Dehi did not know what it wanted to achieve. That is still the case.

Kashmir Committee and Ram Jethmalani

The Kashmir Committee, chaired by Ram Jethmalani, was a non-starter from day one. It began functioning after the elections had been announced. And all its efforts were concentrated on making the different parties in the state polls.

How could they do so when New Delhi had promised only "free and fair election ?" This was relevant till the 1987 polls. That was the last election the Kashmiris wanted to see whether New Delhi or Srinagar had learnt any lesson from the past and whether they would hold an indepenedent election. When it turned out to be a rigged one, a lot of the youth lost faith in the ballot box itself. This was when they picked up the guns Islamabad was too willing to supply.

The expectation from the Kashmir Committee was not the reiteration of free and fair election, but the political package it could offer. It seems that Jethmalani had no brief from New Delhi on that point. He had jumped into the fray on his own. Deputy Prime Minister L.K. Advani did not think there was any harm if he threw in the government's name as long as he talked about elections and subsequent dialogue.

True, Jethmalani got all the publicity and attention. That was because people in Kashmir cling to even a straw of hope in the sea of disappointment. But he has messed up the chances of any other unofficial team which the centre may want to have to talk to the separatists. It would be suspect in their eyes. Talks through unofficial channels have become a joke because New Delhi has used too many—K.C. Pant, A.S. Dulat and Wajiatullah —to offer too little.

The Jethmalani committee has not broken even new ground. The Hurriyat's 'no' or Shabir Shah's, 'conditional no' was already known. To run down the Hurriyat, as Jethmalani has done after the talks, is neither here nor there. Its credentials are not hidden. How representative is the body is in the valley can be judged from the fact that everyone from Delhi makes a beeline to the Hurriyat's headquarters.

That the Hurriyat has Washington's blessings may create problems for New Delhi in the days to come. America's intentions are far from pious. Had it put pressure on the Hurriyat—on Pakistan as well—it would have participated in the elections. Secretary of State Powell's statement that Kashmir is on the international agenda is ominous.

Against this backdrop, it is all the more necessary that the forthcoming elections in Kashmir are credible and look to be so.

But the continuance in office of Farooq Abdullah at Srinagar and that of his son, Omar Abdullah in New Delhi, creates doubts. They must resign to stop the wagging tongues.

The presence of foreign observers will help because they will be to see whether fear keeps away the voters from the polling booths or whether they are themselves boycotting the election. The violence in the valley may make foreign observers appreciate the dangers New Delhi faces because of cross-border terrorism. If the foreign media is there, besides representatives of foreign mission, how foreign observers can have an adverse effect on the Election Commission's autonomy—a point made by New Delhi—is difficult to comprehend.

Jethmalani has also, unwittingly, underlined the separtion of the valley from the rest of the state. The committee never visited Jammu or Ladakh. The Sangh parivar is advocating a trifurcation thesis. He should have denounced it. Dividing the state into Muslim valley, the Hindu Jammu and the Buddhist Ladakh is communal proposition which will damage our pluralistic policy beyond repair. The committee should have made it clear.

The point that New Delhi has to focus on is autonomy. The state joined the Union on certain conditions. In the instrument of accession, the ruler of J& K transferred to the centre only three subjects: defence, foreign affairs and communications. Article 370 was included in the constitution to recognise the separate status of the state. The Union has no authority to hog more subjects on its own. Only the state can do so. Sheikh Abdullah agreed to go beyond the original terms during his talks with Lal Bahadur Shastri and G. Parthasarathy, Mrs. Indira Gandhi's representative. If any more authority is required by the state, the assembly must endorse that.

During the last session of Parliament, both Advani and opposition leader Manmohan Singh said that there was no going back to the original status. That is not for the Union to decide. The assembly's concurrence is essential. New Delhi will be reneging on its promise to the state at the time of integration if the state's autonomy is chipped off without its consent. In fact, New Delhi is mainly responsible for today's state of thing, first having its own nominee at Srinagar and encroaching on the state's right and then not creating the democratic character which the other states in the country enjoy.

Even a person like Jawaharlal Nehru committed the mistake of detaining the Sheikh and running the state as New Delhi's colony for more than a decade. The latter's fault was that he wanted New Delhi to make the undertaking given to Srinagar good. Nehru realised where he went wrong but died before he could rectify it.

Nehru also realised that without the association of Pakistan, the problem could not be solved. Even though there was no cross-border terrorism at that time, the pro-Pakistan feeling was substantially visible in the valley.

When the Sheikh proposed ideas like a condominium or federation at Islamabad, General Ayub Khan, then Pakistan's President rejected them. He reportedly argued that Pakistan would not accept an arrangement where it was at the mercy of the majority. However, before any other proposal could come up, the Sheikh returned to New Delhi because of Nehru's sudden death. Many things have happened since to dent New Delhi's confidence in Islamabad. The latter violated the undertaking it gave—first at Tashkent (1966), and then at Shimla (1972)— not to try to change the status quo by resorting to arms. From the 1965 war to the current cross-border terrorism, Pakistan has defeated the letter and spirit of every agreement.

Probably it is that realisation which has made General Musharraf drop the reference to the Shimla Agreement along with the UN resolutions. Once Pakistan foreign minister Abdus Sattar, when he was the High Commissioner in New Delhi, said that Pakistan had responded to India's protests by mentioning the Shimla Agreement and the UN resolutions together. The change was visible when he was the foreign minister under Musharraf.

By crossing out the minutes of the Shimla Agreement of the Lahore Declaration, Islamabad does not help the situation. It is the violence and cross-border terrorism which must be eschewed whichever agreement gives it validity. One bad thing that has happened over the years is the communalisation of the state. Some of the Hurriyat leaders are as much responsible for it in the valley as are the Sangh parivar in Jammu. Neither Islamabad nor the Hurriyat leaders realise the effect on the subcontinent if the Muslim-majority valley were to secede from

India. Firsty, will any government at Delhi allow it? Secondly, can a government doing so stay in power.

In fact, the main difficulty that the Hurriyat faces is not on the question whether New Delhi is prepared to have a dialogue with it. Its main problem is that ofter promising Kashmiris independence, how does it participate in the election which gives no such hope. The Ram Jethmalanicommittee should have realised the Hurriyat's limitations as well as its own.

II

With due reference to the Kashmir Committee the exercise it is doing has been gone over many a time before. There is little use in repeating it. The Hurriyat stand is well known and so is that of Shabir Shah and others. I have not seen anything which suggests that they have resiled from their position. By covering the same ground, the Committee has unnecessarily evoked hope which has no basis.

The problem is with New Delhi. At one time it said that the sky is the limit. On another occasion it gave the impression as if it would consider a status within India which need not be within the Constitution. Then there was the talk of going back to the status which the state enjoyed before Sheikh Abdullah's arrest. Now the word coined is 'devolution' of power. This is applicable to the rest of India where, after the Sarkaria Commission's report on Centre-state Relations, power should have been decentralised from the centre to the states and from the states to the districts and villages. But the BJP has always favoured a strong centre. Therefore, it is not possible for the states to get more power till the Vajpayee government is at the centre.

The case of Kashmir is, however, different. The appropriate word is autonomy. It joined the Union on the understanding that its integration to India was confined to three subjects: defence, external affairs and communications. Article 370 of the Constitution recognised that fact. What more subjects the state should transfer to the Union is the prerogative of Jammu and Kashmir. Its assembly is the authority. After his release, Sheikh Abdullah conceded some territory to New Delhi. The rest is encroachment.

Unfortunately Kashmiriyat, a secular pull, has weakened in the state over the years. Terrorists have played havoc with it. They have communalised the movement, which was once for a democratic, secular state. Their planned killing of Hindus and Sikhs has contaminated Kashmir. Whether it was Qasim Nagar a few days earlier or Kalu Chowk two months ago, their target was one religious community. Jammu is a Hindu majority region which has largely stayed away from the movements in the valley. Its problems with Srinagar are many but it has been part and parcel of a secular democratic structure. The exit of Kashmiri pundits gave the state a jolt but it was able to hold together. The climate is changing now. The killing by the terrorists and the propaganda for trifurcation are too much for Kashmiriyat. On top of it some in the Hurriyat do not believe in the concept of pluralism. And the Pakistan establishment has seldom shirked from playing a communal card.

Islamabad may have lessened infiltration but the damage it has done to itself and India in supporting religious and *jehadi* elements is irreparable. A new mood has come to prevail, that of fundamentalism. It is a Frankentein's monster and it is now eating up Pakistan. It also has an adverse effect on India's pluralistic society. Muslims are bearing the brunt. This suits the Hindutva forces. They can spread their hate-Muslim policy more effectively.

Assassination of Abdul Ghani Lone: A Warning

The assassination of Abdul Ghani Lone is a warning—this time drenched in the blood of a tall Kashmiri leader—that the problem of Kashmir cries for an early solution. When Prime Minister Atal Behari Vajpayee said in his Kerala musings that he would adopt an unbeaten path, it was assumed that he was conscious of the aspirations of the people of Kashmir. Mr. K.C. Pant may be a good Planing Minister but when he was Home Minister in New Delhi he just followed in the footsteps of his predecessors on Kashmir.

Mr. Vajpayee's predicament is that he does not want to go beyond his esoteric group, which has not been able to bring the problem closer to a solution even an inch. But the main problem is that we have no policy on Kashmir. First when we could have won the plebiscite, Sheikh Abdullah was interned and then when he went to Islamabad to meet General Ayub Khan, his trip was cut short because of the death of Jawaharlal Nehru. The discussion was around a federal structure embracing Kashmir and the rest of the subcontinent but before the Sheikh could mollify the fears of General Ayub—in a federal structure the majority ultimately prevails the Kashmiri leader had to return.

The timing of the recent incident in Jammu seems to have been chosen deliberately. When the country is going through a crisis of communal divide, such an incident can only aggravate the situation. It can be godsend opportunity to those who believe in Hindutva and who are trying to tear asunder the fabric of a pluralistic society of the country. But what does a military dictator care when he is not answerable even to his own people?

Mere condemnation by America is not enough. It has done this before. It has to put pressure on General Musharraf who may be going along with it on Afghanistan but not on India. The policy of Pakistan's military junta (the army has practically ruled the country since its foundation) is to fuel hostility against India so as to justify the denial of democratic structure to the Pakistanis. From General Ayub Khan to General Musharraf, Islamabad's intention has been to see if India can be disintegrated into six-seven parts so that comparatively smaller neighbour can talk to a bigger neighbour on equal terms. But the more is Pakistan's pressure, the greater is the unity in India.

A free and fair election, which Mr. Vajpayee has promised to the state, should have contained terrorism. But when the 1988 election was rigged, the attention of the Kashmiris was diverted from the ballot box to the bullet. I met Lone at Srinagar in 1990. The fire of militancy was spreading at that time. He warned me that there would be a lot of bloodshed because the boys, who had gone across the border, had no faith left in New Delhi's way of running things in Kashmir. New Delhi wanted puppets and the Kashmiris did not want to go along with them since they had become a disobedient lot after several rigged elections. Even then he was optimistic about the solution. He asked me again and again: "How far is India willing to go?" The same question stares us in the face.

The problem has got more complicated because Pakistan has made the compulsions of the first Kashmiri group that went to collect arms from it into an opportunity to dabble in the affairs of the valley. It has been unfair to the movement that the Kashmiri youth had initiated (Yasin Malik leading it and Shabir Shah participating in it) becasue Islamabad inducted foreigners

—people from Sudan, Algeria and the then Afghanistan—into it. But the problem will remain unsolved if Pakistan and the people of Kashmir are not associated with it.

Instead of touching all three points at the same time New Delhi, Islamabad and Srinagar—we should restrict ourselves to New Delhi and Srinagar. This has become all the more important because the state is going to the polls in late July or in early October. But what can New Delhi really do to win back the alienated Kashmiris? The ruling combination in India is opposed to even going back to 1952, when the state held all subjects except Defence, External Affairs and Communications. These three subjects were specifically mentioned in the Instrument of Accession Act when the Maharaja chose integration with India. In fact, the state joined the Union to appropriate more. The ruling National Conference in the state antagonised New Delhi when it passed the resolution of autonomy within India. In fact, it is willing to give more subjects than the original Instrument of Accession.

The problem will take time to sort out. But one thing that should be clear to New Delhi and Islamabad is that any partition of the state on communal lines will rip open the old wounds of partition. The Muslim-majority valley cannot opt for an arrangement, which is not acceptable to the rest of the state. Too much religion is our problem and nothing should be done to aggravate it.

Maybe, a free and fair election in the state will throw up the real representatives who can then discuss the question of autonomy and such other things with New Delhi. Once that process is completed, Pakistan can be brought into the picture. But Islamabad's problem is that it does not want to wait for the process to begin and would rather have a shotgun *nikah* instead of allowing people to express their opinion through the polls.

The National Conference Loses its Charisma

It is nobody's case that elections in Kashmir will solve the 50–year–old problem. But it cannot be anybody's case that they will not straighten some of the creases which the overused formulas have left behind. A new dispensation has taken shape at Srinagar. The National Conference (NC) has lost the majority. It was India's one basket where it kept all eggs. A new beginning is already in the air.

Sometimes I feel that Prime Minister Atal Behari Vajpayee, who kept his promise to hold free and fair elections, wished the non-NC combination to come to power, as Rajiv Gandhi did in 1985 when the Akalis won in Punjab. (The rout of the BJP is not by design but by the voters, rejection).

The Akalis, however, failed to have the central government implement the Rajiv Gandhi Longowal accord which had promised Punjab an autonomy of sorts. The case of the Congress and the People's Democratic Party (PDP) is different because they have yet to talk to New Delhi on Kashmir and other subjects. Still there is no running away from the fact that the PDP, like the Akalis, caught the imagination of the separatists in this elections and made gains.

The Congress may not have come anywhere near the PDP in its appeal to the separatists. But Sonia Gandhi earned attention for her speech at Srinagar that all elements, even militants, would be associated with the talks which would be without any pre-conditions. New Delhi has already said that it is willing to talk to anyone. If the elected representatives do not try to project their pre-eminence because they have travelled through the valley of death to reach the assembly, the ground seems to have been prepared for talks on the future of Kashmir.

The All Party Hurriyat Conference, which is increasingly painting itself into a corner is hoisted by its own petared. It cannot give up its demand for independence or secession. This is the argument the Hurriyat made when several human rights activists from the country pleaded with it to participate in the election. On the other, hand, if the Hurriyat does not relate to India, its acceptability in the eyes of New Delhi will go down still further. Its must have seen that despite its call for boycott, people from the valley voted in greater numbers than they did in the 1996 election

This does not mean that the alienation against India has decreased. But this does indicate that more and more people want to get out of the present state of affairs. The defeat of the NC should confirm this because the party has come to represent the status quo.

That being the case all should move to next stage: talks. It is obvious that no dialogue can take place when the guns are booming. The violence must stop, not only by terrorists but also by the security forces. Human rights violations, interrrogation centres, searches, humiliation of people—all these things have distanced the Kashmiris from the mainstream.

Can this process of dialogue begin without involving Pakistan's relentless pressure, talks with Pakistan are necessary. New Delhi itself feels that the solution of Kashmir is not possible without Islamabad's cooperation. If it had been possible, Jawaharlal Nehru would not have sent Sheikh Abdullah to meet General Ayub. Nor would have Indira Gandhi conceded in the Shimla Agreement that the problem of Kashmir remained to be settled.

India realises that Pakistan, if not associated would continue to meddle with its affairs, as it has been doing in the last 50 years. Kashmir is what gives Pakistan its ethos. How to reach an agreement that does not disturb India's own ethos is the problem. The international support on this point has been verbal, nothing in substance.

Cross-border terrorism has not decreased. Nor is Islamabad willing to give New Delhi an undertaking in this regard. In fact, the manner in which fundamentalists have come up in Pakistan in the military-supervised election may handicap General Pervez Musharraf still further even if he wants to lessen the number of jehadis infiltrating into India.

The crux of the problem is: At what stage should Pakistan be associated? The first priority is the people of Kashmir. Hence the dialogue should begin between New Delhi and Srinagar. Even otherwise Islamabad has said that it will agree to what the people Kashmir accept. However, Pakistan would like to be assured that a final settlement would have its participation.

This scenario makes all the more necessary for New Delhi to talk to all elements, even those who are considered pro-Pakistan. This pre-supposes the release of all political prisoners from the state. The PDP, which has the largest support from the separatists, should take the initiative. Releasing political prisoners may not pose a problem. But convincing them or others who did not participate in the election of New Delhi's bona fides may. This will have to be a long, patient effort.

The PDP may have a problem with the Congress, which would not like to go beyond the Indira Gandhi-Sheikh Abdullah accord of 1975. The Congress would be watching its steps lest the talks should go in a direction where the party's fortunes might be affected in less than two years from now. Probably it would like to position itself halfway between secession, which the separatists demand, and complete integration, which the BJP and a few other political parties want. Does that help?

Probably the new dispensation would do better if it were to begin with the administration first. With a clean and purposeful government, the atmosphere would improve. The demand in the velley is not so much for a representative government as for a responsible government that could give jobs, health, education and the like. Development is what people want.

The NC administrations generally failed in this respect. Can the new government deliver the goods? What the state wants is no different from what others parts of India want. Free and fair election is not an end in itself. It provides an opportunity to the elected government to build up the state economically.

But the many —year—old insurgency makes it clear that development alone will not meet the aspirations of the people. The stir, which began after the rigged election in 1987, has cost thousands of lives. It had cost the people's faith in the ballot box which, thanks to the Election Commission, has returned to a large extent. Roughly 41 per cent voted this time.

Kashmir is beset with a horde of problems. The Hurriyat will continue to ask for a tripartite meeting between India, Pakistan and the Kashmiris. The Hindutva forces, decimated in their stronghold Jammu, will continue to demand for the trifurcation of the state. Islamabad will continue to say that Kashmir is a lifeline for Pakistan. And New Delhi will continue to say that Kashmir is an integral part of India.

To reconcile all these is a tough problem. But elections have aroused hope. People are optimistic about a new beginning. How long that optimism lasts will depend on how much the government can do to win back the people and to span the distance between New Delhi and Islamabad. I do not think any new configuration is possible in the immediate future. But a sense of accommodation may bring something which is not visible at present. Both sides have their compulsions.

Nehru told Zulfikar Ali Bhutto 40 years ago: Zulfi, I know that we must find a solution for Kashmir. But we have got caught in a situation which we cannot get out of without causing damage to the system and structures of our respective societies.'

Kashmir and Emergence of Mohammad Mufti Sayeed

Jammu and Kashmir chief minister Mohammad Sayeed was then the Union Home Minister. Insurgency in the valley was at its peak. The newly appointed governor Jagmohan had his own rough and ready methods for countering it. Complaints about human rights violations by the security forces were piling up on Mufti's table. He was unhappy about one or two points. One, Jagmohan's heavy hand was bringing him a bad name because Jagmohan was supposed to be his appointee. Two, the bottled up grievances of Kashmiris had found an outlet in the shape of militancy that had acquired a Pakistani edge.

"Is there no Tarkunde for the Kashmiris?" Mufti asked me. Tarkunde, a retired judge of the Mumbai High Court, was at the time the chairman of the Citizens for Democracy (CFD), a body founded by Jayaprakash Narayan, to seek remedy against the excesses by the authorities. Mufti said: "You people go all over India, but never to Kashmir. Why do not you find out what is happening there?" Coming from the Home Minister as it did, I was amused by his remark because the security forces were directly under his charge.

Tarkunde led a team and the CFD published report which was not to the liking of the government. But it attracted a lot of attention. Pakistan straightaway picked up instances of human rights violations cited in the report for propagation abroad. Mufti did not have time to discuss the report because the V.P. Singh government in which he was a minister did not last long.

All that come to my mind the other day when Mufti, as the head of the People's Democratic Party—Congress coalition in the state, said that his priority was to assuage the hurt of those who suffered in the last decade or so. Indeed, the healing touch is required to retrieve the alienated Kashmiris. If the new government at Srinagar is serious about pursuing human rights violations it should pick up some of the old reports prepared by the Tarkunde-headed teams. Sending them to the National Human Rights Commission for processing and suggestions may help Mufti.

Another report on human rights violations, I recall was at the instance of Yasin Malik, the Hurriyat's youth leader. Some years ago when he, during his detention, went on fast to death at the All India Institute of Medical Sciences in Delhi, the intelligence men telephoned me at his asking. His demand was that a team of Amnesty International should visit the valley and prepare a report on human right violations. I asked him why he was insistent on the Amnesty team and why he did not trust the Indians. He broke the fast when I told him that some of us would tour the valley and report on the conditions obtaining there. Again Tarkunde led the team.

Neither Srinagar nor New Delhi ever took notice of the reports, much less any action. There was not even an acknowledgement of the communications we sent to the Home Ministry. However, during the investigation we found top officials at Srinagar (not Delhi) and state chief minister Farooq Abdullah extremely cooperative and forthcoming. In this respect, the Home Ministry record under L.K. Advani has been far better. I took up with him one case of an "encounter" in Srinagar where a BSF official had allegedly killed a couple travelling in a scooter. Advani had ordered the inquiry into the case. Whenever I have written him about Yasin Malik's health or proper medical care, Advani has been prompt in his response. He even allowed him to go abroad for medical treatment.

Coming to the release of detenus, there are two categories: those who have committed murder or any other heinous crime will have to face trial. Others who are under detention on suspicion or hold a different point of view have to be treated differently. Any conciliation process will require their release. Mufti's poll plank was that his party would apply balm on the wounds of the state. It should go ahead.

Nonetheless at some stage Mufti will have to be set up an inquiry commission comprising retired judges from outside Jammu and Kashmir to examine the allegations about officers taking the law into their own hands in different cases. He has before him the precedent of Prakash Singh Badal, who after becoming Punjab chief minister ordered a judicial review of doubtful encounters. Nearly 150 from the police are on trial. The NHRC has also identified 550 bodies which are cremated without anyone accounting for them. The state has yet to explain their death and the circumstances leading to them.

I cannot understand the prime minister's defence he gave the other day that during the terrorism which the country faced, some rights had to be abridged. But the government has already done so by having the Prevention of Terrorist Act (POTA). The government can have more laws if it so requires. Still it has to maintain a balance between the state's needs and the compulsions of fundamental rights. In no case should the authorities go beyond the boundary of the law. Otherwise, it can become a jungle raj.

This is the reason why I have felt disappointed over the general reaction to the Ansal Plaza shootout. The argument is: They were terrorist and, therefore, the police was entitled to kill them without bothering about the law. The judicial system is slow to deliver justice. It does not matter even if the encounter is false so long as the terrorist has been killed.

It is a matter of regret that except for a few newspaper, the comment of the print media was motivated. The Sangh parivar moved in to try to silence the anti-Hindutva voices. Even the NHRC's authority was questioned for entertaining the petition. It had to point out that it could take cognisance of the incident under the powers given to it by the law. But more than legal or constitutional justification it is the campaign of vilification against the commission which is frightening. It shows a degree of intolerance, inconsistent with the principles of our democratic polity.

What is important in a democracy is the courage to speak out. No consideration, whether of party or convenience, should keep us quite when we see or suspect a wrong done.' The countries that have earned respect are those where people have preferred punishment for telling the truth to the reward of keeping quiet. "The day we see the truth and cease to speak is the day we begin to die." So said Martin Luther King. I feel something like that is happening to India.

Insurgency in Jammu and Kashmir and Reaction of Vajpayee and Advani

Jammu and Kashmir chief minister Mohammad Mufti Sayeed was then the Union Home Minister. Insurgency in the valley was at its peak. The newly appointed governor Jagmohan had his own rough and ready methods for countering it. Complaints about human rights violations by the security forces was piling up on Mufti's table. He was unhappy about one or two points. One, Jagmohan's heavy hand was bringing him a bad name because Jagmohan was supposed to be his appointee. Two, the bottled up grievances of Kashmiris had found an outlet in the shape of militancy that had acquired a Pakistani edge.

"Is there no Tarkunde for the Kashmiris?" Mufti asked me. Tarkunde, a retired judge of the Mumbai High Court, was at the time the chairman of the Citizens for Democracy (CFD), a body founded by Jayaprakash Narayan, to seek remedy against the excesses by the authorities. Mufti said: "You people go all over India, but never to Kashmir. Why do not you find out what is happening there?" Coming from the Home Minister as it did, I was amused by his remark because the security forces were directly under his charge.

Tarkunde led a team and the CFD published the report which was not to the liking of the government. But it attracted a lot of attention. Pakistan straightaway picked up instances of human rights violations cited in the report for propagation abroad. Mufti did not have time to discuss the report because the V.P. Singh government in which he was a minister did not last long.

All that came to my mind the other day when Mufti, the the head of the People's Democratic Party-Congress coalition in the state, said that his priority was to assume the hurt of those who suffered in the last decade or so. Indeed, the healing touch is required to retrieve the alienated Kashmiris. If the new government at Srinagar is serious about pursuing human rights violations it should pick up some of the old reports prepared by the Tarkunde-headed teams. Sending them to the National Human Rights Commission for processing and suggestions may help Mufti.

Another report on human rights violations I recall was at the instance of Yasin Malik, the Hurriyat's youth leader. Some years ago when he, during his detention, went on fast to death at the All India Institute of Medical Sciences in Delhi, the intelligence men telephoned me at his asking. His demand was that a team of Amnesty International should visit the valley and prepare a report on human rights violations. I asked him why he was insistent on the Amnesty team and why he did not trust the Indians. He broke the fast when I told him that some of us would tour the valley and report on the conditions obtaining there. Again Tarkunde led the team.

Neither Srinagar nor New Delhi ever took notice of the

reports, much less any action. There was not even an acknowledgement of the communications we sent to the Home Ministry. However, during the investigation we found top officials at Srinagar (not Delhi) and state chief minister Farooq Abdullah extremely cooperative and forthcoming. In this respect, the Home Ministry record under L.K. Advani has been far better. I took up with him one case of an "encounter" in Srinagar where a BSF official had allegedly killed a couple travelling in a scooter. Advani had ordered the inquiry into the case. Whenever I have written him about Yasin Malik's health or proper medical care, Advani has been prompt in his response. He even allowed him to go abroad for medical treatment.

Coming to the release of detenus, there are two categories: those who have committed murder or any other heinous crime will have to face trial. Others who are under detention on suspicion or hold a different point of view have to be treated differently. Any conciliation process will require their release. Mufti's poll plank was that his party would apply balm on the wounds of the state. It should go ahead.

Nonetheless at some stage Mufti will have to set up an inquiry commission comprising retired judges from outside Jammu and Kashmir to examine the allegations about officers taking the law into their own hands in different cases. He has before him the precedent of Prakash Singh Badal, who after becoming Punjab chief minister ordered a judicial review of doubtful encounters. Nearly 150 from the police are still on trial. The NHRC has also identified 550 bodies which are cremated without anyone accounting for them. The state has yet to explain their death and the circumstances leading to them.

In a civilized society it is imperative that the basic rights of the people are protected. The police should be accountable for the action they take to maintain law and order. They have no license to kill. Nor can they be a law unto themselves. Article 21 of the constitution says, "No person shall be deprived of his life or personal liberty except according to procedure established by law." The government which came to power after the emergency —it included Atal Behari Vajpayee and L.K. Advani enacted that Article 21 could not be suspended even during the emergency.

I cannot understand the prime minister's defence he gave the other day that during the terrorism which the country faced, some rights had to be abridged. But the government has already done so by having the Prevention of Terrorist Act (POTA). The government can have more laws if it so requires. Still it has to maintain a balance between the state's needs and the compulsions of fundamental rights. In no case should the authorities go beyond the boundary of the law. Otherwise, it can become a jungle raj.

This is the reason why I have felt disappointed over the general reaction to the Ansal Plaza shootout. The argument is: they were terrorists and, therefore, the police were entitled to kill them without bothering about the law. The judicial system is slow to deliver justice. It does not matter even if the encounter is false so long as the terrorist has been killed.

There are umpteen numbers of examples where the police have been high-handed. The Shah Commission, appointed to look into excesses during the emergency, was so horrified over the cavalier behaviour of the police that it drew the government's attention pointedly to the matter and said: "Some police officers as though they are not accountable at all to any public authority."

This makes the silence of academicians, lawyers or artists over the "encounter" at the Ansal Plaza all the more deplorable. I know that political parties come to life only when they smell power. The left, even when prodded, remained silent. Only the BJP and other members of the Sangh Parivar were vocal because they wanted to use the opportunity to attack human rights activists. Their discourse, understandably, was like that of an authoritarian.

It is a matter of regret that except for a few newspapers, the comment of the print media was motivated. The Sangh parivar moved in to try to silence the anti-Hindutva voices. Even the NHRC's authority was questioned for entertaining the petition. It had to point out that it could take cognisance of the incident under the powers given to it by the law. But more than legal or constitutional justification it is the campaign of vilification against the commission which is frightening. It shows a degree of intolerance, inconsistent with the principles of our democratic polity.

What is important in a democracy is the courage to speak out. No consideration, whether of party or convenience, should keep us quiet when we see or suspect a wrong done. The countries that have earned respect are those where people have preferred punishment for telling the truth to the reward of keeping quiet. "The day we see the truth and cease to speak is the day we begin to die." So said Martin Luther King. I feel something like that is happening to India.

A Long Way to Srinagar

If posterity ever apportions blame for conditions in Kashmir, New Delhi will have far more to explain than Islamabad. From the very beginning, we have made hash of things in the state. We jailed Sheikh Abdullah, who was instrumental in the integration of Jammu and Kashmir with the Indian Union. We never allowed the people of the state to choose their rulers as the rest of the country did and saw to it that New Delhi's choice was Srinagar's choice.

And till today, we have not realised that our policy—if there is one—is wrong. Pakistan is a consequence, not the cause. It is always fishing in the troubled waters. Why could not we calm the waters till 1989, the year to which Pakistan's direct complicity is traced?

Islamabad and the Valley. The present phase in the valley is a carbon copy of the last one which Islamabad started as 'Operation Gibraltar' 29 years ago, in August 1965. The difference between then and now is that the Kashmiris did not respond at that time. They, in fact, thwarted Pakistani moves by handing over the first batch of infiltrators to Indian security forces. This time, the Kashmiris have responded and fought with the training and the weapons which they were offered by Pakistan even then. Why have the same people changed is the key to the situation.

Giving information on the 1965 operation, Altaf Gauhar, then Pakistan information secretary, has said in his book, *Ayub Khan, Pakistan's First Military Ruler;* "The decision to send 'freedom fighters' (Mujahids for Pakistan and armed infiltrators for the Indians) across the ceasefire line to start a guerilla war in the Indian-held part of Kashmir, where there was no evidence of any popular stirring at the time, made no military sense."

Singling out Zulfikar Ali Bhutto, then foreign minister, and Aziz Ahmed, then foreign secretary, Altaf has pointed out how some in Pakistan had convinced themselves that they were in a position to dislodge the Indians from Kashmir. That once the trained Pakistani soldiers went into Kashmir, the people of the valley would rise in revolt. India, because of Chinese fear, would not go all out and would thus lose Kashmir as they had done in the Rann of Kutch a few months earlier.

Ayub's Directive. General Ayub's directive, 'Political Aim for Struggle in Kashmir', is revealing: "To expect quick results in this struggle, when India has much larger forces than us, would be unrealistic. Therefore, our action should be such that can be sustained over a long period. As a general rule, Hindu morale would not stand more than a couple of hard blows at the right time and place. Such opportunities should, therefore, be sought and exploited."

The operation failed. Altaf has regretfully noted that "the people in Pakistan had been swallowing stories of the trimphant progress of the 'freedom fighters', purveyed out to them by a euphoric press." The question that New Delhi has to ask itself is why that operation failed and why the current one has not. On that hangs the tale.

The simple answer is that the people in Kashmir at the time were with us. This time they are not. So much so, they want an independent state of their own. Why they have got so alienated is the question to which we have to seek an answer before attempting any solution on Kashmir.

"You did not allow them to rule themselves," Abdul Ghani Lone, now in prison, told me in 1990, when the militancy had taken a concrete shape. "You did not allow them even to win some seats in the assembly elections. They thought that going across the border and getting the arms was the only way out."

Truth in Lone's Statement

There is ample truth in what Lone had said. But the post 1989-90 action do not suggest that we have learnt anything from our mistakes. True, the militancy had to be met. But the law protectors did not have to become the law violators. It is not a weighty argument that the excesses are bound to take place in such situations. Then those who transgress the law should also be punished and the public should know about it. Only accountability does evoke response.

My impression is that the Government of India has been reacting all along to certain situations and taking steps to get out of them. Whatever its pronouncements, it is increasingly depending on force. But the mere use of force cannot be a policy. Ultimately, the people in Kashmir have to be won over.

One would have imagined that New Delhi must be cultivating such elements as are opposed to violence and fundamentalism. But this is not the case. Shabir Ahmed, a young Kashmiri, who is dead against the gun, has been in and out of jail for the last 20 years. He is still behind the bars. Yasin Malik, the JKLF leader recently freed, has been forced twice in the last six months to go on fast upto death.

People of Jammu and Kashmir. The first time his demand was that the people of Jammu and Kashmir should be associated with the talks India would have with Pakistan for a permanent solution to Kashmir. It was not an unreasonable demand. But he had to shake his life to make New Delhi agree. The second was about the removal of bunkers in and outside the Hazratbal shrine. Once the militants, who had taken shelter inside the shrine, were cleared in the last November, the bunkers should have been removed there and then. They were established only to deal with that particular situation, not permanently. The J and K commissioner had even given in writing that the bunkers could easily be removed.

Yasin Malik's Fast. What the government should have done on its own had to extracted from it, again through Yasin Malik's fast. Minister of state Rajesh Pilot worked hard to effect a formula which, it must be said to the credit of prime minister Narasimha Rao, went past even the intransigent governor. The Mazratbal shrine has been restored to the people. I wish the threat to Amarnath yatra would also go because in interfering in the religious affairs of others is against the ethos of Kashmiris.

We made some promises to the people of J & K when they joined the Indian Union. Those promises are incorporated in Article 370, which gives a special status to the state. I can understand the Bhartiya Janata Party line, which wants to abolish Article 370. It is not a moral or principled approach because the J & K joined the Union on the assurance which have been watered down over the years. The right to withdraw those assurances depends on those who got them, not on those who gave them.

Policy of Political Parties. The policy of other non-Congress parties is not at all understandable. They are conspicuous by their silence. At best they look like camp followers of the Congress. They should have come out with a categorical statement that they are opposed to what the Congress is doing in Kashmir. They should have themselves got in touch with the new young, emerging leadership in the state.

The word from the government these days is 'political process', as if it is some switch which can be turned on at will. It is an effort which have to be spread over a long period, with several inputs (Pakistan will have to come into the picture at some stage). Those who confine to mere elections do not realise that the people do not want to go back to the set up against which they rose. What that set up is yet to be decided.

Once Narasimha Rao said that the sky was the limit. That means he is willing to accept any set up that is within the Indian Union but not necessarily within the Indian Constitution. Even preparing the ground for such a formula is not going to be easy. Already, as a Muslim Kashmiri told me in Srinagar a few days ago, the valley was increasingly becoming a vortex of international Islamic fundamentalism where the Kashmiris were counting less?

War is Far from Won

Problems and Battles. You may win battles but you can lose the war. This may be a cliche. But it needs repetition in the context of Kashmir. No doubt, New Delhi has rolled back militancy to less than half a dozen pockets. The 63 groups have been reduced to three. Bunkers are fewer than before and soldiers are generally not visible on the streets.

Equally pleasant sight is the return of life, if not confidence. Bazars in Srinagar are full of people. Shops are loaded with goods. The Boulevard is gay with boys and bareheaded girls without any fear of fundamentalists. Moghul gardens are once again blooming with flowers and visitors.

Yet the people's mood is sour. Their alienation has not decreased in any way. The continue to be distant from India. If they are going about normally, it is apparent that they are taking life as it comes. Frankly speaking, they are tired. Something within them was died. They have seen murder and worse. They want to be left alone.

In the last 10 years, people have undergone untold sufferings. There is hardly a family which has not lost a near and dear one. Hundreds of people are still going from pillar to post to inquire about the missing relatives. Interrogation centres are the same old torture chambers. Many recall nostalgically the past when the valley would be agog to receive tourists. And then they pose the question which they have posed again and again in recent months: What did they get from the sacrifices they have made? This is an indication of the several battles New Delhi has won. But it is retreating rapidly on the human rights front. And this may make the proverbial saying of losing the war come true. The men in Khaki, whether state or the Centre, lay down the law. They are arrogant in deportment and rude in behaviour. So much so that a remark to a rash driver to slow down the vehicle's speed brought wrath against a press photographer, who is still in plaster. I am reminded of a poem by famous Urdu poet, Faiz Ahmed Faiz.

Nisar main teri galyon, ke, ai watan, ke jahan / Chali hai rasam ke ko / na sar uthake chale / Jo ko I chahane-wala tawaf ko nikele / Nazar churake chale, jism-o-jan bachake chale; / Hai ahl-i-dil ke liye ab ye nazam-e-bast-o-kushad / Ke sang-o-khisht muqaiyad hain aur sag azad . . . (May I be a sacrifice to your streets, O fatherland, where it has become a custom that none shall go with lifted head, and that any lover who comes out on pilgrimage must go with furtive look, go in fear of body and life; Applied to the people of heart now there is this method of Administration. That stones and bricks are locked up, and dogs free . . .)

Law and Order. Hundreds of people have been picked up by the authorities without any explanation. Even the court's order for the release has no effect. The Kashmir Bar Association has tabulated the number of missing persons. It averaged 200 a month in 1997 and 225 in the first three months of 1988. Custodial deaths last year were 588, according to the Bar. Instances of someone missing, someone getting electric shock or someone receiving merciless thrashing are so many that after hearing the complaints for some time you become numb. Incidents become numbers and the victims a subject. And when you are told how S. Hamid, a political activist, was brought out of his house around midnight last month and shot dead at point blank range, you give up in despair. Yet you realise that you cannot abandon the people who you claim are an integral part of your nation.

Special Operation Group. All put the blame on the

Special Operation Group. The group goes out of the way to "harass" relations and friends of a 'suspect'. It is inhuman in its punishment. And there are allegations of corruption against it. Chief Secretary Ashok Jaitley says that the state has constituted Human Rights Commission, headed by a retired judge, for the redressal of complaints by victims. Chief Minister Abdullah feels helpless. He says he follows the incidents brought to his notice. "I do not come to know all," he says.

"The gun is not an answer to our problems," admits Shahid-ul-Islam, who was supreme commander of Hizbullah, a pro-Pakistan militant outfit. In the last nine years, he celebrated the Idd with his family members for the first time. Shabir Shah, a Kashmiri leader, who is in the midst of floating a political party, says he never believed in violence from the beginning. Many young boys, who were once committed militants, feel the futility of killing. Indeed, an average Kashmiri has turned his back on militancy. He has even stopped giving refuge to militants. Some go to the extent of informing the authorities if they spot them. The number of locals joining them is lessening day by day. According to top officials at Srinagar, there is "practically no response in the valley to militants, who are now coming mostly from across the border. "The Jammu region still provides them with 15 to 20 per cent locals," say the officials at Jammu.

The Hurriyat does not join issue on this point. Its claim is that the militancy is "below the surface at present." Significantly, it does not talk about Jammu or Ladakh. But then it does not even talk about the Kashmiriyat. Moderate Yasin Malik, like the outgoing president, Omar Farooq, is an odd person in the party. "But it is policy, not the person who matters," says Yasin, while explaining why he did not leave the Hurriyat when the hardliner Sayed Ali Gillani became its head.

Attitude of Hurriyat. The lessening of Hurriyat's credibility and the decrease in the militants' sweep should have made New Delhi happy. But this is not so because of several factors. One is the difficult terrain along the Chenab, within the whispering distance from Pakistan, which has come alive. Militants are operating here, with all the assistance and guidance from the other side. This is the area where the Hindus feel insecure and some of them have migrated following the recent killings at Paranpur in the upper reaches of Jammu. The few migrants I met a Riasi, 55 kilometres from Jammu, are reluctant to go back.

Another factor is mistrust. This has not only increased the cleavage between Kashmir and Jammu but has also created more distance between Muslims and Hindus. For the first time since independence, the BJP has won all the Hindu-majority Assembly and Parliament seats in the Jammu region. Neither the Muslims in Kashmir shed tears over the travails of people in Jammu nor do the Hindus in Jammu sympathise with the Kashmiris over the excesses committed in valley. Linking the two regions emotionally is a big problem, which the governments at Srinagar and New Delhi continue to underestimate.

The Way to Reconciliation

Probably, New Delhi's worst defeat has been in the political field. An elected government was expected to set into motion a process of reconciliation. It is not yet there. Instead, the MLAs are generally afraid to go into the field. People feel let down because roads are full of potholes as before. No doctor or teacher goes to the countryside. Unemployment is rampant. Conditions are no better than before. The administration is generally lax and corrupt. "From where do I get officers?" says the chief secretary. Things went haywire during Governor's rule is the general belief.

Kashmir Problem at the Summit: India's Policy

Talbott's Efforts. Truth is stronger than fiction. Nothing else can describe why Pakistan agreed to India's proposal for a meeting between Prime Minister Atal Behari Vajpayee and Prime Minister Nawaz Sharif. Islamabad was at one time determined not to have any dialogue until New Delhi made prior commitment for 'substantial talks' on Kashmir. Knowledgeable circles in Pakistan claim that it was Washington's pressure, which made Islamabad, write a letter to New Delhi to say 'yes'.

US Deputy Secretary of State Strobe Talbott was seen the man behind the scenes. Whoever made the summit at Colombo possible has done a favour to the two countries. They have gone so apart that it is difficult to imagine normal relations between them, much less friendly. If they do not span the distance, they will be spending so much on weapons in the months to come that their peoples will mostly starve.

Role of Political Parties

The meeting between the two Prime Ministers does not come a day soon. In a way, it is good that the Muslim League-run government is negotiating with the Hindu nationalist BJP-led government. Otherwise, both would have denounced an agreement by any other party. That does not, however, mean that the secular polity that India has built over the years will be diluted or ignored during the discussion. I did not, however, met many people in Pakistan appreciating the point.

This is also evident from the prevalent view in political, government and some other circles that the best solution of Kashmir is to divide the state on the basis of religion, the Muslim-majority area, the Valley, coming to Pakistan and the Hindu-majority area, Jammu and Ladakh going to India. "After all, this was the basis on which the subcontinent was divided 50 years ago." they argue.

I do not know whether their formulation is correct. I believe that the Muslim majority states, which did not want to stay with India, seceded and constituted a separate sovereign country, Pakistan. Parts of Punjab and Bengal also went either side for the same reason. Since the NWFP was under the Congress government in 1947, a referendum was held to ascertain the option of the people living in the state.

Whatever were the considerations at that time, it would be suicidal to revive them, religious passions, while settling Kashmir. At least India cannot afford to go back to the basis of partition, whatever it was. It is a secular country, which cannot allow religion to be mixed with the state. Its very stability will be endangered because it is based on pluralism. Some political parties may be trying to undo it. But they are not in a majority. Nor does their philosophy fit into the country's ethos. Even they interpret *Hindutva* as a secular concept, realising that composite culture is what animates the nation.

India's Policy

How can India accept the division of Kashmir on the basis of religion, I argued with some of those who advocate such a bifurcation. "It will amount to playing into the hands of fundamentalists, who continue to torment Indian Muslims for partition even after 50 years." From Pakistan's viewpoint, the division of Kashmir on the basis of religion is understandable because it strengthens its theory of two nations, Hindus and Muslims. But for India, which does not believe that religion is the basis for nationhood, the proposal is ruinous. It is also unfair to Indian Muslims particularly the Kashmiris, who do not entertain the idea of religion having the focus once again.

The proposal brings before my eyes the horrors of partition. Millions left their homes—Muslims for Pakistan and Hindus for India—with whatever they could carry. The exodus included all; rich and poor, landlord and the landless, employers and workers, the brutal and the compassionate. The worst affected were the two punjabs, where migration in either direction was wholesale. Five million were butchered and 20 million uprooted during partition.

The pent-up feelings in the hearts of Hindus and Muslims in the wake of communal propaganda and riots found a vent in an administration, which was itself, divided on the basis of religion. The men in the military, the police and the other services had got contaminated over the years. To have expected them to be impartial and punish the guilty from their own community was to hope for the impossible, particularly when they knew that they would go scot-free in their "own country." So they connived at the killings.

The two countries cannot risk a situation where religious zealots will take over. The scenario becomes still more dangerous when you think that both sides have nuclear bombs. This does not mean that Kashmir should remain unsettled. The very willingness of the two Prime Ministers to discuss the problem indicates that they relise how sensitive and critical is the situation. Still, both sides are groping for an honourable way out.

Attitude of Farooq Abdullah. Jammu and Kashmir Chief Minister Farooq Abdullah's suggestions to freeze the problem is not as outlandish as is considered in Pakistan. The late Zulfikar Ali Bhutto made the same proposal when I met him at Rawalpindi before the Shimla conference in 1972. Much water has flown down the Ravi since. But it is not possible for Sharif to freeze the situation because of domestic compulsions. He cannot stay in power if he does not indulge in ritualistic rhetoric that Kashmir is the core of the problem.

What can unhinge the talks in Pakistan's insistence on associating a third party, the UN or some other country or both with Kashmir. On the eve of the summit, Defence Committee, which the highest body to recommend to the Prime Minister on the use of bomb, has announced that "the effective involvement of major powers and the UN was essential for progress towards the just and final settlement of the Kashmir issue." New Delhi is diametrically opposed to this. It wants to stick to the Shimla Agreement, that is, bilateral talks.

That foreign secretaries should pick up the thread from where it was left off is a good beginning. The level may have to be raised, ministers taking the place of secretaries after some time. But the talks should continue, however much time they take and however frustrating the entire exercise may become. In the meanwhile, the working groups, suggested at the last summit between former Prime Minister Inder Gujral and Nawaz Sharif, should take up the other outstanding problems already identified.

A situation may arise when any one of the groups finishes its task before the one on Kashmir does. Obviously, everything cannot wait till an agreement is signed on Kashmir. Trade, contacts and other things will have to begin as soon as the groups discussing them reach an agreement. Otherwise, the problem will get more tangled.

Effort by SAARC. However, I have not been able to know what the team of eminent people, appointed by the SAARC at Male, have been doing to tackle the issues between India and Pakistan. Even after one and a half years, there is no word from them. They, non-officials as they are, should have come with some concrete proposals instead of holding a meeting there, including the one in Mauritius. It is as if they have been having a good time. If this body has been only crossing the t's and dotting the i's, it should be disbanded sooner than later.

The failure of talks should be avoided at all costs. It will give wrong message to peoples of India and Pakistan. The latter are particularly expecting something concrete to emerge from Colombo. Even if there is no brakthrough on Kashmir, there should be some agreement in the nuclear field to spread the message that progress has been made. The meeting between the two Prime ministers, taken to the highest pitch, should not end up in the warnings that the late Bhutto made at a press conference, after he returned from Shimla. He said that "India had never utilised opportunities for friendship in the past; this was the last one."

The Talk Must Go On

"Defence against whom?" This was Jawaharlal Nehru's reply to Pakistan's chief martial law administrator, General Mohammad Ayub, who had proposed on April 29, 1959, that in the event of external aggression both India and Pakistan should come together to defend the subcontinent. Nehru's 'no' was understandable but unfortunate because the beginning of a lasting friendship ended there and then.

Nehru had in his mind Pakistan's membership of the CENTO and SEATO defence arrangements against the Soviet Union, which was India's close supporter in its stance of non-alignment. Had the joint defence against forces coming from 'north—wards,' the word used by Ayub been effected, India would have been better off three and a half years later when it was attacked by forces from northward, that is, China. When Ayub offered the joint defence, Islamabad and Peking stood apart, although Delhi was lost in the *Hindi-Chini bhai bhai* euphoria. But the roles changed a few months later, China becoming Pakistan's ally and India's main rival.

The proposal for joint defence died with Ayub. Yet the suggestion of a no-war pact has been renewed off and on. It is not one country but both of them have taken the initiative to propose no-aggression treaty over the years. But either procedural wrangling or just cussedness has come in the way of understanding on the banning of war. That may explain why there has never been a serious discussion on the proposal.

Sharif's Suggestion. Pakistan Prime Minister Nawaz Sharif's suggestion can form the basis. At the UN General Assembly session he said: "I offer India today from this rostrum to open negotiations on a treaty of non-aggression between the two countries." He put no conditions. Nor did he say that the pact would be dependent on the solution to Kashmir.

It is not understandable how BJP spokesperson Sushma Swaraj has rejected the no-war offer on the ground that it presupposed a solution on Kashmir. In fact, the sequence is the other way round. Nawaz Sharif said that a non-aggression treaty should be signed to facilitate resolution of Kashmir dispute. This is how Lahore's daily, *The Nation,* has reported. How can the BJP twist words to suit its purpose? I expected a person like Atal Behari Vajpayee to welcome the proposal. I thought he would see the difference between the earlier proposal and this one. But the party's ideology is squeezing out liberalism from anything it has.

For the last few years there has been no progress on any front between India and Pakistan because the letter would make Kashmir 'the core issue'. First Kashmir, then anything else has been Islamabad's refrain. The talks between foreign secretaries of the two countries have again got stuck on Kashmir. New Delhi is willing to discuss the problem, alongwith the other pending issues. But Pakistan foreign secretary wants to make a 'show' of talks on Kashmir. This is understandably difficult for the Inder Gujral government to accept because even the mention of Kashmir is not to the liking of the anti-Pakistan lobby which is quite strong in the country. Does Islamabad want a solution or the sham of propaganda.

Mistake by Pakistan. Pakistan is, however, making a mistake by insisting on a separate, visible discussion on Kashmir. Once New Delhi agreed to discuss Kashmir in a substantive way, Islamabad should have left it at that. It is no use pushing it beyond a point. What is important is content, not the form. After a lapse of many years the talks have been held and Indian foreign secretary has given an undertaking that New Delhi would discuss the problem in depth, covering all aspects. By accelerating or by abusing India, which Nawaz Sharif did while referring to Kashmir. Pakistan is spoiling the case.

Mercifully, the third round of talks in Delhi has been 'adjourned', not ended. The two sides are bound to pick up the thread again, particularly after a meeting between Nawaz Sharif and Inder Gujral in the UK towards the end of October. The two seem to be of the same opinion that the dialogue should continue and they have brushed aside objections to the resumption of talks between the two foreign secretaries.

Yet the best thing that has happened since the last meeting of foreign secretaries is Nawaz Sharif's offer of non-aggression pact. And for the first time in the history of India-Pakistan relations, the pact is offered without any prior understanding on Kashmir. Even the Pakistan press has pointed it out.

But it is not understandable why Indian officials are determined to sabotage the proposal. The vested interests of some of them is known. But that they would go to the extent of giving a new twist to Nawaz Sharif's proposal was not expected. In fact, they made fool of themselves in New York when they rejected the proposal. Islamabad had a propaganda victory when Indian officials were cool towards the proposal.

Centre's Attitude. New Delhi should see the opportunity with both hands. Any quibbling or further elucidation from Pakistan may give it an excuse to put conditions. It is already under pressure at home. One Pakistan daily has written that "the offer by Nawaz Sharif may attract some in India because it would appear to leave India in possession of Kashmir plus the freedom to continue the genocide of the Kashmiris. The offer is not as open-ended as may seem at first glance. The offer is for opening negotiation on a treaty of non-aggression,' which is quite different from an offer to sign a no-war pact without preconditions."

The mere holding of talks will be a positive thing. It will open still another track. Suppose the talks between the two secretaries on various matters, including Kashmir, get derailed, there will be another track, that of no—war proposal, for movement. The effort to reach an understanding will not be stalled. Both sides will be talking.

Things as they stand today do not look healthy at all. There is mistrust. Whatever one side does is suspected by the other side. Motives are sought where there may be none. True, the two foreign secretaries will resume the talk because both governments are determined to continue the dialogue, come what may. But the baggage of the past is too heavy. There is not much likelihood of progress on the actual problems between the two countries.

That is why the no-war pact offer assumes great importance. There is a possibility of the two countries coming to some understanding on keeping hostilities out while grappling with such issues as have defied solution for the last 50 years. Peoples on both sides will welcome a no war pact because their present thoughts are dominated by the fear that there may still be another war if the Kashmir problem remains unsolved. A no-war pact will assure them that whatever the outcome of discussion on Kashmir, the two will not begin shooting. What a relief a no-war pact will be!

Meanwhile, both countries must seriously consider the proposal by Mahbool-ul Haq, a Pakistan expert, to scale down the military expenditure by five per cent and to divert the amount to the programmes to eliminate illiteracy. His estimate is that both countries will come to have at their disposal $6 billion, more than Rs. 2,000 lakh. This is a lot of money. More than the money, the cut in defence expenditure may set into motion a process that may ultimately banish hatred if not estrangement, between the two.

Hurriyat's Frustration in Kashmir

Go back to the last Lok Sabha election in the valley of Kashmir or one before. It is the same old story. The all-parties Hurriyat Conference leaders go around Srinagar and such other cities and ask the voters to boycott the election. And as usual the militants from across the border kill a candidate here and a security man there to create a scare. They succeed in keeping people indoors, allowing the ruling party to indulge in gerrymandering.

Is low-polling a criterion of success? Had it been so, the action of the Hurriyat leaders would have made sense. But it is the same exercise they go over every time elections are held. Probably they too have come to the end of the road. They have no other alternative. New Delhi does not care to talk to them. And they find that people are gradually moving away from them because they have not brought the Kashmir problem anywhere near to solution.

There is hardly any local mujahideen fighting for independence or the right for self-determination. The battle has come to be confined to the Pakistanis, the Afghans, the Sudanese and some other mercenaries on one side and Indian security forces on the other. How does it help the situation? It only brings more misery to the already afflicted population. More and more innocents are killed in the valley and in other parties of the state.

The Hurriyat Leaders. The frustration of the Hurriyat leaders is clear from the 32-page pamphlet they have issued to criticise Pakistan having concluded the Tashkent and Shimla Agreements with India. They believe that "in doing so, Pakistan has done irreparable damage to Kashmir's cause during the 50 years." If they were to analyse, they would find that Pakistan was helping them by trying to settle the Kashmir problem through force. But it could not succeed.

By blaming Pakistan, they do not wash away their own mistakes. Apart from pursuing negative politics or encouraging fundamentalism, what else have they done? Islamabad's case is that for Kashmir it has fought two wars with India in 1965 and 1971 and has conducted two "adventures," the first in 1948 through tribal people and the second in 1999 through the armed forces in Kargil.

It is another matter that Pakistan was defeated. What Islamabad forgets is that it can have an initial advantage, as it had in 1965 and then in Kargil this year, through intrusions or secret placement of forces. But India will always undo it however long it takes. With the size it has and resources it commands, there cannot be any other outcome. More Pakistanis, like the Hurriyat leaders, operate under a wrong assumption. To put it in the words of a seasoned Pakistani commentator, "there is a general belief that the Indians are too cowardly and ill-organised to offer any effective military response which could pose a threat to Pakistan."

Views of Ayub. General Ayub Khan went a step further. He genuinely believed that "as a general rule, Hindu morale would not stand more than a couple of hard blows at the right time and place." Former Information Secretary Atlaf Gauhar, Ayub's confidant, has quoted him in his book, *Ayub Khan: Pakistan's First Military Ruler.*

After the 1971 war, which resulted in the liberation of Bangladesh, Ayub was so demoralised that when I met him at Islamabad in early 1972, before the Shimla Conference, the first thing he asked me was "when are you going to conquer this part of Pakistan?" I told him that even the lunatic fringe in India did not demand it.

What surprises me is that every government at Islamabad has propagated that India has not accepted Pakistan. Many people there believe to be true. Although Islamabad has lost in wars and misadventures against India, the information disseminated is that Pakistan won them initially but lost them later because of "circumstances beyond its control."

Problem of Kargil. Take Kargil. It is being claimed that Pakistan had won the war there but Nawaz Sharif "chickened out" and conceded defeat. That is not true. That Pakistan's intrusion surprised India is correct. It is also correct that New Delhi's intelligence failed and there was no timely action. So much so, the Indian army prepared "the war blueprint" only in early July when it was all over.

True, Pakistan took advantage of India's negligence. But once New Delhi sent its forces and heavy equipment to Kargil and threatened Bhawalpur in Sind by moving troops to the desert border, Islamabad's advantage fizzled out. It was bound to happen. The defence of the Line of Control (LoC), as Brigadier Surinder Singh had warned in mid-August, 1998, nearly one year earlier, had gaps. But they were filled when the counter-action operation began to roll. A substantial contribution was made by the airforce, which hit the Pakistani force sitting on the hills of Kargil. India did not have to even cross the LoC, a step which the army vigorously advocated.

It is an open secret that the Kargil operation was sought to be initiated by the Pakistan army in 1987 during the martial law rule of General Zia-ul Haq. But then the Foreign Minister, Shahibzada Yaqub Khan, once a serving army officer, stalled it. His argument was that the posts sought to be occupied were covered by snow most of the year and that the Pakistani soldiers had already died in trying to stay there.

Views of Sharif. Sharif appears to have agreed to the old plan "some time after the Lahore Declaration was signed in February, 1999". (There are also allegations that "Sharif gave the go ahead before signing the Lahore Declaration".) A group of senior intelligence and army officers, including chief of army staff General Pervez Musharraf, is said to have persuaded the Pakistan Prime Minister to say 'yes.' The argument reportedly used was that the occupation of Kargil was necessary because India was sniping through artillery into the Neelum valley on the Pakistan side of the LoC. Sharif was assured military success and he did think that he would be the first Pakistan ruler to defeat India. Things turned out to be different and he had to fly to Washington to save his face.

Whether the Kashmir problem has been internationalised it is for all to see. No country is interested in it. Instead, the LoC has become the international border. It is obvious that the international community will put its pressure against either of the two countries if it violates it. Once again Islamabad's step to solve it through force of subterfuge has failed. Pakistan shuold have learnt from its earlier mistakes.

Similarly, the Hurriyat leaders have not learnt anything from the past. Now they want to cross the LoC. How does it help? That the security forces have indulged in human rights violations in the valley is known. Indian activists have themselves prepared reports, which Pakistan has quoted in the world forums. What the whole thing emphasises is that the Pakistan-aided militancy in Kashmir should end so that there is proper atmosphere for negotiations. New Delhi has already made it clear that there can be no talks so long as there is cross-border terrorism.

Hurriyat Leaders. Do the Hurriyat—leaders youthful leaders like Yasin Malik and Shabir Shah really believe that any meaningful dialogue between India and Pakistan or between them and New Delhi is possible in the atmosphere of violence? They have only damaged their stock by welcoming the mujahideen, who comprise mercenaries. Desperation will not bring any results. It will only harden New Delhi's stand.

The Hurriyat leaders have lost another opportunity to enter Parliament which they could have probably had if they had not boycotted the election. Parliament could have given them an opportunity and the stage to present their point.

Kashmir—How to Begin?

Peace Required. The talks on Kashmir are of little use if there is no peace in the state. This is what I told Yasin Malik, the Kashmir youthful leader, when we met soon after his release from jail. He was the first to have raised the gun. But he abjured violence some years ago and has now even become a vegetarian. He calls himself a follower of Mahatma Gandhi.

I placed before Pakistan Foreign Minister Abdul Sattar at Islamabad the same proposal regarding peace a few weeks ago. He did not say 'no'. But he wanted the suggestion to come through official channels as if I was carrying a message from the Atal

Behari Vajpayee government. The point I was making was probably lost on him.

The recent round of killings, including that of a Jammu and Kashmir minister, indicates that the idea of peace is yet to seep in the minds of militants and those who are sustaining them. If the press reports are correct, the Hurriyat too has discussed peace as one of the pre-requisites for holding talks at its marathon meetings. Some intellectuals from Pakistan have also supported the move that all guns, direct or indirect, open or secret, should stop firing for creating an atmosphere of peace.

True, there is much ado about parleys on Kashmir, but without anything in substance. Home Minister L.K. Advani has said that the government favours talks with "the alienated members of the society, particularly the youth." Leaders in Kashmir, especially from the Hurriyat, have welcomed the 'offer.' The matter rests at that.

This is, however, not the first time such words have been said and hopes built. The difference between then and now is that the atmosphere is fraught with so much distrust that even honest brokers are suspect. Most militants are outsiders and the security forces are becoming more ruthless under pressure. And people, although exasperated, have become indifferent as they have learnt to live with the situation. A new approach is necessary.

It is a healthy development that New Delhi has realised, rather belatedly, that it should talk to "its own Kashmiris." But it is still stuck at a solution within the constitution. It is probably difficult for the BJP, which leads the government, to change. The abrogation of Article 370, that gives a special status to Kashmir, is on the party's agenda. But it is strange the BJP should still plug the line which Advani seems to have forsaken. When he said in Parliament that his government was prepared for a solution within the parameters of the constitution, he more or less accepted Article 370 and the special status of J and K.

To break the ice, Advani could have gone further and said that any settlement within the Indian territory will be acceptable even if it is outside the constitution. When the entire document is under review, the constitution has lost its sanctity. What is sacrosanct is the country's territorial integrity.

If the Hurriyat leaders are the ones Advani has in mind for

talks, he should have seen to their care in jail. According to Yasin, they were treated worse than criminals. Even his sister was not allowed to meet him when he was seriously ill. That the Hurriyat leaders were detained under the orders of the Farooq Abdullah government does not absolve the centre of its negligence or complicity. Even Yasin's medical certificate was fudged to show that he did not require any special treatment for heart.

This should not, however, embitter the Hurriyat. Whichever the government, the system takes over. The bureaucracy and intelligence agencies have the mindset of the British days. They have not changed. Political prisoners are treated in the same manner as they were during the Raj. The Kashmir problem should not, however, be linked with the deficiencies in jail.

How to clear the decks for talks is the problem. Just as the government of India has to get out of the South Block-made status quo syndrome, the Hurriyat too has to face the reality. The reality is that the situation in the state has got communalised as well as regionalised. The success of the talks will depend on the extent to which the Hurriyat is willing to repair the situation.

"If you want to save Jammu and Kashmir as an entity, you should revive the *Kashmiriyat,* the state's secular ethos." This was my advice to Yasin. He seemed to agree with me. However, Hurriyat chief Gillani has broached the proposal on dividing the state into three parts: Jammu, the Ladakh and the Valley. True, his thinking is not shared by many Hurriyat leaders. But Yasin, Umer Farooq or someone else should have rejected the proposal and said that Gillani's views were his own. Otherwise, it is being taken that the present stand of the Hurriyat is in line with what Gillani had said.

Gillani is a hard-liner. But his utility is that he is acceptable to Islamabad. This may be the reason why its foreign office spokesman said the other day that Pakistan would accept whatever the solution was reached between the government of India and the Hurriyat. The statement has in any way obviated the insistence by the Hurriyat to have the presence of Islamabad during the talks on the settlement.

However acceptable the Hurriyat in Pakistan, it has to put its act together in India. It has very few supporters in the country. In fact, it still has more contacts with foreign missions than with the Indian parliamentarians. Whatever changes in the constitution for any settlement will have to be passed by the Lok Sabha and the Rajya Sabha.

Apart from some worn out slogans in place of demands, there is nothing in the Hurriyat case, which anyone can bite on. The right of self-determination is an old hat. It does not go down well in India. Even the world powers are veering round to the viewpoint that a plebiscite to decide the fate of the state is outdated and it does not fit into the exigencies of the situation.

This argument may not be acceptable to the Hurriyat but it must ask itself: "Does it want to represent the state or a part of it, the Valley?" So far the Hurriyat is linked with the valley. But if it wants to expand its horizon, it has to fight against communal or regional elements. It should unequivocally stand on the side of secularism. However, the record of both Gillani and Hurriyat's spokesman Abdul Ghani Bhat has not been clean in this respect. They have been opposed to the return of Kashmiri Pandits to the valley until the overall problem of Kashmir was solved.

The talks with the Government of India do not mean that Pakistan will be keptout of the picture. Both the Shimla Agreement and the Lahore Declaration say that New Delhi and Islamabad will hold talks for "a final settlement." But it is neither practical nor politic to touch the three points at the same time: New Delhi, Islamabad and Srinagar.

A beginning between New Delhi and Srinagar is easier and more tractable. And Srinagar does not mean the Hurriyat alone. Farooq Abdullah's National Conference, Shabir Ahmad Shah's People's Democratic Freedom Party and Mehbooba Mufti's People's Democratic Party have to be associated with the talks at some stage. The purpose is to break the imbroglio and this requires everyone's cooperation.

In the Name of Autonomy

Views on autonomy. "Autonomy is what you promised us," says Chief Minister of Jammu and Kashmir Farooq Abdullah. "Azadi does not literally mean independence . . . Autonomy may not be a solution, but it can at least be a starting point for debate," says Mir Waiz Umer Farooq, a leader of the Hurriyat Conference. "The autonomy resolution, if implemented, may take the wind out of our sails," says a Pakistan leader. The three points of view, heard at Srinagar and Lahore in the last few days, cover practically the debate in favour of autonomy.

But first a word to explain autonomy. After partitioning India into two countries, the British advised the 550-odd princely states to join either India or Pakistan. One such state was Jammu and Kashmir.

The Jammu and Kashmir accedded to India. But the ruler, in 'the instrument of accession,' indicated that he was giving up control over only three subjects: defence, foreign affairs and communications. The state held its own constitutent assembly in November 1952 to ratify the accession and New Delhi's hold over the three subjects. This is what is generally referred to as the pre-1953 status.

India after receiving the instrument of accession on October 26, 1947, conferred the special status on Jammu and Kashmir through Article 370 in the constitution. The power of Parliament to make laws for the state was restricted to defence, foreign affairs and communications.

The state, if it wanted, could extend any law operating in the rest of India. But the assembly had to indicate so by passing that law. In other words, Jammu and Kashmir enjoyed autonomy, self-governance, in all central and concurrent subjects listed in the constitution except the three.

Bakshi Ghulam Mohammed, who succeeded Sheikh Abdullah, when the latter was detained, 'worked' with the centre on the Constitution (Application to Jammu and Kashmir) Order, 1954, to extend its rule beyond the three subjects. Many provisions of the Indian constitution and laws were extended to the state, a couple of them by the then governor, Jagmohan, after the dissolution of the state assembly.

The furore over the state's resolution on the autonomy report is understandable but unreal. It is understandable because the Farooq government placed before the nation a *fait accompli,* which took everyone by surprise. True, the report on the autonomy is as old as 15 months. The debate, now raging should have begun then. But the report have gone unnoticed. Hardly anyone had read it, not even the Home Minister. Farooq Abdullah himself hardly talked about it till the state's special assembly session last month.

The debate is unreal because the state is within its right to reiterate that its accession to India was confined to the three subjects. Whatever was done during the Bakshi regime or later was 'wrong'. The centre's reaction that the clock cannot be turned back is considered by the Farooq government a one-sided statement with no legal backing. If New Delhi wants control over other subjects, the state's plea that the centre has to hold talks with it and reach an agreement.

An influential segment of opinion says that if the pre-1953 status is reviewed for Jammu and Kashmir, it would evoke similar demands from other states. The argument is fallacious. It is J and K which joined the Union, not the other way round. It is up to Punjab, Tamil Nadu or Assam to demand any status at any time but they cannot cite the example of J and K in their support. They and other states constituted the Union while J and K joined it.

No doubt, most of the princely states gave defence, foreign affairs and communications to the centre to begin with. But then they themselves agreed to merge with the Union. J and K did not. Nor did the Union amend Article 370 to indicate that the state's special status had not changed. So much so, the BJP set aside its demand for abrogation of the Article to head the government at the centre.

Where the autonomy report can be faulted is that it does not take into account the accord reached between Sheikh Abdullah and Mrs. Indira Gandhi in February 1975. The accord does not figure even in the terms of referene of the committee on autonomy.

The 1975 Accord. The accord should have formed the bedrock of the relationship because the Sheikh has sanctified it. He took over the reins in 1975 itself. He was the one who agreed to span the distance between 1952 and 1975. The committee on autonomy should have begun its journey from the 1975 milestone.

The 1975 accord authorises Parliament to make laws to prevent "activities directed towards disclaiming, questioning or disrupting the sovereignty and territorial integrity of India or bringing about cession of a part of the territory of India from the Union or causing insult to the Indian national flag. The Indian national anthem and the constitution." Why should the Farooq government feel shy about it?

Apparently, there were differences over the interpretation of the 1975 accord. In a letter to Indira Gandhi, the Sheikh had said: "As you are aware, it is my view that constitutional relationship between the centre and the state of Jammu and Kashmir should be what it was in 1953. *Nevertheless,* (italics are mine) I am happy to say that the agreed conclusions (the 1975 accord) provide a good basis for my cooperation at the political level and for centre-state relationship."

Sheikh's Views. Sheikh's went on to say: "The accession of Jammu and Kashmir to India is not a matter at issue. It has been my firm believe that the future of Jammu and Kashmir lies with India because of the common ideals that we share." Farooq Abdullah has used more emphatic words than these. But by ignoring his father's accord, he has created doubts about his political strategy. Did he want this only as a plank for the assembly election next year?

The hostile posture that the RSS has adopted against him and the special status conferred on J and K would have annoyed a pro-autonomy person. And it is a pity that the RSS has succeeded in its endeavour. The BJP members in the cabinet buckled under the RSS command to reject the autonomy resolution without delay. Some ministers like Nitish Kumar wanted the government to appeal to Farooq Abdullah to reconsider the resolution. But the BJP-headed government did not allow any dispassionate scrutiny. Even the plea to place the report before Parliament was rejected. The worst part of the autonomy report is the regionalism of J and K on communal lines. This recommendation tallies with the views expressed by the RSS and some of the Hurriyat leaders. Yasin Malik is said to have slapped Prof. Gani on his insistence that the state's division on communal lines was the Hurriyat's policy.

The states should, however, be happy over the cabinet resolution, which reaffirms the government's commitment "to evolve a broad consensus on the implementation of steps for wide-ranging devolution of power to the states." Central minister S.S. Dhindsa from Punjab was most vocal on this point in the cabinet. Surprisingly, DMK's Murasoli Maran did not attend the meeting. The Cabinet's support to the Sarkaria Commission recommendation on the centre-state relations is adding insult to injury. The report has been accumulating dust for the last 18 years and nothing has been done so far. The Cabinet should have referred the matter to the Inter-State Council or to the Constitution Review Committee.

Indeed, the straight rejection of the report has disappointed and the people in the valley generally. I heard them expressing their unhappiness. Farooq Abdullah has yet another reason to be unhappy. The centre is holding secret talks with the Hurriyat leaders. The reported offer to them is to head the state government. Is it the solution? New Delhi has not learnt a simple thing: those who live in glass houses should not change their clothes with the lights on, as Bernard Shaw put it.

A Ray of Hope in Kashmir

Suffering of leaders. It was their triumphant hour. For years, they had struggled to get recognition. New Delhi's invitation gave them that attention. So has Islamabad's realisation that they, not the tripartite conference, came first. The All Party Hurriyat Conference could not have asked for more.

True, their leaders and workers have borne untold sufferings. There is probably no Kashmiri family which has remained unscathed. If ever a cause has forced the rulers to reckon with the realities, Kashmir is the one. Still, the Hurriyat have not risen to the occasion. They have been found wanting in their hour of glory.

It is not the scuffle outside the Hurriyat meeting place which forbodes ill. The age–old crack between the pro-Pakistan elements and the pro-Azadi forces was bound to appear, sooner or later. The slogan-mongering and the stone-throwing episodes were a natural fallout. The statement issued after the meeting indicates the pressure. The Hurriyat leadership had to speak in general terms. "The conglomerate will join any meaningful political process for a permanent legislation of the Kashmir dispute."

Views of Hurriyat. Even if the differences have been spanned only temporarily, it suits New Delhi. A divided Hurriyat would have been still more a difficult proposition that the Hurriyat that has now emerged .The tragic point, however, is that it is not going about in a manner it should have.

By its acts of omission and commission, the Hurriyat confirms that it is interested only in the Valley. No doubt, their leaders' contact, not to speak of the hold, in Jammu and Ladakh is nominal. But they are not even making an effort to associate their representatives or those who count in the two regions. By this time, the Hurriyat should have sought them and tried to assuage their fears.

Kashmiri Pandits. I recall when I broached the subject of Kashmiri pandits' return to the Valley with the present Hurriyat chairman, Abdul Ghani Bhat, at Srinagar a few years ago, his reply was that their future would be decided when the Kashmir question was settled. It was unfair on his part because the pandits are the warp and woof of Kashmir. Still he, and even Syed Ali Shah Gillani, stuck to those views, not realising that they were unwittingly giving support to the communal divide. They may have changed by now but they have never made their position clear.

It is still not too late for the Hurriyat to reach out to people in Jammu and Ladakh. They may want regional autonomy, their aspiration, which the Hurriyat fighting for the Kashmiri identity, can appreciate. Talking to Jammu and Leh directly will be far better for them than going through New Delhi.

Even within the Valley, the Hurriyat should talk to others, like Shabir Shah, Mehabooba Mufti and the National Conference, because they represent different points of view, ranging from near independence to autonomy. Their support, however limited, may help the Hurriyat present a consensus which New Delhi cannot take lightly.

Attitude of Centre. At present, the central government is obliged to hold talks with various elements in the Valley, Jammu and Ladakh. The Hurriyat, no doubt, represents the dominant opinion in the Valley. But there are others who cannot be ignored. Before making up its mind, New Delhi will have to hold talks with the non-Hurriyat elements, particularly the National Conference, when it is part of the ruling National Democratic Alliance at the Centre.

Presuming the Hurriyat insists on representing the Valley solely, what about Jammu and Ladakh? The Indian people, whatever be their views on the RSS proposal, will not agree to trifurcate the state on religious grounds because it will spell ruin to the secular polity, already shaky. Some leaders within the Hurriyat, like Yasin Malik, are wholly opposed to the idea of splitting the state into Kashmir, Jammu and Ladakh. At present, it is not even clear who are the real leaders of the three regions.

Local Politics. Perhaps, fresh elections in the state may become inevitable. The Farooq Abdullah's government is only a 12 per cent government. The Hurriyat's boycott had made the state polls a mockery. Even the Jammu and Ladakh did not go the National Conference way. The Hurriyat may insist on the UN supervision if the idea of fresh election is mooted. But it should realise that no sovereign country can agree to such a suggestion. Were the Hurriyat to ask the election to be supervised by the Indian human rights activists, New Delhi would find it hard to say no.

The Hurriyat has to do some hard work. It has succeeded—thanks to many in India, Pakistan and elsewhere who have articulated the Kashmir problem so much in the world—that the government had no choice except to concede to the talks without any pre-condition. The same Home Minister L.K. Advani, who refused to have any truck with the Hurriyat leaders only a year ago, is now keen to hold a dialogue.

Still the Hurriyat will have prepare the ground and start devising a formula which may find acceptance in New Delhi and Islamabad. The Hurriyat leaders' travel to Pakistan presents no difficulties. They would help establish their credentials and cause far better if they were to force militants in the Valley and elsewhere to stop firing guns. A complete ceasefire, to begin with for six months, would create the necessary climate:

The association of Pakistan is only a matter of time. The situation will automatically lead to it. The Hurriyat took some time to realise this. Islamabad appears to have played a positive role from behind the scenes. The immediate point which Pakistan and the Hurriyat have to attend to is to silence every gun, in the Valley and across the border. In fact, the Hurriyat have to attend to is to silence every gun, in the Valley and across thbe border. In fact, the Hurriyat has to build an atmosphere where any individual or group violating peace would be denounced by all.

Kargil Operation. This does not look so difficult at present as it did some months ago, particularly after the Kargil operation. In fact, the problem is not that of ceasefire, not even of talks. The real issue is what should be done to sustain the talks. Maybe, one way could be to go slow on Kashmir. Both India and Pakistan, after breaking the ice through official level talks, will be well advised to take up the nuclear safeguards and free trade. The progress on these subjects may be quicker and may generate understanding which will stand a solution on Kashmir in good stead.

It has to be admitted that Track Two, people to people contact, has brought about the thaw, not Track One, between the governments. Now is the time for some persons from Track Two, both from India and Pakistan, to meet and hammer out some alternatives on Kashmir and other matters. If they, likeminded and liberal as they are, cannot agree among themselves, the officials with their mindset will never be able to do so.

Really speaking, the governments in the two countries are prisoners of their own actions. Even the non-officials working behind the scenes are acting on their brief. New Delhi and Islamabad have to tear away from the web they have woven around them that they cannot sell to their people anything beyond a particular stand. The two should show determination and stamina because peoples of both countries are sick of hostility and hiatus.

Hurriyat Leaders. What is important is to find a common denominator to reach a settlement. The Hurriyat leaders are in a better position to do so. But if they too continue to indulge in rhetoric, or live in the world of their own, as most of them do, they will waste the opportunity which their blood and sacrifice, and many of those like them, has brought about.

Attitude of Islamabad. Pakistan's reaction to India's unilateral ceasefire is churlish. Once again there is an undue haste for a tripartite conference. This is an exercise which Islamabad has gone over before it. It still has not understood its futility.

India cannot solve the Kashmir problem without Pakistan. If it could, it would have. This is the reason why Jawaharlal Nehru sent Sheikh Abdullah to meet General Ayub in 1964. And this is the reason why both the Shimla Agreement (1972) and the Lahore Declaration (1999) said that the two countries will find "a joint settlement of Jammu and Kashmir."

Pakistan's reiteration of its demand for a tripartite conference is nothing sort of putting the cart before the horse. There has to be the cesation of violence. Only a peaceful atmosphere can prepare the ground. How is a meaningful dialogue possible after the Laskar-e-Toiba's threat to the life of India's Prime Minister? The outfit is operating from Pakistan. *Jihad,* presently less mentioned by General Pervez Musharraf, is the Laskar' war cry. Such a frenzy by fundamentalists can destroy any effort at peace.

Views of Vajpayee. By extending the ceasefire—third in a row—Atal Behari Vajpayee has once again indicated his resolve to solve the problems between the two countries through peace, not war. I wish Musharraf had also reciprocated the gesture by stopping the supply of arms and giving refuge to militants. He should realise that patience in India is wearing thin.

The ceasefire does not mean that one country has accepts the viewpoint of the other. It only means that both want to give peace a chance. There is no other option. Pakistan has to rein in the *jihadis* on its soil. If Musharraf can declare a ceasefire on the Line of Control (LoC), what stops him from having it all over? He had agreed to such a proposition six months ago during a conversation with me. If that were to happen, I can visualise a meeting between India and Pakistan at the highest level. What I cannot visualise is how the two will sort out the Kashmir problem unless one of them or both change their outlook.

True, Jammu and Kashmir is a Muslim majority state. But that does not give Pakistan the legitimacy to demand it. Had the state gone to Pakistan when India was partitioned on the basis of the two-nation theory, the latter would have taken it in its stride. Now, after 55 years of independence, how can it negate the ethos of its freedom struggle: a secular polity? What does it do to the *Hindutva* forces which will be emboldened in its efforts to convert India into a *Hindu Rashriya?*

Sheikh Abdullah

Leave aside Hari Singh, the Hindu ruler, who signed the state's instrument of accession to India. Sheikh Abdullah, the state's most popular leader at that time, too, chose to align himself with New Delhi. A staunch follower of Islam as the Sheikh was, he saw the reflection of Kashmiriyat in India's pluralism. The ties between New Delhi and Srinagar are that of secularism.

I am amazed to read an interview by Syed Ali Shah Gillani, a prominent leader of the All Party Hurriyat Conference that there is "no place for secular parties in Kashmir." He says that "'the present struggle (in the Valley) is part of Islam and cannot be separated from religion." Gillani has, in fact, maligned the 12-year-old movement, which is meant to register Kashmir's entity and its demand for autonomy. He is also a wrong person to represent the Kashmiris. But if the Hurriyat has selected him to go to Pakistan, New Delhi should not come in the way. The purpose of the Hurriyat delegation is to persuade the militants to stop firing, not to negotiate any settlement between India and Pakistan.

Since Islamabad likes Gillani, one wonders whether it shares his views as well. If so, it is living in a make-belief world. India will never accept the two nation theory. Most Indians did not even contribute to it when the subcontinent was divided on that basis. The 130 million Muslims in India are part and parcel of the same nation. In any case, New Delhi cannot afford to settle the Kashmir issue on such a theory because its own unity and integrity will become a question mark. There has to be another formula.

Demand by Hindu Fundamentalists

The demand by Hindu fundamentalists is precisely the reverse of what Gillani and the like-minded in Pakistan cherish. They are far more powerful today than they were a decade ago. If religion were to determine the future of Kashmir, it would be disastrous for us. How do we stop Hindu fanatics from going to town with the argument that, even after 53 years of independence, the Muslim majority areas in Jammu and Kashmir want to join Pakistan because it is an Islamic country?

I can visualise the horrors of partition repeating themselves. Once again the wounds would be reopened. Whatever India has been able to do, probably not much, to inculcate the spirit of secularism among people will come to a nought. We are already weak and exposed. We cannot jeopardise our composite culture by accepting the principle of separateness.

Gillani's interview has made it clear to me why he was opposed to the return of Kashmiri pandits to their homes until there was an overall settlement of Kashmir. Gillani believes in a theocratic state. Kashmir without the Kashmiriyat. He is no different from the RSS which too believes in a state based on religion.

In fact, when the RSS talks about trifurcation of the state into the Muslim majority valley, the Hindu majority Jammu and Buddhist majority Ladakh, it traslantes the sentiments of Gillani. Why have the two not made a joint front remains a mystry to me because there is hardly any difference in their the thinking.

Many in Pakistan have reminded me of Jawaharlal Nehru's promise to hold a plebiscite in the state after things had settled down. So many new factors have come into play since. For example, the induction of the US arms in Pakistan in 1954 when it became America's ally during the cold war, changed the balance of the subcontinent. In any case, a plebiscite is bound to take a religious turn. It would be the *Quran* versus the *Gita,* as happened during the referendum held in the North West Frontier Province to decide after partition whether it should go to India or Pakistan. New Delhi cannot risk a proposition which has religious overtones.

It is a pity that Pakistan has gone away from the principles which its founder had enunciated after its creation. I was still in my home town, Sialkot, when Mohammad Ali Jinnah said on August 13, 1947: You ceased to be Muslims and Hindus, not in the religious sense but otherwise. You were now either Pakistanis or Indians. This was indeed a secular thinking. Had he lived, he would have established in Pakistan a secular, democratic society. Maybe, the migrants would have returned to their homes as they had imagined they would do after the disturbances had subsided. Maybe, fundamentalists on both sides would have had no opportunity to exploit the religious sentiments.

Still the fact is that neither Jinnah in Pakistan, nor Gandhi in India could stop parts of the subcontinent from going up in flames. Killing and looting in the name of religion went on for days without any check. Nearly one million were killed and 20 million were uprooted from their home in the two countries.

Whatever the solution to Jammu and Kashmir and however long it might take, India, for one, can never agree to divide the state on the basis of religion. The sooner the likes of Gillani in Kashmir and in Pakistan realise this, the better it will be for them. Religion strengthens faith in the principle of accommodation, not separation. In the moment of prayer, every man is at his best.

Facing the Facts

We delude ourselves if we believe that Kashmir has remained a bilateral problem or that we have been able to keep away the association of a third party. Our claim may be correct rhetorically but not factually.

Kashmir is all over the front page of newspaper in the world. TV networks report on developments every hour. Even ordinary remarks abroad shows deep concern over the confrontation between India and Pakistan. Not many understand the rights and wrongs of the Kashmir problem. But their fear is the two countries have reached a flashpoint where the first nuclear war in the world can start. We may not like it but the problem has been internationalised.

Again, we go on saying that we will not accept mediation or arbitration because it impinges on our sovereignty. This is true in principle. No independent country can be forced to accept what it does not want to. Yet if we do a reality check, we will see that we have opened the door to anyone who knocks in the name of assessing the tension between India and Pakistan. There has been a caravan of top officials and leaders from all parts of the world, stopping first at Islamabad and then at New Delhi. Washington and London are constantly in touch with both of us through the phone or otherwise.

No doubt, foreign countries are talking to us separately. But they are the ones who are trying to devise an ever new formula to get our or Islamabad's assent. The formula is chiselled and chopped in the light of the reaction of the two countries and to see how far the two countries are willing to go. None of us are visiting each other's country. It is the third party that is going back and forth to find out a common ground. What else is mediation if not effecting an agreement or reconciliation? At least that is what the dictionary says.

Take the verification proposal for infiltration. It was Washington that initiated the move. British Foreign Secretary Stern gave content to it by suggesting that 150 helicopters, manned by British and American soldiers, oversee the Line of Control (LoC) to check if there is any infiltration. Prime Minister Atal Behari Vajpayee was amenable to the suggestion and agreed to a joint patrolling by India and Pakistan. But he is still squeamish about associating any other country.

I do not find any harm in having some force under the aegis of the UN alongwith Indian and Pakistani troops to oversee the borders so that there is no infiltration. One advantage is the recognition of the LoC. If UN forces are part of the patrolling parties, the LoC, which has become a *de facto* border, might one day become *de jure*.

There is a point when we say do not want any third country. Its association may complicate the Kashmir problem. It may assume ramifications which are not acceptable to us. At least Washington knows that we can never accept formulations which may harm our polity. I wonder whether certain proposals have been conveyed to us unofficially or whether we have ever sounded America on what the solution it has in view.

I am not saying that we have not been wronged. Nor am I suggesting a dialogue with Islamabad if it does not stop the cross-border terrorism. But we should not shut our eyes to the fact that Kashmir has not remained hidden in the closet of India and Pakistan. The international community knows that the problem has been hanging fire for a long time. It believes that there has to be an amicable settlement if the two countries are to live in peace.

Our response has been that of a self-righteous person, who has been sinned against. True, Islamabad has been up to one trick or another to irritate us and keep the problem alive. For some years, it has trained and armed thousands of young men and sent them across the border to indulge in terrorism, not only in Kashmir but also in other parts of India. In a way, we have faced an undeclared war for more than a decade and have lost thousands of our men. Probably we have not explained to the world properly to make it realise how we have been at the receiving end all these years. But that is the failure of our diplomatic endeavour. Whatever the objective reality, the international community wants India to sit across the table with Pakistan to sort out all our problems, including Kashmir. Already some signs of exasperation with New Delhi are beginning to appear in the American and British press.

Unfortunately, there has been practically no condemnation in Pakistan of cross-border terrorism. Even when there were elected governments at Islamabad, we found very few eyebrows were raised. The military junta has increased the level of infiltration knowing well that the intelligentsia would keep quiet in the interest of the country. Surely, it is not anybody's cause that there is wide support for cross-border terrorism. Yet, there is hushed approval of what terrorists do as if they are freedom fighters or the ones who keep Kashmir on the front burner.

The Pakistan intelligentsia should feel embarrassed over President General Pervez Musharraf's admission of infiltration. He has himself announced that he has issued orders to end it. That means there must have been infiltration which he has stopped. I thought the disclosure would evoke some critical articles in the Pakistan press. There is hardly any. On the other hand, I have seen many responsible people appreciating Musharraf's compulsions and asking New Delhi not to ask for more than he has done. But has he done enough? That is the question. And that is what that India has been asking.

If terrorism was over, Vajpayee had said in his Kerala musings, he would settle the problem of Kashmir. His promise was to go beyond the "beaten track." He should pick up that thread again when he is convinced that Pakistan has stopped exporting terrorism to India. What Vajpayee can offer to Musharraf is difficult to quantify because Vajpayee has lost the stature he had even six months ago. The hardliners in the BJP are the real rulers. But they too realise that the status quo cannot continue.

The continued detention of Yasin Malik is not understandable if the peace process has to begin. Nor does the arrest of Iftikhar Ali, the journalist son-in-law of Syed Ali Shah Gillani, makes sense. His writings could be outspoken but freedom of expression is one of our fundamental rights. If there are other 'charges' against him, he should be tried in an open court.

This is not the way to proceed to retrieve the Kashmiris most of whom are alienated from India. There have to be talks. During the regime of Nawaz Sharif the two countries had almost reached a settlement. Vajpayee had told me that time that they had nearly found the formula. Musharraf reportedly pushed out Sharif at that time because the formula was not acceptable to the military, the real rulers of Pakistan. How would it agree to a settlement on those lines now?

There is, however, one difference from the old days. Washington never had so much clout in New Delhi as it has today. If American Deputy Secretary of State Richard Armitage could make Pakistan stop infiltration and tell India to respond, it must be admitted that America has the leverage to nudge both the countries to a settlement. Its main ingredients may well be autonomy for the valley, something New Delhi promised when it included in the constitution Article 370, which gave a special status to the state of Jammu and Kashmir.

5

Militants and Refugees: Concern of India

What Rajiv and Zia must Answer

When Mehbub-ul Haq, the Pakistan Finance Minister, was in Delhi recently, he told some of us that a hotline had been installed between the Foreign Secretaries of India and Pakistan to ensure quick contact in case there was anything untoward happening which might raise fears in either country. After checking with the Indian Foreign Secretary's office, I find that there is no hotline. Probably there is a proposal to instal one, but it is yet to be implemented.

This is a typical example of good intentions going awry that litter the history of Indo-Pakistan relations; Mehbub-ul Haq's own trade package, announced with much publicity, is still on paper. And it may remain there for long. In the words of an Indian diplomat who is familiar with Indo-Pakistan problems, "so many commodities have been on approved list for years, but the problem is how to make Pakistan import them."

There is no lack of agreements. If one were to look back, right from the Nehru-Liaquat pact in 1950 to the Tashkent accord between Lal Bahadur Shastri and General Ayub Khan in 1966 and the Simla Declaration, which Mrs. Gandhi and Zulfikar Ali Bhutto signed in 1972, there have been many attempts to bury the hatchet and start afresh. But every time optimism flickered only for short period before both countries found themselves back to square one.

Distrust. The problem is that of distrust, which mere signing of pacts and treaties cannot erase. To some extent, it is the fault of bureaucrate, who try to score points against each other; but more to blame are political and religious leaders who have developed a vested interest in estrangement between the two countries, because it yields them dividends. Rajiv Gandhi and General Zia-ul Haq, who have been meeting on an average once in two months in the last one year, cannot go very far if they continue to depend on the same men to find ways to ensure better relations. They have to go directly to the people, who on both sides are far ahead of governments and leaders in their desire for peace and friendship.

Rajiv Gandhi and Zia. The question to which Rajiv Gandhi and General Zia have not attended to is how to facilitate contact between the people on either side. The beginning may have to be modest. The two countries have built within their borders walls of fear and suspicion. The young particularly are given distorted information. In Pakistan, for school children history has been mutilated to denigrate the common heritage of the subcontinent; in India, though the text-books are more truthful, there is a tendency to extol the "Golden era" of Hinduism. Fortunately, the young are beginning to feel that they should not be burdened with the past. Why not allow free contact between them and relax restrictions for others?

Visitors from two Countries. At present, visitors from either country to the other have to report to the police within 24 hours of their arrival and cannot go to more than three cities. And one has only to travel by train between Lahore and Delhi to know the indignities that visitors are subjected to by police and customs men on both sides. Everyone is suspected to be a spy or smuggler. Even the known academics, doctors, lawyers and businessmen have to undergo much humiliation. No newspaper, journal or book of the other country is allowed to be brought in and this too is a barrier that has to be broken. Hordes of subcommittees have met to relax these rules but little has been done.

I have vainly argued with Foreign Ministers in India to have restrictions lifted unilaterally and treat Pakistani visitors like those from other countries. For example, a visa issued to a non-Pakistani is for the entire country. The stock reply I have got is that we should wait until Pakistan is ready to extend reciprocal facilities. I have heard the same argument in the Pakistan Foreign Office. If they cannot do this simple thing, what is the use of Rajiv Gandhi and General Zia holding any number of meetings?

Cultural contacts could also bring the two sides closer to each other. However, the Pakistan government is opposed to allowing in Indian cultural troupes having women in them. Once, when I drew General Zia's attention to it, he said that Islam did not allow "exhibition of women". But troupes from Turkey and China visiting Pakistan have had women dancing on the stage in shorts.

No War Pact. Since the fear in Pakistan is that India, a far bigger and more powerful country, may one day gobble it up, a no-war will help in allaying it. An agreement on the nuclear bomb also is necessary. If we are not going to produce one even if Pakistan were to do it, General Zia's proposal for mutual inspection of nuclear installations has merit. It is hard to believe that Pakistan is not making the bomb—all the evidence is to the contrary. Only the other day two Pakistanis were caught in Houstan, US, trying to smuggle out 50 devices for triggering the nuclear bomb. But Pakistan's suspicion that India already has the bomb or can produce it in a matter of days will have to be met to pave the way for a better relationship.

On the other hand, one is unable to understand why the Pakistan government is encouraging Sikh extremists if it honestly wants to come to a settlement with India. Eight extremists who were arrested in Punjab after the series of killings recently have confessed that they were trained by Pakistan. According to them, one thousand more extremists who have been trained there are waiting to slip into India.

Views of Extremists. The extremists have admitted that the Pakistan authorities wants them to create in Punjab the conditions of insecurity that erupted before operation Bluestar. And it is now proved beyond any doubt that the pistol the hijackers of an Indian Airlines Boeing were given at Lahore last year was imported by the Pakistan intelligence agency from West Germany. The Pakistan police also connived at the happenings in Nanak Sahib last year and they adopted the same attitude when recently some Canadian Sikhs manhandled two Indians diplomats at Dera Sahib, near Lahore.

It is difficult to believe that such happenings can take place in a country like Pakistan, which is completely in the grip of the military, without official complicity. This is having its repercussions in India and until Pakistan changes its attitude all the cooing of peace by General Zia cannot be taken seriously. At the same time, a running battle over the Siachin glacier in the Ladakh region cannot but escalate bitterness on the two sides. Both countries have lost men and have vainly tried to reach an agreement through local commanders. Why cannot the status quo prevail? In fact, there is a case for converting the present line of control in Jammu and Kashmir into international border, even though the paper Pakistan distributed at the SAARC summit at Dhaka renewed the demand for self-determination.

And it is no use harping on the past. Whether or not the division of the subcontinent was tragic, it was inevitable. When I was writing the book, *Distant Neighbours* in 1972, I had met Mountbatten and his press secretary, Alan Campbell-Johnson, "I tried to argue for a United India," Mountbatten told me, "but Jinnah replied that even though nothing would have given him greater pleasure than to see such unity, it was the behaviour of the Hindus that had made it impossible for the Muslims to share it." Campbell-Johnson recalled how Jinnah, during a dinner at Viceroy's House, was to worried about Pakistan eluding him when he said: "The Congress would accept even Dominion status to deprive me of Pakistan."

Hindus and Muslims. I think that the differences between Hindus and Muslims had become so acute by the beginning of the forties that something like partition had to be considered. Khurshid, Jinnah's secretary, told me once in Lahore that after 1942, Pakistan and Pakistan alone could have satisfied Jinnah and there was no question of his even considering something else.

In fact, what plagues the relationship between the two countries even now is the old communal question. How to erase that is the problem they should solve. One should remember what Jinnah said after the creation of Pakistan: "Some nations have killed millions of each other's and yet an enemy of today is a friend of tomorrow. That is history." The two countries can find their own destiny according to their own genius if left alone and if the peoples are allowed to look within, not without. With time, they may forget their quarrels.

Fear and Distrust. I do believe that the high walls that fear and distrust have raised on the borders will crumble one day and the peoples of the subcontinent, without giving up their separate identities, will work together for the common good. But for that the two sides must go away from their policy of trying to embarrass each other and turn a new leaf.

Brew of Trouble in Kashmir

Perhaps nowhere else have people said to be troubleshooters done more to help troublemakers than in the Kashmir Valley. A succession of ill-considered steps over the past couple of years by the powers that be in New Delhi has given a great opportunity to secessionists and fundamentalists to win a following.

No wonder then that many students in Srinagar and other places in the Valley are enthralled by the movie, Omar Mukhtar which has as hero a Libyan revolutionary who led an armed struggle against Italian oppressors and a dream of a similar struggle against "Indian oppressors". That there is no such oppression is not the point, but that they have been led to believe there is.

Role of Youth. Some young people have slipped to the Pakistan-occupied area of Kashmir, the rulers of which have openly assured them "help"; several of them have even returned, trained and armed, to commit sabotage and foment communal trouble. Their threat is not only to Hindu temples but also to Muslim mosques, for what they want is trouble. The administration fears that the saboteurs may even try to blow up the Shahi mosque, where the Prophet Mohammed's hair (Muay-e-muqadas) is kept, to create a worse situation than what prevailed after the hair was stolen in 1963.

Militants. The militants are becoming bolder day by day because increasing Islamic "fundamentalism" in the Valley not only gives them a cover but a cause, which the more gullible can be made to believe, is in the interest of Islam. The Jammiat-e-Islamia, flushed with Gulf money, is their anchor and it also brainwashes them. Never has Kashmir seen so much communalism as it does today and the Jammiat is going all out to link all the troubles of the people, whether it is the fall in tourism or trade, with the accession to "Hindu India".

The Jammiat has three organisations, one for tulaba (students), another for women, including girl students, and the third, the main one, for men. They are exhorted to be "true Muslims", saying their prayers regularly and doing what they are told to be their "Muslim duties". There is also an emphasis on the solidarity of the Muslim world, where India does not fit in but Islamic Pakistan does.

Books, pamphlets and journals, pegging this line are distributed free and even some teachers, first secretly and now more openly, talk of secession from India in the name of protecting Islam against the onslaught of secularism.

Unchecked theocratic preaching has made the secessionist and anti-Indian elements vocal. The pro-Pakistan All J&K People's League and pro-Plebiscite Front (Mahaz-e-Azadi) openly give vent to their anti-Indian and secessionist feelings. These organisations take pride in having perpetrated several ugly incidents, including the digging up of the pitch during the one-day international cricket match of India against the West Indies in Srinagar on October 13, 1983.

The Intelligence Bureau of the Central Government has repeatedly underlined the need for "a very close watch" on the activities of leaders and workers of secessionist and anti-national groups and organisations but there have been only perfunctory attempts to deal with the problem. Farooq Abdullah, because of his differences with New Delhi, never took the IB's warnings seriously.

G.M. Shah. G.M. Shah, his successor, did take some action at first but has been inactive from the time he realised that his regime may not last long. In fact, he now attacks New Delhi to win cheap popularity and often refers in his speeches to the arrest of Sheikh Abdullah by Jawaharlal Nehru in 1954 "because the Sheikh wanted the Kashmiris to rule themselves".

Farooq Abdullah does not minimise the threat that fundamentalism coupled with secessionist propaganda can pose; in fact, he feels that unless remedial steps are taken "very soon the situation may become irretrievable". He holds New Delhi responsible for "playing politics" and creating situations where anti-Indian elements have a field day. "You know secessionists and fundamentalists could have taken advantage of any agitation I would have begun to create violence and communal riots to defame me and my party, the National Conference," Farooq Abdullah says.

Militants and Abdullah. The militants also use the dismissal of Farooq Abdullah as an argument to allege that when it comes to Kashmir, the yardstick applied by New Delhi for democracy is different. They say that Sheikh Abdullah was kept out of the state for two decades because the people wanted him, though not the Government of India. And their suspicion is that Farooq Abdullah will not be allowed to return to power until he has made some deal with the Congress (I). Even some of Farooq Abdullah's followers are beginning to believe this.

There are reports that Farooq Abdullah's arm is being twisted to come to an understanding with the Congress (I). Over the years, particularly in the last two or three years, the Congress (I) has become so synonymous with the anti-Kashmir attitude that the people may denounce any combination which has even a trace of Congress elements. The Sheikh was always popular but there was a rise in it whenever he chose to underline his distance from New Delhi. Farooq Abdullah attained the height of popularity, not when he was chief minister, but after New Delhi dismissed him.

Even Farooq Abdullah admits—and he has conveyed this to the powers that be at the Centre—that any alliance, official or unofficial, with the Congress (I) will not only ruin his reputation and that of his party, but also favour in the elections the secessionists and fundamentalists from the Kashmir Valley and the Hindu chauvinists from Jammu.

Rajiv Gandhi and his Advisers. Indeed, it does appear that if Rajiv Gandhi, on the advice of M.L. Fotedar, his political secretary and Arun Nehru, Minister of State for Internal Security—the two who influenced Mrs. Gandhi to dismiss Farooq Abdullah in early 1984—force an electoral arrangement on Farooq Abdullah, the National Conference may not win a majority. However, after the polls, the two parties could probably come to an arrangement similar to the one there was during Nehru's time when the Sheikh and subsequently his successors had made the National Conference an associate party of the Congress.

The Fundamentalists. The secessionists and fundamentalists harbour this fear and some of them have begun to question the Sheikh's lead in Jammu and Kashmir's decision to India in 1947 when the Maharaja has fled from the state. They are playing scores of tapes of the Sheikh's alleged speeches and interviews, made long before the accession, in which the Sheikh reportedly talked of independent Kashmir.

This is not factually correct. He often said—and I quote

from one of his speeches—"Muslims were flung all over India and they would face more difficulties if certain portions were taken away from the country and declared independent. If they (the Muslims) were not safe in the entirety of India, how could they be safe in a smaller portion?"

But too many changes at Srinagar at the behest of New Delhi have generated a feeling that the Centre does not want Kashmir to be ruled by the Kashmiris. In fact, as days go by, they are increasingly asking themselves: What is their identity?

Farooq Abdullah and like him many others believe that the search for an identity may have been helped by merging the Kashmiris into the mainstream. More and more contacts would have helped; for that New Delhi should have made more efforts than it has. "But all that New Delhi wants is a stalking horse in Srinagar," says Abdullah. "How can this work?"

The Disinherited People

Plight of Pandits. Way out, in the open, beyond the crowded streets of Jammu, there is a jumble of tattered tents, beneath which thousands of pandits from Kashmir live. It is a haggard life. But they have been braving every adversity for the last four years in the hope that one day they will return to their homes.

When they left or made to leave the Valley—nearly 1.25 lakh—they were at a high scale of affluence, human life. Today they have entered the ranks of labourers, shop-keepers and drifters. Some of them retain their old job and get the salary wherever they are. But most of them are on a dole from the government, a sum of Rs. 1,000 a month per family.

"We want to go back." This is the refrain of their conversation, whether you meet them in Jammu, Delhi or elsewhere. It is not a tall or unjustified demand because they are Kashmiris. Like the Muslims in Kashmir, they speak the same language, eat a similar food and share a common history. Their argument that they are refugees in their own country is unassailable.

I have not met a single Kashmiri Muslim who does not deplore the treatment meted out to the pandits. Nor does anyone deny their share in the Kashmiri ethos. The Jammu and Kashmir Liberation Front (JKLF) has said that they are part of Kashmiri identity. Still there is no one who will lead the flock back. The militants have never issued any dictum against their return. The general impression is that at least the Hizbe Mujahideen does not want them back.

Role of Muslims. Nearly two years ago, some Muslims from Baramulla invited people from Jammu to return. A family of eleven, including women and children, responded to the call. They stayed in a dak bungalow for more than two weeks, waiting to be allowed to relive where they once did. But they were force to return.

I asked this May, Ali Shah Gillani, a leading figure among the Kashmiri Muslims at his residence near Srinagar, why he did not prepare the ground for the pandits to come back. He admitted they were sons of the soil, "our brethren." But he added: "They will have to wait till there is a final settlement of the Kashmir problem."

He was honest to give his mind. But this does not rectify the wrong done to the pandits. How can a human problem be linked with a political one? Kashmir has been hanging fire for nearly 45 years and there is nothing on the horizon to suggest an early solution. Does it mean that the pandits—and their children—are doomed to live on the periphery of life indefinitely?

The Secular Outlook. The Kashmiris are known for their secular outlook. Sufism has tempered fundamentalism and elevated the religion to higher values; tolerance and compassion have come to prevail in the valley. The Kashmiri identity has spanned the distance between the Muslims and the Hindus. Even in the worst days of communal rioting in the country, they remained unaffected. In August, September 1947, when religious frenzy took over the subcontinent, Kashmir was an example of amity and brotherhood.

It is true that many among the pandits, who languish in camps and elsewhere were initially influenced by the Bhartiya Janata Party's philosophy. But they have learnt their lesson and come to realise that communalism is an antithesis of *Kashmiriat*.

That way many Muslims in the Valley have also got contaminated. They have destroyed the houses which the pandits occupied. And they damaged several temples when the Babri Masjid was demolished. This is unlike Kashmiri Muslims, who have never allowed religious passions to dominate their faith in secular principles.

Pandits in Dilemma. The problem of pandits is also human. They are a victim of political exigencies. An international jurists team which visited the camps in Jammu recently was horrified to see the conditions in which they live. Their report does no pride to Kashmiri Muslims. The Government of India's policy is not to rehabilitate the pandits but to sustain them till peace prevails in the Valley. The pandits realise this. But what happens to them in the meanwhile? They continue to be in a mess.

"Kashmir, a Report to the Nation," prepared by the Peoples' Union for Civil Liberties and Citizens for Democracy, says: "Living arrangements have to be considerably improved; imagine a set of latrines which do not have doors in front of them. This was the situation in the camp that we visited. Water is so scarce that the place stinks from a distance."

At a recent seminar in Delhi, a Muslim journalist said that the Muslims were bound by the *Hadith* (traditions relating to the deeds and utterances of the Prophet as recounted by his companions). It enjoins upto Muslim not to oust the minority. I wish those militants who are not letting the pandits to return follow the precept.

Complex Property Problem. However, it is significant that the property of Kashmiri pandits is not being purchased by anyone as if some sort of unstated ban exists. Nearly 20,000 pandits still live in the Valley and they are quite safe. They tell how Kashmiri Muslims are at pains to make them feel secure.

The Pandits' question has also come in handy to the BJP. It is poisoning the atmosphere by playing on the emotions of Hindus, pointing out how the pandits were turned out of their houses by Kashmiri Muslims. This is not entirely true because many pandits left on their own or at the instance of the then governor, Jagmohan.

Views of Balraj Puri. According to Balraj Puri, a Jammu leader, Kashmiri Muslims had guaranteed protection to the pandits as back as in March 1990 when the militancy was at its height. But soon after H.N. Jattu, chief of pandits, landed in Jammu, who also gave him air ticket, there was panic among the pandits when he left. "Once Jattu, the leader, quitted there was no stopping of pandits," says Puri.

But how long the faults of Jagmohan are going to visit on the pandits? They have suffered enough for their part of the mistake. It is ironical that on one hand the government and some political parties had made capital out of their plight and, on the other they have used them as a political football. The pandits have lost both ways.

The Muslims in the rest of India can give a new turn to the situation by taking up their cause, putting pressure on Kashmir Muslims to get the pandits back. So far the matter remains communalised, the Hindu zealots, particularly the BJP, making it a fallout of Hindu-Muslim clash and most Kashmiri militants propagating that the Hindus who left were opposed to their "movement."

The pandits were in the forefront of the struggle for independence against the maharaja, who was a Hindu. They have been part of the Sheikh Abdullah headed National Conference, which once stood for Kashmir's separate identity. It was a Kashmiri pandit, B.K. Nehru, who joined issue with Indira Gandhi, then the prime minister, and left the state when wanted to replace an elected set-up in the state.

Several Kashmiri pandits, for example, H.N. Wachoo, an activist, have been on the side of the "renewed movement" since 1990. He was murdered by one group of militants. But his family has not swerved from its faith in the Kashmiri identity.

The Muslims in the rest of the country have to raise their voice for the return of pandits because that will give roots to the Kashmir identity and weaken communal forces in the Valley. Once the pandits begin to trek back, it will set in a new trend, not only in the valley but all over the country, a trend that will defeat the BJP and its ilk and strengthen secularism.

From Rao to Rao (General Krishna Rao and P.V. Narasimha Rao)

The government is barking up the wrong tree in Kashmir. For some time it has been doing so because of lack of policy. The problem is the alienation of Kashmiris, which has only deepened with the destruction of the Charar-e-Sharif shrine.

Mistakes of New Delhi. Till today New Delhi has not realised its mistakes. The burnt site of Charar-e- Sharif was first handed over to the army. What message was sought to be conveyed? It is not the iron fist that is needed, but an effort to understand and heal the hurt the Kashmiris have carried for years.

A person like General Krishna Rao was never the answer. His misdeeds in Nagaland are well known. To expect that he had changed was at best Prime Minister Narasimha Rao's indulgence for a Telugu brother. All political parties in Jammu and Kashmir state, including Congress, have demanded his replacement at one time or another. But the Prime Minister has continued with him apparently because he too believes that force is the only way to deal with the Kashmiris.

Governor Rao's assessment is that a Low Intensity Conflict (LIC) is raging in Kashmir. And it can be tackled in the same way as he handled the situation in Nagaland. (Insurgency has broken out again in Nagaland). With no contact with people, Rao sits in his palatial bungalow pouring over the map of Kashmir as if he is giving shape to a military strategy. And when it comes to the field, he miserably fails.

The Proxy War. The Government of India's jargon is that the Kashmir situation is the result of a proxy war between India and Pakistan. No doubt, Islamabad is arming and training militants, as well as instigating Afghans and those Kashmiris it controls to cross into the valley. But these people would not have found any response if New Delhi had not lost faith with the Kashmiris. In 1965 it was the Kashmiri shepherds who reported to the army about infiltrators from Pakistan.

The fact is that somewhere along the line the link between New Delhi and ordinary Kashmiris has been severely strained. The policy should have been a political strategy, how to retrieve them. But instead of that the administration, which has failed to provide even the basic amenities, has relied on the indiscriminate use of force.

The Hazratbal. The manner in which the government handled the earlier crisis at Hazratbal shrine underlines the point that force is not the answer. Human rights activists were brought into the picture at the time and they were able to persuade JKLF leader Yasin Malik to break his fast unto death. Governor Rao was vehemently opposed to the settlement and tried his best to sabotage it.

But Prime Minister Rao overruled him and ordered the redeployment of security forces, which should not have been there in the first instance, so that the shrine was accessible unhindered to pilgrims. Governor Rao's warning that the Hazratbal shrine would become a den of militants has been proved wrong and the shrine has returned to its age-old glory.

Rao's follows Governor's Advice. When it comes to Charar-e-Sharif, Prime Minister Rao apparently followed the advice of the hawkish Governor Rao, who made it a prestige issue. Some bureaucrats in Srinagar and Delhi are of the same bent of mind. The entire handling was wrong. For six months militants were allowed to have a free run. Three months later the security forces were put at a distance of one and a half kilometres to ensure that no weapons would be carried in to the shrine. Obviously, this was no way either to stall militants or the smuggling in of arms. The result is known to all.

The government depended completely on force. No human rights activist was contacted. Even Yasin Malik and another popular young Kashmiri leader, Shabir Shah, as well as veteran Kashmiri leader Abdul Ghani Lone, were stopped from going to the shrine and contacting militants to find a way cut.

Who burnt the Charar-e-Sharif is not so relevant as is the ability of militants to be a focus of attention. Yesterday they were at Hazratbal shrine, today they are at Charar-e-Sharif and tomorrow they may be at some other shrine. The government's responsibility is to seek the root cause of militancy. And we come back to the attention of people. At least, a Supreme Court judge should have been appointed straightaway to hold an inquiry to find out why set fire to the shrine. Whatever the propaganda, the country must know the truth.

People are Tired of Gun-culture. Kashmir is back to square one. Whatever little New Delhi had gained—people were getting tired of the gun culture—have been frittered away. Once again there are demonstrations and instances of defiance even in the face of tear gas and lathi charges. Muslim fundamentalists are exploiting the situation; they have demolished six Hindu temples and set fire to some 20 vacant houses of Kashmiri Pandits. Even otherwise, they are polluting the atmosphere.

What is surprising is that the government insists on holding assembly elections before the middle of July. It will be quite a spectacle. Not even one per cent of the electorate in the valley is expected to participate. Aviation Minister Ghulam Nabi Azad is said to have cautioned the prime minister that the polls might turn out to be a referendum against India and the prevailing impression that none in the valley is on India's side may be confirmed. The Border Security Force chief, whose men bear the brunt in the operations, has reportedly advised against the elections.

Periodical Elections. No doubt, periodical elections are the only way to know the people's attitude towards their rulers. But they are only a means to an end. The end is man's sovereignty. We talk of the good of Kashmir. Is this something apart and transcending the good of the individuals composing it? If the Kashmiris are ignored or sacrificed for what is considered the good of India is that the right objective to have? The touchstone should be how any political process enables the individual to fulfil his aspirations.

Even if the government has to have elections, it must prepare the ground for them. That means initiating a political process that will culminate with the polls. One important ingredient is transparency so that the Kashmiris are seen to be determining their own destiny without any pressure from the state, militants or the people across the border.

It would have been credibility to what the government faced on the fateful night when Charar-e-Sharif was demolished if the media had been given free access. The reason why Operation Black Thunder went down well in Punjab was that the flushing out of militants was done in the full glare of TV cameras, photographs and other press representatives. The government conducted a press party to the Charar Sharif site, but did not allow journalists to go on their own. The request by human rights organisations to visit the site was rejected.

The debate in Parliament, where Prime Minister was a glum spectator, should have come to grips with the guts of Kashmir problem. The trouble did not start in 1990 when Farooq Abdullah resigned (he regrets that he should not have taken former Prime Minister Rajiv Gandhi's advice and quitted because that aggravated the situation). It is a series of acts of omission and commission since 1953, when Sheikh Abdullah was arrested, which has led to the present situation.

By putting the blame on others, or dubbing them as 'enemies within', the Congress party cannot absolve itself of the responsibility of making a mess in Kashmir. None, not even Congressmen, know what is the government's policy beyond sending more troops to Kashmir and extending newer repressive laws. One minister complained to me on the debate in Parliament that where was no briefing on Kashmir and that he did not know what he was supposed to say.

During the debate, much was made about the disappearance of Mast Gul, the Afghan who reportedly masterminded the Charar-e-Sharif incident. Many other militants also disappeared. The security forces could not act on their own because the entire operation was conducted on the instructions of Raj Bhavan, which is said to be in constant touch with the Prime Minister's office in New Delhi.

Author's Views

Essentially, the Kashmir policy is between the Raos, the state Governor and the Prime Minister. Whatever that is, it has failed. Not only that, it has given India a bad name. Someone has to be held accountable. At least one of the Raos will have to be sacrificed to atone partially for the mistakes in Kashmir. It is obvious who that Rao should be.

6

India and Nawaz Sharif: Efforts for Reconciliation

Pakistan's Third Chamber: The Armed Forces
How to delineate civil and military fields is the biggest problem that Pakistan faces after the election. The congratulatory message that General Mirza Aslam Beg, the Pakistan chief of army staff, sent to Benazir Bhutto, the Pakistan People's Party (PPP) chief, and Nawaz Sharif, the Islamic Jamoohri Ittehad (IJI) chief, the two who have staked their claims to be prime minister, indicate the patronising attitude that the armed forces have come to acquire after 30 years of rule.

Still more telling is General Beg's suggestion of "a broad-based government". If he can make such a proposal after the people have elected their representatives freely, it means that Pakistan still has to reckon with a third chamber, the armed forces. Had the proposal been made before the election, it might have been taken as merely a suggestion made in good faith to the people.

But after the election to the National Assembly (Pakistan's Lok Sabha), the General's expression of a preference for "a broad-based government's sounds ominous. It is a revival of the same old idea of partyless government that the late General Zia-ul Haq had pushed. Had the Supreme Court of Pakistan not intervened on Benazir's Petition, the election would have been on that basis.

General Beg's statement has yet another dimension. He has made it knowing well that the chief of army staff is a mere officer under a civilian prime minister. And he could not have done this without having the supreme confidence that he is strong enough to face any repercussion. In fact, the way Ghulam Ishaq Khan, the Pakistan President, is dragging his feet in transferring power to the majority party, the PPP, shows that the armed forces are active behind the scene to make sure that they have the "right type of prime minister".

This is precisely the kind of thinking that the civilian government will be up against. By dint of having been at the helm of affairs for so long, the armed forces have acquired a status which no democratic government can allow it. Mere withdrawal to the barracks is not enough; the armed forces have to realise that they are no longer the masters. General Beg's attitude does not reflect acceptance of the supremacy of an elected government.

Any Pakistan government will have to assert itself and prove publicly that the armed forces are no longer the privileged. But at the same time it will have to tread warily. While it may be able to cut their representation in the Pakistan foreign service—at present more than 50 per cent—and some other sectors, it would be rash to touch their emoluments and some of their perks. Benazir was realistic when replying to a question whether the generous allowances of the armed forces would be cut, she said: "Do you want martial law to return?"

In fact, the PPP and the IJI were both eager during the election to placate the armed forces. Both parties nominated several former military brass as their candidates—the PPP fielded two army generals and a retired air marshal and the IJI two retired generals. One can understand Nawaz Sharif's bias for the armed forces because he was all for "Ziaism" and saw "benefits" in military dictatorship. But even Benazir had to be discreet and did not criticise the armed forces lest they should hold that against her when the time for handing over power came. In a post-election interview, she has been equally generous: "The role of the armed forces has been critical to restoring democracy".

Apparently, the dynamics of power work in a curious manner. After meeting Ishaq Khan, before whom Benazir laid her claim on formation of government, she went straight to General Beg for dinner and reportedly assured him that the generals would have nothing to fear from an administration headed by her. Her supporters see in her meeting with the army chief a pragmatic move. But it has, unfortunately, made it clear where the power lay and what kind of administration she would give if the generals were to overlook her shoulders?

Reports from Pakistan that the armed forces asked Benazir to accept some ground rules and that she has accepted them are ominous. My friend, Mushahid Hussain, former editor of *The Muslim*, has reported that one of the major demands of the military establishment was that a new civilian government "must not disturb the country's secret nuclear weapon programmes". Another demand was support for Afghan resistance and close ties with the West and Arab nations. Benazir, according to Mushahid Hussain, has accepted the demands. As for Nawaz Sharif, he has already said publicly that he will follow General Zia's path.

The armed forces' warning may be the reason why Benazir has changed her instance on Pakistan's nuclear programme. During the election campaign she said that she would not pursue the effort for acquisition of the bomb. But after the elections her statement is that she would continue the nuclear programme already chalked out. She has also gone back on her announcement that she would open the Kahuata plant for inspection by America.

In fact, Benazir would have done better at the polls if she had broad-based her appeal and directed the campaign towards the common man. The slogan that attracted the people towards her father, Zulfikar Ali Bhutto, was *Roti, Kapda aur Makan*. The PPP then was a left-of-centre party. Benazir has moved it to centre. In the PPP manifesto she even made the specific commitment that there would be "no nationalisation of industry".

To quote a Pakistani intellectual: "Today the landed gentry appears to be pretty evenly divided between the two principal contestants—with a slight tilt in the PPP's favour in Sind." Benazir's support is the Wadera in Sind, the zaminder in Punjab and the sardar in the NWFP. Neither the landed aristocracy, nor the industrialists, can be expected to stand up to the armed forces because usually they support the establishment. The lower half has been left high and dry.

The election results also show that the hold of the armed forces in Punjab—Punjabis concentrate 90 per cent of Pakistan's military—is strong. Out of 115 seats in Punjab Benazir got only 52, a little over 45 per cent. What it implies is that the Punjabis did not wholeheartedly with Benazir because of the suspicion that she might try to settle scores with the military, which had her father executed.

The hold of the armed forces could lessen if the party in power were to cut them to size, numberwise. But "the Indian threat" is considered so real that no attempt to reduce the strength of the armed forces can be made. "Increasing Indian aggressiveness", in fact, may bring demands for further expansion of the armed forces.

The Rajiv Gandhi, though it often talks of closer relations with Pakistan, has been hawkish. Its policy reflects the same big brother attitude and wants Islamabad to look up to it, recognising India's pre-eminent position in South Asia. The history of the subcontinent is such—with the continuation of the Congress-Muslim League confrontation of the pre-independence years—that the two countries will take years to normalise their relationship.

During the last stages of the election campaign India did become the whipping boy. The IJI was inciting the anti-Indian lobby from the beginning but even Benazir towards the end said that those who described her as pro-India should remember that it was her father who had talked of a 1000-year war with India. But election rhetoric is not to be taken too seriously. I do recall that nearly two years ago, when I interviewed her in Karachi, she said: "Let us start from scratch; we have had enough of enmity".

A friendly approach by India and reduction of tension will no doubt help a civilian Pakistani government to face the armed forces with confidence. But it is mainly for the Pakistani public to restrict the military. It is for it to answer the challenge by the armed forces not to come in their way of acquiring sophisticated weapons from America. Such challenges impinge on the government's freedom in its dealings with Washington. Democracy and dictation by the armed forces cannot co-exist.

In 1972, soon after the creation of Bangladesh, when Bhutto was in the midst of reorganising the armed forces, he told me in an interview at Rawalpindi: "When you are pruning an institution like the armed forces, you can prune them (sic) on two grounds; one is, that they are inefficient, and the other that they have politics in them".

From all accounts, the efficiency of the Pakistan armed forces is an established fact. But there is no doubt that the bug of politics has bitten them. I do not expect Nawaz Sharif to follow Bhutto's advice. At least Benazir should.

A Martial Law Culture

Politics knows no forgiveness. Otherwise, the winner Nawaz Sharif, after the National Assembly was restored by the Supreme Court of Pakistan, and the rebuffed President Ghulam Ishaq Khan would have started afresh, letting beyond be bygones. Their rapproachment would have averted immediate dangers that looks like overwhelming infirm democratic structure in Pakistan.

But the moment Nawaz Sharif reassumed power he said that the repeal of the eighth amendment was "high on the political agenda." Very few people will disagree with him that the amendment, through which General Zia-ul-Haq consecrated his martial law rule, is a drag on a prime minister. A President, voted to office by members of national and provincial assemblies, should not have authority to dismiss a prime minister who has a majority in the popularly elected National Assembly.

What is right may not, be politic or at least not opportune. In the rush of effusive slogans of victory, Nawaz Sharif has forgotten that it is a troika that rules Pakistan. the president is as much an integral part of the ruling triumvirate as the prime minister himself. The third horse, the strongest, to the vehicle is the army, which has felt perturbed because the existing constitutional arrangement is sought to be disturbed unilaterally.

True, the eighth amendment is an arbitrary source of power, a factor of instability in Pakistan's political system. But this was not the time when Nawaz Sharif should have joined issue with the President. After several political agitations, including the opposition leader Benazir Bhutto's long march and Nawaz Sharif's demonstrations in the wake of dismissal, the people saw a poetic justice—and relief—in the Supreme Court's judgment. They wanted peace. Nawaz Sharif himself told the court that he would work with the president jointly. But he did not go to meet him till recently.

The President also did not rise above the discomfiture of defect in the Supreme Court. His ardent supporters, the provincial heads in Sind and Punjab, was conspicuous by their absence when Nawaz Sharif visited the states after becoming prime minister once again. There are many other irritations which Nawaz Sharif has faced. To quote a Pakistan daily, *The Nation,* "the President employed every trick in the book, including pitting the provinces against the federal government to dislodge the prime minister even after the Supreme Court verdict."

Punjab appears to have proved the proverbial last straw on the camel's back. Nawaz Sharif was justifiably angry over the manner in which the state government of his supporters was bundled out and the assembly members were forced to change their loyalty after his dismissal. But should he have thrown the gauntlet the day he came back to power, knowing full well that Ishaq Khan, being a Pathan, would pick it up. The President's refusal to go by the National Assembly's resolution on the dissolution of the Punjab assembly was expected.

Had Nawaz Sharif stopped after the Lahore High Court threw out the dismissal order and restored the assembly, things would not have come to such a pass. In democracy, particularly when it is at a fledgling stage, discretion is the better part of valour. How the Lahore High Court decides on the dismissal of the Punjab assembly is no so relevant as the response of the prime minister and the President. The question is political, not legal. Much will depend on whether the two are willing to stop fighting till December when Ishaq Khan's term expires.

That is probably the reason why General Abdul Waheed, chief of the army staff, is reported to have met Ishaq Khan and Nawaz Sharif a number of times in the last few days to emphasise upon them to carry on till December or hold the general elections. Leave aside the fact that General Waheed was appointed by Ishaq Khan over the heads of several lieutenant generals and in the face of Nawaz Sharif's murmurs. What choice does the army chief have if he does not want to rule himself? The eighth amendment as well as the extraordinary powers of the President is a reality. He cannot wish them away. They have to go but there is a set procedure for that. Already working on it is a committee which, ironically, was constituted on the proposal by Benazir Bhutto's law minister. Nawaz Sharif should have waited for its recommendations.

His political opponent, Benazir Bhutto, who was also a victim of the eighth amendment when she was dismissed nearly three years ago, has played her cards for better. She had lost considerably in moral stature by appointing some of her Pakistan' People's Party (PPP) men on the Mazari interim government in the wake of Nawaz Sharif's dismissal. However, by not adopting the posture of a confrontist, she has gained some ground. The people do not want to bring down the democratic structure, however rickty; nor do they like to see the army back. Benazir Bhutto, compared to Nawaz Sharif, looks like a person who is trying to find a way out.

Nawaz Sharif has every reason to be irritated over the demand for a fresh poll when he has half of his five-year term to go. But his demand that Ishaq Khan should also resign does him no credit. In fact, he should seize the opportunity to go back to the electorate and tell them how he was wronged. He can make the abolition of the eighth amendment as his poll plank, the point on which even Benazir Bhutto has compromised.

In an open letter to Nawaz Sharif, she has talked about the redistribution of power between the President and the prime minister. All the power to the prime minister can make him authoritarian and the President of his choice may lead to a fascist rule, Benazir Bhutto has argued. This is not a dilemma for Pakistan alone but the democratic countries world over. That is the reason why it is often said that democracy is only upto the polls.

But unless Benazir Bhutto has some other form of democracy in view, there is no going away from the system where an elected person by the free will of the people has the last word. He is expected to be responsible. That is the reason he is called the leader of the House—the President and the prime minister sharing power—does not work. Pakistan has itself seen it. If both are directly elected, there will be a clash. The only check on the prime minister are the institutions: parliament, press, bureaucracy and the judiciary. They have to be strengthened.

India is still not fully on the track after its system was derailed by Indira Gandhi in 1975 when she imposed the Emergency. Pakistan cannot recover from the 25 years of martial law so quickly. The tradition set by Ghulam Mohammed, the prime minister, of handing over power to the army—General Ayub Khan was the army chief at that time—has not yet gone out of fashion. Vested interests are once again in the field.

Curiously, when everyone was looking for Nawaz Sharif after the government's revival, he was offering *fateha* at the grave of General Zia-ul-Haq.

General Mirza Aslam Beg, former Pakistan army chief, has given a timely warning by expressing fears about eventual army intervention if the contending politicians are unable to work out their differences. Speaking from experience, he said that the pressure on the army chief was intense. The lobbying in Pakistan in the recent days testifies this.

"Unfortunately, over the years we have developed a martial law culture," he has said. There may a grain of truth in the statement because whenever politicians have tried to break up the system, there has been a cosy feeling among the people that the army will pick up the pieces. Indeed, it does. But every time Pakistan has paid dearly. Will it be different this time?

Left to the army, it would not like to intervene lest it should spoil the professional profile it is beginning to acquire. But if the country cannot be governed, as is the impression, what should the armed forces do? Zia had a solution. He would often say that the role of military should be spelt out in the constitution itself, like in Turkey. The armed forces should be able to intervene when wrong and return to the barracks after setting them right. The only danger in such an arrangement is that the big forces do not go back. Zia ruled for more than 11 years!

Talking to Pakistan Prime Minister

Pakistan Prime Minister Nawaz Sharif is looking forward to the meeting with Prime Minister Atal Behari Vajpayee for "moving forward" as he puts it. He is keen on "burying the hatchet once and for all." But he has his doubts about the Bharatiya Janata Party, which is considered anti-Muslim in Pakistan.

"In all my speeches, I have used word like the BJP or the Indian government, but not India," said Sharif. "The Indian people are not responsible for the bomb." Nonetheless, he singles out, from among the BJP leaders, the Indian prime minister. He recalls that Vajpayee made "a good impression on him" when he, as Punjab chief minister, met him.

I spent nearly one hour with the Pakistan Prime Minister at Islamabad a few days ago, asking him questions on nuclear tests, Kashmir and the related subjects. He used all the three languages, English, Urdu and Punjabi, while replying to me. He has shifted from the sprawling, spruced PM house to a small bungalow and he uses part of PM house for meeting foreign dignitaries, top businessmen and journalists.

Why did the BJP do it, Sharif went on asking his again and again. His brother Shabaz Sharif, the Punjab Chief Minister, whom I met at Lahore subsequently, was more explicit. He said that the BJP was "trying to cover up its weakness through the bomb." This would not help, he said. In fact, the BJP is Pakistan's *bete noir*. Main criticism is against it. Everybody asks how long the Vajpayee government will last as if they believe that a new government in New Delhi will try to undo the effects of the bomb. Everybody is certain that the BJP exploded it for "domestic political compulsions" to increase its electoral support. And everybody is unhappy that by doing so New Delhi has pushed the people of the subcontinent to a situation where both countries face the danger of ghastly nuclear war.

"I feel personally hurt and let down," said Sharif. His argument was that the talks he had initiated with former Prime Minister Inder Gujral were deadlocked but had not broken down. But then came New Delhi's nuclear tests, which conveyed an 'anti-dialogue' message. Everything came down crashing.

Sharif admitted that tension in the subcontinent had increased and he favoured immediate measures to bring it down. But he did not spell out any. It was as if he wanted to know the mind of New Delhi. Asked why he did not accept the "no first use" agreement offered by India, Sharif said: "I would like to discuss the matter first with the Indian prime minister when I meet him in Colombo. I am not opposed to it but I expect the announcement to emerge from the meeting between the two of us."

The Pakistan prime minister was confident that the command and control system he had built ruled out the possibility of any accident or misadventure. (The system works under Pakistan Defence Council over which the Pakistan prime minister presides. The three service Chiefs are members without the voting right. Finance Minister, Defence Minister and Foreign Ministers are full-fledged members). Sharif wanted to know whether the National Security Council, which India was in the midst of establishing, would have the three Service chiefs as full-fledged members. Foreign Minister Gohar Ayub, whom I also met, complained that New Delhi's system at present was concentrated in one person, the prime minister. "It's not a happy situation," he said.

Whatever the topic, Home Minister, L.K. Advani, considered 'hawkishly hawk,' is brought in for most of the blame. More than New Delhi, he is held responsible for "forcing" Pakistan to conduct nuclear tests. His statements were "particularly provocative", as Sharif said. "Using words like Pakistan will be brought to its knees or giving the warning that the Azad Kashmir will be conquered created an atmosphere of insecurity and panic in Pakistan," said Sharif. "We had to take steps to defend ourselves. We had no other option."

"Travelling for Pakistan for six days and talking to many people at different levels, I found that Advani's statement had raised real fear in Pakistan. There was nervousness and even demoralisation when Sharif was weighing the pros and cons of exploding the bomb. "Had not Advani made provocative statements we would not had probably gone for tests," said Finance Minister Aziz Sartaj. "Once he threw the gauntlet, we had no choice except to pick it up."

My view is that Advani's statements, however irresponsible, were a contributory factor. Once India conducted the tests, the pressure of public opinion and that of middle rung officers in the armed forces was so strong in Pakistan that Sharif had to exercise the option. His own party would have probably denounced him if he had said 'no'. One editor of an influential Urdu paper made it clear to him on the phone if he did not explode the bomb, the people would 'explode' him.

There is, however, a growing debate in Pakistan whether it should have detonated the bomb at all. Intellectuals, human rights activists and journalists are participating in it. A few of them were beaten up when they aired their objection in public. But the discussion behind the doors is fierce. According to them, Sharif had the best of opportunity to establish Pakistan's credentials of "not a maverick country" before the world. "For once he could have shown that Pakistan's policy was not a carbon copy of India's," they say. However bold and committed this lot, its influence is limited.

An average person feels happy that Pakistan has achieved parity with India. Gohar Ayub gloats over the fact that "India has helped us to be at par." This feeling may have been one reason why Islamabad is dragging its feet on the no-first-use pact. It does not want to go back to the conventional weapons where India enjoys superiority. Pakistan foreign office has even said so.

Of all the ministers I met, I found Gohar Ayub, although soft spoken, the most hawkish. Even in Pakistan, many compare him with Advani. Sharif is also said to be unhappy over his speeches. Ayub talks about the nuclear war with India as if it is the question of numbers, not human beings. He told me: "You have populated cities where people will die in lakhs. Our cities are small and the population is spread all over. We will have far less casualities." Gohar Ayub says that the two countries have to "live like good neighbours." But he is not unnecessarily worried over confrontation or hostilities, unlike the other ministers I met.

On Kashmir, Nawaz had no formula to offer. He said he was open to suggestions. But he had no doubt that "this is the core problem which has to be solved." He was, however, particular to mention that the Kashmiris would have to be "consulted" if and when India and Pakistan found a mutually acceptable solution.

On my return, I saw Vajpayee's statement in the Lok Sabha that India did not accept the line of control in Kashmir as the international border. People in Pakistan will feel disappointed over the observation. Not that many consider it an ideal solution. But their respect for Jaswant Singh for having made suggested to convert the line of control as permanent border showed that they were not stuck on any one formula. One Pakistan minister even said: "Jaswant Singh is probably the type of person who should be talking to us."

Bus to Lahore

The Prime Minister's secretary rang me to inform that I was to board the bus going to Lahore. A crowd of memories surged within me. I recalled the days in the Law College where Khushwant Singh used to teach me. I thought of September 13, 1947, when I crossed into India through Lahore, traversing a distance of 120 kilometres from my hometown, Sialkot.

Then it looked as if the entire population in the two Punjabs was on its feet. People did not know what had happened. None cared. What did it matter when they had left the homes they had lived in all their life and the friends they had cherished. I was a refugee.

This time I was one of the 22 "eminent" people travelling to Pakistan on a mission to retrieve soiled relations. Chief Minister Parkash Singh Badal joined us at the Amritsar airport. he hugged me and said: "Your efforts are bearing fruit." Indeed, he was referring to our effort of lighting candles at the Wagah border since 1996 to send a message of friendship to the other side.

Badal disappeared in the crowd of tall, turbaned Sikhs awaiting Vajpayee's arrival. But some of us moved towards the bus, standing lonely near the tarmac. Flags of India and Pakistan were painted on its body. Thank God, there was no slogan, which would have spoilt the bluish colour that stood out in the afternoon sunlight. Dancing and singing men and women in colourful costumes provided an ideal backdrop. Policemen looked out of place, even though they were not many.

As soon as the Prime Minister sat in the front seat, the bus began its journey to Lahore. A ticket collector first gave me a ticket and then tore half of it, which I retain as a souvenir. Another attendant offered cold drinks. The TV and mobile telephones were there—all part of service as it would be at the time of regular service. Right up to the border, a distance of 35 kilometres, people were lined up on the both sides. Children waving yellow flags and bands playing loud tunes reflected the enthusiasm that the meeting between the Prime Minister of India and Pakistan had generated.

The mood in the bus was relaxed. But very few exchanged words with one another. A feeling of expectancy hung in the air. Some nervousness was visible, and it got heightened with very kilometre-stone going past. How will the visit go was the thought writ on everyone's face. Still they were conscious of the history they were making.

"It was a courageous step," I remarked when I sat next to the Prime Minister briefly. He only smiled. I persisted with my questions: "What made you respond to Nawaz Sharif's off-the-cuff remark to take a ride in the bus?" What about your party, the BJP?" He said: "I thought: Let me do something to be remembered. After all, the Prime Ministership does not last long." And then he mentioned the killing of Hindus at Rajori. He was disturbed. "Certain elements always do it to sabotage the talks." I wanted to talk to him further but there was a long queue. I returned to my seat.

Before long, we were out of Attari and then at Wagah. The sun was setting but I imagined that a new one was rising to shed the light of love and friendship. Never before had the Prime Ministers of the two countries met at the border. The iron gates on the Pakistan side were still closed, although the welcome sign in Urdu was visible. People were milling around the Indian side. I spotted BJP chief Kushabhai Thakre in the crowd. I wondered whether his presence was meant to convey his party's solidarity or to make a bid for the vote of Muslims.

There was the usual guard of honour, a large contingent of policemen. I do not know why Badal did not think of having eminent writers, artists and academicians of Punjab to welcome Vajpayee. It would have been more fitting. The guard of honour is a beaten path, covered again and again, even 51 years after the British rule. The *Bhangra* team was, however, a relief. So was the *gidda* party by girls, which conducted the bus right into the Pakistan territory.

The mood of abandon on the Indian side changed into somberness. Pakistan Rangers stood rows upon rows, to attention. There was silence and the air was heavy. Nawaz Sharif's smiling face broke the monotony. Some of his colleagues, dressed in *achkan,* too were a relief.

"Kush ammded (welcome) to Pakistan," were the first words Nawaz Sharif spoke before he embraced Vajpayee. Pakistan ministers also lined up to shake hands with Vajpayee. The three Service chiefs were not there. I wonder if they were supposed to be. I came to know about it when, on arrival in hotel, a newspaperman asked for my reaction to a story published that the three had refused to salute the Indian Prime Minister. This seemed farfetched. The story did not appear in any other paper. However, the fact that the military in Pakistan's third chamber should not be forgotten.

Once again there was the guard of honour on the Pakistan side. This was understandable because the Indian Prime Minister had to be accorded a formal reception. Vajpayee and Sharif left by a helicopter, and we boarded the bus again.

People had lined up both sides of the road leading to Lahore. There were women without veil. Many friendly hands waved towards us. It was a spontaneous welcome. A few yards from our hotel, there were some people who had held aloft black flags. They belong to the Jamiat-e-Islami, a body that has never won a single seat in elections.

It was again Jamia-I Islami followers, who delayed the banquet given by Sharif in the historic Red Fort. The Indian National anthem was played there for the first time since Independence. The roads had to be cleared before Vajpayee's cavalcade could move from the Governor House where the Prime Minister was staying. One policemen died of bullet fired by the Jamiat supporters. The general reaction was that the Afghan war had given access to arms to all and sundry. Pakistan has the problem of unlicenced arms, which are in lakhs.

However unpopular, fundamentalists have a nuisance value. They have silenced the voice of liberals. The common man is afraid of them and of their religious clout. Still people have liked Vajpayee" visit. None from India has spoken to them so well and so frankly. Even otherwise, they argue that it was but logical that a Hindu-backed BJP should have come to an understanding with the Islamic Republic of Pakistan.

What the two Prime Ministers have achieved may seem very little in concrete terms, particularly when Pakistan weights everything in the scales of Kashmir. Even there Vajpayee has said, at least three times during his visit, that the problem of Jammu and Kashmir had yet to to be settled and that the two sides would continue to have talks until they resolved it. In other words, he has conceded that it is a dispute. The fact that he has not mentioned that Kashmir is an integral part of India during his visit is something which the Pakistanis have noticed.

Both Prime Ministers have shown courage and both may go down in history for having tried demolishing the walls of distrust and hatred that have come up in the last five decades. The iceberg of hostility could not have melted in 24 hours, the time that Vajpayee spent in Pakistan. But there is thaw, as Sharif put it.

At least both can say that they have not missed the bus. Much depends on how the mindset bureaucracy builds on the foundation, which Vajpayee and Sharif have laid so carefully and so cautiously. One redeeming factor is that foreign ministers on both sides will be constantly in touch to see how far officials make progress. In a way, the talks have been raised to ministerial level.

The bus was deluxe. But the message was simple: neighbours should never be distant. It has taken India and Pakistan as many years to span a distance of 51 kilometres between Amritsar and Lahore. Still it is a one-time ride. The road is yet to be smoothened and the passengers are too edgy.

It is the same border on which we have lighted candles since the 50th anniversary of India's Independence, although people from the other side have not reciprocated so far. It is the land to make way for people coming from the other side. They were Muslims, we the Hindus and the Sikhs. None spoke— neither they or we. But we understood each other, it was a spontaneous kinship. Both had seen murder and worse; both had been broken on the rack of history. We were refugees.

As the bus carrying Prime Minister Atal Behari Vajpayee and some of us rolled over to the Pakistan side, I felt a new beginning had been made. Whether we were making history or no but we were conscious that it was in the making. Could we be path-breakers? The border bristling with fear and distrust has become chastened. The police that always adopted a martial posture looked like sentinels standing at attention. Something had changed. It seemed as if the peoples of the subcontinent, without giving up their separate identities, would work together for the common good. Would the bus be ushering in an era beyond their dreams—the faith to which I have clung in the sea of hostility and hatred that has for long engulfed the subcontinent.

Vajpayee's speech in Hindustani at the civic reception in Lahore held hope. It was the highest point of his 24-hours stay. He spoke from the heart, as Pakistan foreign minister Sartaj Aziz put it. Vajpayee did not hide the feeling that he had been against partition. Many in his entourage did not want to visit the Minar-e-Pakistan, built to commemorate the memory of March 23, 1940, when the resolution for the formation of Pakistan was endorsed at Lahore.

He not only admitted the pressure exerted on him not to visit the place but also declared that he wanted to allay the fears of those who believed that India had not accepted Pakistan. He announced that the integrity of Pakistan was *sine qua non* for India's unity. Vajpayee was at his best, poetic in expression and lofty in thoughts. He assured the Pakistanis that the "outstanding problem of Kashmir" would be resolved peacefully. What he said implied that it was a dispute, which must be settled—something which even liberal Pakistanis have been wanting New Delhi to say.

Surely, the Pakistanis were not serious when they linked Vajpayee's visit to a solution on Kashmir. They deluded themselves if they believed that the 51-year-old problem could be sorted out in 24 hours. It will take time. That Vajpayee has described more than once Jammu and Kashmir as a problem shows how far he has travelled from his earlier stand that J and K is an integral part of India. It means he is talking in terms of give and take. I am glad that Nawaz Sharif said more or less the same thing while declaring that the "traditional stand" on outstanding problems would have to be changed.

I was surprised over a proposal by Punjab Chief Minister Shahbaz Nawaz, brother of Pakistan Prime Minister, to Parkash Singh Badal, Chief Minister of India's Punjab. Shahbaz suggested that India could take Jammu and give Kashmir to Pakistan. The hardcore Pakistanis had made this suggestion. The reason why it is not acceptable to New Delhi is the thinking it delineates on communal lines. India is a pluralistic society. It cannot accept the thesis that the Muslim-majority Kashmir should go to the Islamic state of Pakistan and the Hindu-majority Jammu to the Hindu-majority India. This will give a fatal blow to the policy of secularism that India upholds. Some other formula has to be worked out, which includes the say of Kashmiris. Both countries have suffered enough from partition on the basis of religion. For them to go back to the days of religious divide is to invite disaster.

Islamabad has disappointed me by not reciprocating New Delhi's offer of no first use of nuclear weapons. The argument that they give equality to Pakistan, which is weaker in conventional weapon war, is fallacious. The bomb has, in fact, ruled out wars between India and Pakistan. Can Islamabad use it on India without exposing itself to the consequences of the fallout? Even if Pakistan could not afford to have a no-first-use pact because of domestic compulsions, it could have had a no-war pact. This would not have jeopardised its defence in any way. Had Vajpayee and Sharif signed such a pact a sense of relief would have swept across the subcontinent. The two countries could have then been cut their military expenditure and divert funds to education, health and hunger, the vision to which they referred during their speeches.

Maybe, they will work towards that now in the days to come. The core problem is trust and confidence, not Kashmir. That has to be built first. One way to begin it is to look at the history books. And this cannot be done until they are rewritten and a biased approach to problems is changed. The two Prime Ministers can do that because one represents the party of Hindus and the other that of Muslims. Strange, the two should forget to lift restrictions on newspapers and books of one country entering the other. More contacts between the peoples will help. But without free flow of information, contacts begin to languish. Maybe, foreign ministers will rectify the lapses whatever the two Prime Ministers have failed to identify.

With all its deficiencies, the Lahore declaration has opened up many avenues for cooperation and amity. Once again there is an opportunity for the two countries to generate goodwill, which will help them solve all outstanding problems. But if the atmosphere built by Vajpayee's visit and Nawaz Sharif's generous approach is allowed to be dissipated, events will meander to the same old situation. Even if there is no conflict, there will be no settlement, even if no hostility, no harmony and, even if there is no war, there will be no peace. Both countries would have missed the bus.

After Lahore Declaration What ?

I asked Home Minister L.K. Advani the other day whether the Lahore Declaration had led to the lessening of interference in Kashmir from the other side. He said: "No." I persisted in my question to find out if there was a slight change, even though not very significant. He reiterated, "No."

That the problem of Kashmir is yet to be settled goes without saying. That Prime Minister Atal Behari Vajpayee conceded this categorically at Lahore more than once and later in India needs no elucidation. That he has never mentioned

Kashmir as an integral part of India since his return from Lahore is known to even the Pakistanis.

In other words, the basic demand of Islamabad to regard Kashmir as a dispute has been accepted. I recall how the Pakistan officials would say during the discussions in public or private that the mere recognition by India of the dispute would meet half their claims. This should have made Islamabad reciprocate and stop, for at least some time, the arms and armed men coming from its side into India. Even otherwise, the Lahore Declaration has mentioned at more than one place that the problem will be settled peacefully, through bilateral talks. Prime Minister Nawaz Sharif has repeated the assurance even after the declaration.

It is understandable that Pakistan is reluctant to stop giving its 'moral and political' support to the Kashmiris. Islamabad and the Pakistanis are so obsessed with the problem that they cannot easily separate the reality from fiction. For politicians, it is still more difficult because of the mileage that Kashmir gives them. Support through statements or resolutions is one thing but to set up centres for recruitment and training and help the Afghans, the Sudanese and others cross the line of control to get into India is another.

It is no use entering into a sterile discussion on whether the assistance Pakistan gives is moral or military. Many foreign assessments have shown that it is involved knee deep in armed activities. Even America has said so publicly. Therefore, denials and counter-denials will not take us anywhere. What Pakistan has to analyse is the repercussion of military involvement on the peace process.

After many, many years, the two countries have reached a stage where Kashmir is sought to be discussed seriously. The Prime Minister and the foreign minister of Pakistan have themselves admitted in their statements that they feel India is genuinely wanting to find a solution. How does Islamabad's policy of gun-running fit in?

New Delhi has come a long way in recognising Kashmir as the most important subject that requires tackling by a separate committee out of six constituted towards confidence-building measures. It is but fair for India to expect that the Pakistan government should suspend the assistance to militants in Kashmir so long as the talks continue. Very few will buy the argument that it is an operation of the Inter Service Intelligence (ISI), which is not under Islamabad's control. Pakistan can at least stop the use of its territory.

No doubt, the pressure on Sharif's is much more than that on Vajpayee. Some people in Pakistan are determined to sabotage any conciliation with India. In our country, the climate is different: the anti-Pakistan lobby has crashed. But New Delhi also is not above pressure. What happens in Pakistan has its reaction in India. How meaningful will the talks when one side of Pakistan is at the negotiating table while the other is working with militants and supplying arms to them?

The constant attack on the security forces in Kashmir can affect the talks. After the injury to DIG Police, state chief minister Farooq Abdullah has said that the interference in Kashmir was to be fought like a war. He is volatile person. But his message that peace cannot be achieved when the war is on is unexceptionable. Senior officials of the armed forces in India have also been making the same point.

Islamabad should realise that it cannot run with the hare and hunt with the hound. It is unproductive. War and peace are two contradictory situations. The presence of the one is the absence of the other. The Lahore Declaration has provided Pakistan with a fresh opportunity to depart from the path it has taken in the past.

An unofficial proposal reaching India is that New Delhi should be prepared to withdraw its forces from the valley if it wants the interference from the other side to stop. How far the Sharif government is willing to back the proposal is not known. But it is not an outlandish one. That can form a basis for discussion. The point to keep in mind is that the strength of security forces in Kashmir is in proportion to the danger faced or perceived by India. Once the interference from the other side lessens, the strength of security forces in the valley will automatically go down.

There is no doubt that the armed forces will return to the barracks once militancy ends. And whether the Pakistanis believe it or not, the insurgency in the valley has come down considerably. The embers get re-ignited when the valley receives fresh supply of arms and armed men. And the Afghans and the Sudanese, who come through Pakistan, communalise the situation.

Even if Pakistan does not see the reason behind the discontinuance of its involvement, India should take the initiative to settle the other aspect of Kashmir: the Siachin glacier dispute. Nearly 10 years ago, both New Delhi and Islamabad had reached an agreement, which was initiated by foreign secretaries of the two countries. An indiscreet announcement at that time sabotaged the entire exercise. The draft can perhaps be retrieved for further discussion, if not for straight implementation.

I believe that our army is against the old agreement. But the retired top brass that I have talked to tell me that the Siachin glacier is of no strategic importance. If so, the political leadership should not leave it to the army and order the withdrawal of forces from there on the condition that Pakistan also does so. The word, redeployment, was used in the draft agreement.

Primarily, there is a lack of confidence on both sides. The suspicion is that if one side were to vacate, the other would step in. Surely the agreement can be endorsed by America, Britain, Russia and France to guarantee its full implementation.

In fact, the Lahore Declaration should build mutual confidence. There is no need for a third party. Maybe, as the days go by, the trust will increase. But there is no doubt that the Declaration has made a new start possible. Living in the past will only bring back bitter memories. If Great Britain and France could be friends after fighting wars for 100 years, why not India and Pakistan?

My only fear is that Vajpayee's bus journey may go to waste if the two sides are not careful about what they say. Foreign officials in both countries have to show more responsibility because they hold press briefing almost every day. Politicians may say that they are quoted out of context, officials cannot. Many a time in the past, I saw the beginnings of a new era. It happened after the Tashkent Agreement in 1966 and after the Shimla Agreement in 1972. But then, distrust and suspicion overlook the two countries. And they became distant neighbours again. I trust that politicians and bureaucrats will this time resist the temptation of stoking the fire of their vested interest. The people on both sides are sick and tired of being enemies. They want to live in peace so that their children and their grandchildren grow up in an environment of security and confidence. Is it too much to ask for?

LoC Becomes International Border

There is never a good war. So said a US President. Pakistan thinks otherwise. It does not realise the harm it has done to itself or to the peace process in the region. Some day it may. One only hopes it will not be too late by then.

Take the aspect of the harm Pakistan has done to itself. The Line of Control (LoC) in Jammu and Kashmir is what it has been seeking to alter through negotiations or wars. And that is where it has spoilt its case. The LoC has become the international border.

Islamabad's incursions into the Kargil area have shown the vehemence with which its violation has been opposed. The demand all over is that the Pakistan's intruders must go behind the LoC. No one in the world supports its violation.

Whether it is President Clinton or the Group of Eight nations, they have the inviolability of the LoC in view. They have demanded that it should be respected. And what they have condemned is its violation. America has even asked Pakistan by name to withdraw its men and restore the status quo ante.

In other words, the LoC is permanent. Pakistan has to respect the line if it does not want to be singled out as an aggressor. It may cloud the issue, as it has been trying to do through diplomatic manoeuvres. It may train and arm infiltrators and send its own forces as it has done in the Kargil area. But it has to withdraw them because they are on the Indian side of the LoC, the border. The sanctity which the LoC has come to acquire after incursions is India's gain, which has not yet seeped into Pakistan.

New Delhi has been trying for years to make Islamabad accept the LoC as the international border. Zulfikar Ali Bhutto, then Pakistan's Prime Minister, gave a solemn assurance to the late Prime Minister Indira Gandhi at Shimla in 1972 on the conversion of the LoC into the internatinal border. But he could not sell the idea to his defeated armed forces and he went back on his word.

What could not be achieved then has been made possible through Islamabad's military adventure. Unwittingly, the Pakistan armed forces have themselves converted the LoC into the intenational border which they had opposed. Lt. Gen. (Rtd) Syed Rafaqat in Pakistan had something to do with the drawing of the LoC. He has said in Islamabad that the line was demarcated, not delineated, lest it should become an international boundary. But whatever the technicalities, the Pakistani forces have done what India had failed to do.

True, it will take time for the Indian forces to clear the Kargil heights. They have done well to warn the nation that it would be a long haul. But the target they have set before themselves is the LoC. That is the border beyond which the Pakistani forces are sought to be pushed.

The Pakistani armed forces have not only firmed up the LoC but also made talk on Kashmir difficult. Now that the LoC is the border, what is there to discuss except the opening of the Srinagar-Rawalpindi road for better contacts between the two sides of Kashmir and laying down the ground rules for the haulage of timber through the Jehlum? All the Kashmiris who have certain other ideas about the state will have to reckon with the reality of the LoC. The Pakistani forces have given *de jure* recognition to the *de facto* situation.

Still the worst thing that the Pakistani force have done is to defeat peaceful options on Kashmir. New Delhi was prepared to sit across the table to discuss the problem. The two foreign secretaries had even begun talks solely on Kashmir, as was the condition laid down by Pakistan for any dialogue. Now all that has been destroyed. The confidence which had got built after the Lahore Declaration has been rudely shaken. Who will pick up the thread and from where?

Indeed, after the Lahore Declaration, a new chapter in India-Pakistan relations had opened. People all over India and Pakistan were beginning to look for a solution on Kashmir to normalise relations between the two countries. There was an atmosphere where there were serious efforts afood to try and bury the hatchet. And it looked as if the 51-year-old gulf was beginning to be spanned. Trade, culture exchange, easy travel between the countries—all seemed a possibility. The meeting between Prime Ministers Atal Behari Vajpayee and Nawaz Sharif at Lahore promised new vistas. Apparently, the Pakistani armed forces have a vested interest in war against India. They have no faith in peace. They want to sustain the atmosphere of ill-will and hatred.

Still the situation is not all that grim. The Prime Ministers of the two countries pick up the phone and talk to each other. The bus, which Vajpayee rode first, is plying between Delhi and Lahore. The Indian mission in Islamabad and Pakistan in New Delhi are issuing visas and people are travelling back and forth. The Samjhota Express steams out of Lahore and Delhi three times a week. Only recently did some 50 intellectuals and journalists from both sides issued a joint statement to appeal to the rulers not to escalate the situation. The armed forces in Pakistan may be furning over all this. But the people of Pakistan want peace.

Even the Group of Eight nations has not named any country as an aggressor. It wants the two to sit across the table to sort out their differences. India is ready once the infiltrators withdrawn from the Indian side of the LoC. Will they do so for the sake of peace? That is the question.

One feels sorry for the people of Pakistan because the armed forces had never allowed them to rule themselves. For more than four decades, there had been martial law. Even when the army returned to the barracks, it kept a close watch on political rulers. Now it has taken over without sitting in the chair. Democracy has receded further into the background.

General Parvez Musharaff, the chief of army staff, is reportedly wanting a national government in Pakistan. It means that even Sharif's days are numbered. Even if the military does not have a direct role, it has established its unquestioned supremacy by starting the hostilities. Musharaff is reported to have said, while talking to his troops in the forward areas, that they were engaged in *jehad* (religious war). He should know that the Indian troops include Muslims. A Muslim officer and some Muslim soldiers have died in the operation at Kargil. Whatever name he may give to their fighting, they have sacrificed their lives for their motherland.

The armed forces in Pakistan are living in a world of their own. In an Urdu journal which they run, they have argued that "unstable conditions in India" have weakened the control of rulers in Delhi. This is mere wishful thinking. In fact, the incursions of the Pakistani forces have created in India a sense of solidarity which was lacking before. Political parties have criticised the BJP-led coalition for not keeping them in the picture. But all of them stand behind the government in operations in the Kargil area to vacate the aggression. The armed forces in Pakistan do not know how strong the united will of a nation in a democracy is.

What worries one is the desperation of the armed forces in Pakistan. Realising that they have made the LoC sacrosanct, they may widen the conflict. This will be a tragedy. Dr. Abdul Qadir Khan, the father of Pakistan's bomb, warned me during an interview in 1988, in which he disclosed that Pakistan had the bomb, that "if you ever drive us to the wall, we will use the bomb."

Nawaz Sharif's Ideology

Nawaz Sharif seems to have tied up all in his mind: Benazir Bhutto will sweep the polls in Sind and he, in Punjab, the NWFP giving 60 per cent to Benazir and Baluchistan 60 per cent to him. He may not first put in his claim to the Prime Minister's chair and instead let Benazir occupy it first. Both are in touch with each other on the phone regularly.

For a person who has been in the wilderness for more than three years, Sharif sounded resolute and determined. There was not a note of despondency during the conversation I had with him in Jeddah for five hours spread over two days last week.

The deposed Prime Minister had no doubt that the military rule in Pakistan had run its course, once and for all, no matter what people say. He, for one, was convinced of this. He seemed willing to wait till whatever time it took but he would never come to power on the shoulders of the military.

Sharif resides in an old palace. He not only looks corpulent but also opulent. But then he has always been known for his regal style. He keeps a lavish table. Ornate furniture, carpeted floors and glittering chandeliers, you just name it and it is there. Two guards open the front gate one of them is a Saudi Arabian policeman and the other is from one of the many servants he carried in the jumbo jet when he flew from Islamabad to Jeddah to take refuge in Saudi Arabia. He would have visited other countries but his passport has not been renewed for the past one year. Several reminders to Islamabad have not evoked even an acknowledgement.

Sharif feels let down by Prime Minister Atal Behari Vajpayee's initiative on Pakistan. The former Pakistan Prime Minister is all for rapprochement, but not when the real power is in the hands of the armed forces. Any agreement with the military would have a question mark against it.

A co-architect of the Lahore accord, Sharif is personally hurt because Vajpayee was supportive of him and had reportedly said after he was overthrown that Sharif was ousted because of his efforts to make up with India. Sharif, however, feels that the Indian Prime Minister has let General Pervez Musharraf off the hook when he was under tremendous pressure from within Pakistan and the world powers. Even otherwise, it did not behove a democratic India to talk to those who had usurped power through a coup. Such seems to be Sharif's thinking.

I believe that a leading editor from Lahore some time back met him with a message from Musharraf for a compromise. Even at Islamabad, his Muslim League (Nawaz) Party has been approached by the military. There have been persistent efforts to wean away from him his brother, Shahbaz Sharif, at present in the US. But Nawaz Sharif does not want to have anything to do with the military.

While in detention, Sharif was treated worse than a criminal. For months, he was kept in solitary confinement. When flown from Islamabad to Karachi for trial, he was handcuffed to his seat. His son, who is running a steel plant which Sharif has established near Jeddah, was also put behind bars. His story is no different.

Sharif seemed particularly bitter about the way in which the army kept him in the dark on Kargil. He was not aware that the Pakistani troops were fighting till Vajpayee rang him up to complain. He had been told by the army that the mujahideen were up in arms. Sharif sounded categorical when he said he was not on board, the allegation which Musharraf had made after the failure at Kargil.

Musharraf's repeated requests to Sharif to ring up President Clinton to intervene was to get Pakistan out of the situation in which it had got embroiled. But before going to Washington, Sharif tried to send his minister, Sartaj, to New Delhi. Vajpayee was so angry that he refused to meet him. Clinton brought about the ceasefire by requesting Vajpayee on the phone to allow the Pakistani troops to withdraw. Sharif must have felt utterly humiliated.

The abortive Kargil action, which took place without his

knowledge, angered Sharif. He seemed to have made up his mind to punish those who were responsible for it. Musharraf was on top of the list, followed by Lt Gen Mehmood and Lt Gen Aziz. The three got an inkling of it and began preparing for the coup.

It was only after the defence secretary was sent with Musharraf's dismissal order, signed by the Prime Minister and endorsed by the President, did the army top brass swing into action to remove Sharif. The Navy and Air Force chiefs did not know anything about the coup till the army informed them.

Musharraf was at that time on a flight from Colombo to Karachi. Islamabad instructed the pilot to delay the landing of the plane or not to land at Karachi airport which had been taken over by the army by then. The pilot expressed his inability because he was short of fuel. Whether he landed at Karachi because he was short of fuel or whether Musharraf's service revolver forced him to land would never be known. Musharraf had apparently come to know of his dismissal and the coup on the plane itself. Sharif was sure of one thing: he had miffed on the timing. The rest is history.

Sharif and Musharraf had decided to oust each other. Musharrtaf struck first. But in the process he knocked out an elected Prime Minister. I do not know why in the midst of our conversation Sharif abruptly brought in former Prime Minister Narasimha Rao and inquired whether the cases of "corruption" against him had been over. I told him I did not remember. Probably one was still pending. Was Sharif thinking of the cases of corruption against him in the Pakistan courts?

But the unkindest cut came at the end of the conversation. Are you from the BJP? he asked.

7

Farooq Abdullah and His Politics: An Appraisal of India's Stand

Dr. Farooq and Indira Gandhi

I hope that Kashmir does not go the Punjab way. But the fear that it might is very much there. Nor Mrs. Gandhi seem to be employing similar tactics in the state. In Punjab she rebuffed the moderates among the Akalis and did not concede even their genuine demands, with the result was that they lost much of their following to the extremists and Jarnail Singh Bhindranwale, though he ordered the killing of innocents and desecrated the Golden Temple, became the most important Sikh leader.

In Kashmir now she is out for the blood of Dr Farooq Abdullah, the J&K chief minister, and her attacks on him are creating a situation where the extremists are gaining ground.

Popularity of Farooq

True, Dr Farooq is still very popular and the more she troubles him the more he gains support. But in the process, anti-national elements are gaining ground. For example, the Jamiat-e-Islami, which had a negligible following even about a year ago, has become a force to reckon with. Her constant pressure on Farooq has given some credence to the Jamiat Islami line that Kashmiris are not accepted as Indians.

If Dr Farooq, who repeatedly says that he is an Indian and the state's accession to India is a closed chapter, is not trusted, how will other Kashmiris be? And the Jamiat has the readymade emotional argument that this is so because Dr Farooq is a Muslim.

Tactics of Mrs. Gandhi

Mrs. Gandhi's tactics have also made Dr Farooq turn a blind eye to the Jamiat's doings. Probably he feels he may need its support if and when Mrs. Gandhi decides to turn him out. The Jamiat, of course, is taking advantage of the confrontation between the two. Had Mrs. Gandhi accepted with grace the defeat of her party in the 1983 state assembly election, things would not have reached such a pass.

The situation in Kashmir is not, as yet, comparable to what it was in Punjab when Mrs. Gandhi took drastic action. But one should remember that in Punjab also, just a couple of years ago, no one would have dreamt that things would deterioriate to the extent it did. And what caused such deterioration? Mrs. Gandhi went on stalling a solution at least thrice the Akalis agreed to a settlement, the first time one negotiated through Swaran Singh, the second time to one negotiated through political parties and the third time to one negotiated through Mrs. Gandhi's own emissary Pranab Mukherjee, Finance Minister. Every time she went back on her assurances at the last minute.

And when the moderates had nothing to show for their moderation, the extremists took over. And Mrs. Gandhi could have saved the situation from becoming explosive, as it did, if she had agreed at least to handing over Chandigarh to Punjab. (At one point the Akalis even went to the extent of accepting the partition of Chandigarh).

Mufti Syed. In Kashmir Mrs. Gandhi first built up Mufti Syed, the Congress (I) chief, as a rival to Dr Farooq. This was when Mir Qasim, a respected Congressman, refused to toe the line in the state; he was a party to the accord with Sheikh Abdullah and resigned from chief ministership to make room for him in 1975.

Now Mrs. Gandhi has G.M. Shah, Dr Farooq's brother-in-law, who has been able to wean away at least 25 per cent of National Conference members and has formed a separate party under the leadership of his wife, the Sheikh's daughter, Khalida. The Congress (I) is making husband and wife its stalking horses because it cannot face the anti-Congress sentiment openly.

Extremists. All these manouvres may be part of politics but they are strengthening the extremists. To what extent one can see from the Intelligence report on the activities of some of the anti-Indian forces, which says:

"Members of the pro-Pak and secessionist all J&K People's League and the militant Islamic Jamaat-e-Tulba (IJT) indulged in violent demonstrations and looted a number of shops during an anti-liquor agitation in Anantnag (March 1-11, 1982). They also exploited the firing incident in the Al Aqsa mosque in Jerusalem and resorted to violent activities (April 14, 1982) at Srinagar against shops and establishments of minorities. Police had to open fire to control the situation in which one person was killed. The activists of the League again indulged in acts of lawlessness in July 1982 and January 1983 by attacking some shopkeepers and their employees at Anantnag town on the plea that they were engaged in clandestine sale of liquor.

Meanwhile, Sheikh Tajmul Islam, Nazim-e-Ala, IJT had been continuously exhorting the Kashmiri Muslims to work for the 'liberation' of Kashmir from 'Indian subjugation'. Some of his recent inflammatory utterances including the observation that the prime objective of the Tulba and the League was to ensure that there was no non-Muslim in Jammu and Kashmir, was calculated to generate communal tension in the Kashmir Valley. A procession led by him at Anantnag on January 30, 1983 raised pro-Pak and pro-Zia-ul Haq slogans.

"The communal and secessionist propaganda by the J&K JEI continued unabated. The party held its triennial conference on August 6-9, 1982 at Srinagar. During its recent annual iztemah held at Srinagar (Feb. 1983) the party reiterated that its primary objective was to achieving Islamic revolution in J&K and to 'liberate' the State by an armed struggle."

New Delhi and Dr. Farooq. Even if ultimately Mrs. Gandhi is able to oust Dr. Farooq, how will that help the country? The Congress (I) may get another state under its umbrella but at what cost and to what purpose? The experience of Punjab is before us; it may take a long time for the wounds it has inflicted on the nation, especially the Sikh community, to heal. In Kashmir any drastic action will have even worse repercussions. There the very settled question of accession may become "unsettled" and anti-centre feelings may develop into anti-India feelings. The Sheikh was a tall man, the product of Kashmiris' struggle against the Maharaja Hari Singh's tyranny. He could always retrieve the situation.

Farooq, a lesser man, may not be able to do that if New Delhi persists in its policy of making trouble for him and his state merely because he had the temerity to defeat Mrs. Gandhi's party at the polls. One hopes the army will not be called in to flush out a chief minister from his office nest.

Farooq Abdullah Critical of Mrs. Gandhiji's Policy

If the Jammu region were to reject him, he would ask for its separation from Kashmir, the chief minister of Jammu and Kashmir, Dr. Farooq Abdullah, said this in an interview with me here. He was visibly upset over the reports that his party, the National Conference, might fare badly in the Jammu region, which has 32 seats in 76-member House.

Dr. Farooq Abdullah said that what he and his father (Sheikh Abdullah) have done for the people of Jammu was known to them. If they still did not want him, "then I do not want them either".

For Fresh Poll. Dr Abdullah said that he would ask for fresh poll if no party secured a clear majority. Asked if he would form the government with the support of the Congress (I), he said he would rather retire than do so.

On National Alternative. He alleged that Mrs. Gandhi has communalised politics in Jammu and Kashmir if she continued that way, as he believed she was doing, she would disintegrate the country. He said she was placating Hindu sentiment and dividing the people of the state "for a temporary gain at the poll".

Dr. Abdullah said that the country must be "saved" from Mrs. Gandhi and there had to be a national alternative to do so. He said he for one would try to help create a national alternative.

Dr. Abdullah said: "Does it behove the Prime Minister to exploit the Resettlement Act when she herself referred to the Supreme Court for its opinion?" He said that Mrs. Gandhi while in Jammu pointed her finger towards the border and told many gatherings that the Pakistanis would come from the other side to occupy their homes and plough their fields. How could she say such things? Did she realise its repercussions?

When pointed out that the National Conference was also indulging in communal propaganda in Kashmir he said, he himself had depreceated this talk. "But my point is that Mrs. Gandhi is doing it herself, not only her partymen. But I have gone out of the way to hit hard the communalists", Dr Abdullah said.

Asked if he had compromised his position by joining hands with Maulvi Farooq, Dr Abdullah said that he was not responsible for his "politics". The state was an integral part of India and there was no question of any plebescite of self-determination. Many elections had been held in the state and the people had given their verdict in favour of India more than once. He said that he was proud to be an Indian and those who are trying to reopen the question "were not serving the interest of Kashmir and the country."

Preference for Mir Qasim

I could never figure out why Mrs. Gandhi turned against Sheikh Mohammed Abdullah. Both having Nehru as a link, she as a daughter and he as a friend, should have been close to each other but they were not. And until a few months before his death, she appeared to considering ways to oust him from office. But for Mir Qasim, a respected leader in Kashmir, Mrs Gandhi might have done just that.

Mrs. Gandhi's Attitude

It was Mir Qasim who told her that it would only add to her troubles. She should not think of any changes in Kashmir in his time, and he was a very sick man. She listened to him and flew to Srinagar to visit the ailing leader. But the relationship between her and the Sheikh had by then become too frozen to be melted by the visit. In fact, his family members, except Dr. Farooq, were more hostile than the Sheikh.

Abdullah's Reception for Mrs. Gandhi

What brought a changes in Mrs Gandhi towards the end only she tell. Here was the Sheikh who annoyed Mr. Morarji Desai, then Prime Minister, by inviting her to Jammu and Kashmir when she was in the political wilderness and according her a VIP reception. The Sheikh even told her at that time that he, having been a close friend of Jawaharlal Nehru, thought of her as his own daughter and his house was always open to her. When she returned to power, there was a good equation between the two—but it lasted only for a short time.

Efforts to Establish Congress (I)

I have not been able to find out why there was coolness on her part. Some Congress (I) leaders have told me that the Kashmiri crowd surrounding her, poisoned her ears because most of them could never have any say in their state. Some have attributed the estrangement to Mrs. Gandhi's all-out efforts to establish Congress (I) in the state and the Sheikh's determination to foil them.

Annoyance of Abdullah

However, the Sheikh, with whom I spent a whole evening three months before his death, told me that the main reason for Mrs. Gandhi's annoyance was that she wanted to treat him as a "door mat" and he would not be one. Since she had got used to chief minister raising their hand at her bidding and had sychophants around her, she could not tolerate any one treating her as an equal. "Now who is this Fotedar, because he is one of her advisers?"

Criticism of Mrs. Gandhi

Part of this interview I have already used in *Sunday*. The Sheikh said: "She would like to throw me out. But I am not an Antulay or Anjiah who sits or stands at her orders. I am elected by my people and I am answerable to them. She thinks everyone has to play court to her. But I alone am not her target. She does not like any non-Congress (I) chief ministers. She does not like the chief minister of West Bengal nor that of Tamil Nadu. She said once that she would like the entire country to be ruled by the Congress (I).

Pinpricks for Abdullah

What hurt the Sheikh were the many pinpricks she inflicted on him. He told me of the visit of Mr. Venkatasubbaiah, Minister of State for Home Affairs, to Kishtwar, and how he had not had the courtesy to call on the state chief minister. Instead of expressing regrets for not having called on the Sheikh, Mr. Venkatasubbaiah, wrote in his report that he submitted to Mr. Gandhi: "I had talked on telephone to the chief minister who was at Jammu on my arrival at the airport to convey my regards to him. He did not inquire anything about my visit to Kishtwar."

Azad's Visit to Srinagar

Another thing which rankled the Sheikh was the visit of Mr. Ghulam Nabi Azad, then the President of the Youth Congress (I), and Mrs. Rajender Bajpai to Srinagar. The Sheikh said that Mr. Azad, who would not even get 10 votes in Kashmir, came with 'that lady' and held a public meeting in Srinagar only to shower abuse on him. The Sheikh felt that Mrs. Gandhi was at the back of this.

Abdullah felt Depressed and Upset

The Sheikh was even more upset by the report that Mrs. Gandhi said at a public meeting in Jammu that the minorities were not safe in the state. Even though she denied having made such an observation, the Sheikh believed that she did. What hurt him was that a person like him who had fought communalism all his life was being branded as a communalist. When I told him that Mr. Atal Behari Vajpayee, then the Foreign Minister, had suggested to Mr. Desai after the exit of Mr. Gharan Singh from the Janata cabinet that the Sheikh be inducted as Home Minister, he said that it was for Mr. Desai to make such a decision.

He did ask me about the preparations for the World Urdu Conference, which I had discussed with him more than once. I told him that there had been no progress since the return of the Congress (I) to power. He offered all help and was keen that the Conference be held. I wonder if we can pay him a tribute by holding the conference.

Mr. Qasim's Politics

Mrs. Gandhi is said to be considering giving the Bharat Ratna postumously to the Sheikh. This may be her way of atoning for her mistakes. But one person who was caught in the cross-fire is Mir Qasim. The Sheikh was willing to offer him a Rajya Sabha seat in 1982 biennial election. But he wanted Mrs. Gandhi to ask for it since Mr. Qasim is a Congress (I) leader. She would not ask him for a favour. Mir Qasim did not got the seat. However, he may now make it to Parliament since Dr. Farooq wants him as a bridge between New Delhi and Srinagar.

8

Indian Leader's Views: Indo-Pak Relations

Siachin Glacier: Pakistan's Refusal for Joint Survey
Pakistan has refused to accept joint survey of the Siachin glacier to find out which side was the aggressor and where, according to authoritative quarters. They also allege that the proposal drafted by the field commanders of India and Pakistan has been turned down by the top brass in Islamabad.

Pakistan's Viewpoint
Pakistan wants India to vacate the territory, but the latter is not prepared to take the risk since it suspects that Pakistan will occupy it, as it had tried to do around April 1984 when the glacier was still a no-man's land, but under India's overall control.

The Siachin glacier sprawling in the north of Ladakh, has been a scene of hostilities between the two countries for nearly two years now and the firing from both sides did not stop even when Prime Minister Rajiv Gandhi and President Zia-ul Haq had discussed the subject at Omman and more recently, at Dhaka, for a settlement.

With only two days remaining before General Zia's arrival in Delhi, the situation has not changed in any way. After checking with defence source in Delhi, one finds that there is yet no word from political masters for a ceasefire or anything else.

In any case, the Indian army is totally opposed to the vacation of the glacier on the ground that Pakistan's occupation of it can expose the Noubra Valley and the terrain below, both disadvantageous for India from the strategy point of view.

Losses
Both countries have lost nearly 200 men and the figure of the injured is around 500. If preparations at the height of

20,000 feet on the two sides are any indication, they want to fight it out. There is no hesitation in deploying more men and material. While Pakistan is fighting from below, carrying supplies and men at night under the cover of darkness, the Indian forces, perched at height, are not allowing any movement during the day.

New Delhi first became suspicious in 1983 when an American map showed the Siachin and places like Lyogme and Lagongma as part of Pakistan. Subsequently, the Indian army came to know that a Japanese mountaineering expedition team was seeking Islamabad's permission to scale certain mountains in the area. The Indian embassy in Tokyo told the team that it was New Delhi which had to give the permission. Consequently, the Japanese called off the expedition.

In recent years, India first sent a patrol to the glacier in 1983; it returned without encountering opposition. But intelligence reports later said that Pakistan was planning to post troops there. In fact, India was able to beat Pakistani troops by about three weeks, acting swiftly after India learnt from an international firm that Islamabad had purchased heavy winter outfits by the thousand. One thing is, however, clear that both sides are more interested in sustaining their claim over the area than in killing one another.

Kashmir Can Thaw Indo-Pak Ties

Meeting with Top Pak Leaders. By a quirk accident the top two in the political field of Pakistan came to Delhi recently. Prime Minister Nawaz Sharif was there and so was Opposition leader Benazir Bhutto. Both met the top in India's political scene. They reportedly felt relieved after talking to the Bhartiya Janata Party leaders, who are perceived anti-Muslim in Pakistan.

Such meetings at the top are always welcome because they evoke hope in a perpetually dismal scenario of Indo-Pak hostility. At this time, when the two countries are doing their utmost to harm each other, except going to war, any talk, however cursory and rambling, indicates that all is not lost.

But this alone is not enough. If they do not bury the hatchet, they are bound to clash. They did so in 1948, 1965 and 1971. The hatchet is Kashmir, which joined the Indian Union after partition and which Pakistan claims should have come to it on the basis of the Muslim majority in the state. Nawaz Sharif said openly and privately in Delhi that the key to friendly relations between Pakistan and India was the solution of the Kashmir problem.

I do not think it is entirely true. The key to the issue lies in the confidence we build among the Muslims in the country so that they have a feeling of security as well as equality. If we are able to curb Hindu-Muslim riots and establish a secular society, we will find the people of Pakistan responding. This does not mean that Kashmir's solution must await until we are able to put our house in order. Nawaz Sharif is quite right when he says that most of tension between the two countries was because of Kashmir. How do we sort it out?

Domination of Religion

Surely, it cannot be done on the basis of religion. India did not accept partition on the basis of religion. Some Muslim-majority areas did not want to stay with India. They opted out and constituted a separate country, Pakistan. Had religion been the arbiter, the exchange of population would have been inevitable. To accept the thesis of religion in Kashmir now, after 44 years of independence, and to allow secession on the ground that the Kashmiris are Muslims will only amount to questioning the very basis of Indian polity.

Presuming all Kashmiris are on one side, how do we reconcile the demand of 3.5 million people with the compulsions of a society which is constitutionally obliged not to mix religion with the state? To ignore them at a time when Hindu chauvinism is on the rise may strengthen communalism and fundamentalism further in India.

I am willing to concede that Pakistan is a consequence and India a cause of what is happening in Kashmir. After all, when conditions were normal in 1965, the Kashmiris themselves reported to the authorities about the infiltration from across the border. There was no uprising even when the infiltrators reached the outskirts of Srinagar. The same people are alienated now and some youths among them have gone to the extent of seeking training and arms from Pakistan.

Islamabad under Pressure

That Islamabad is under pressure is also understandable. The Pakistanis, who were never reconciled to Kashmir being part of India, are worked up after hearing or reading about the running battles between the Indian security forces and the Kashmiri militants. If a liberal leader like Benazir Bhutto can revive her father's battle cry of waging a 1000-year war with India on Kashmir, an average Pakistani must be boiling with rage. But how does this help? Another round of hostilities is no solution to the problem.

Still the Kashmir issue cannot be left where it is if the climate in the subcontinent is to be improved. The two countries must discuss it, without minimising the cruel realities of the situation and, at the same time, keeping in view the aspirations of the Kashmiris. After the new government has been sworn in at New Delhi, its first task should be to hold talks on Kashmir.

Both sides should, however, prepare their peoples that the solution found may not be the one which will satisfy them. In a give-and-take settlement, there is nothing black or white; it is a compromise. So far the leaders in the two countries have taken extreme positions; they have not appreciated each other's compulsions. The embarrassment of one country has been the grist to the propaganda mill of the other. If they are to be, to quote Nawaz Sharif, "honest and realistic", they may be able to find a common ground.

One possible solution is the Trieste-type agreement provided for the partitioning of the Free Territory of Tireste between Italy and Yugoslavia among the then existing demarcation between the two with minor changes. The agreement guaranteed free travel between the two sides. Perhaps this type of arrangement can make the basis for talks between India and Pakistan on Kashmir.

I discussed the formula with Zulfikar Ali Bhutto in Rawalpindi in 1972, before the Simla Agreement, when he was Pakistan's President. He was not averse to it. Asked if he would accept a similar solution for Kashmir, he said: "I was thinking partly of Trieste." But he refused to say more, except: "I have given you a peep into my mind. If I say too much on it, or if we go too much into it, here also we have our Jana Sanghites who will start saying 'betrayal' and such things. But what I am telling you in essence is that taking into account this and other world precedents, we can start moving and I believe that there is great room for it." (This is part of an interview on tape which I possess).

A New Formula

I believe a formula on the lines of the Trieste agreement was on the anvil when General Zia-ul-Haq was killed. Rajiv Gandhi mentioned this in his last interview to the *New York Times* and the *Gulf News*. "We were close to finishing agreement on Kashmir, we had the maps and everything ready to sign and then he was killed," he had said. In 1960 when Rajeshwar Dayal was India's High Commissioner to Pakistan, he discussed with General Ayub Khan, then chief martial law administrator, a similar formula. But Jawaharlal Nehru did not want it to be pursued.

Whether it is a Trieste-type agreement or some other formula, it would be hard to sell it in India. It means concessions at a time when the BJP has gone ahead in northern India, the party's main area of influence, saying that the special status which Kashmir enjoys should go. For countering the propaganda, the Indian people must be convinced about Pakistan's bona fides. One way to prove it is to stop assistance to the militants in Punjab.

I again concede that Pakistan is a consequence, not the cause. But there is no denying about Pakistan's complicity in Punjab. Last year when the two countries almost came to fighting, President Bush's special envoy Gate was able to assuage New Delhi's anger by conveying that Pakistan had closed 30-odd camps for training militants. Any help Islamabad renders to India to curb terrorism in Punjab will influence New Delhi's attitude on finding a way to accommodate Pakistan on Kashmir. To begin with, Islamabad can withdraw the sanctuary it has given to the leaders of militants.

Politics of India and Pakistan

The politics of both India and Pakistan is dominated by small men who are playing small games. The money the two countries have spent on buying arms and armaments to kill each other could have been spent on those who have grown up without hope: unemployed, uneducated and given to violent criminality. Sometimes I wonder whether the disputes between India and Pakistan are there because of leaders or whether leaders are there because of disputes.

The European nations have come together, forgetting the bitterness of wars they fought against themselves for hundreds of years. There is no doubt that some day the same feeling would come about in South Asia. The high walls that fear and distrust have raised on the borders will crumble and the peoples of the subcontinent, without giving their separate identities and countries, will work together for the common good. This might usher in an era fruitful beyond their dreams. But if suspicions are allowed to plague the relationship between the two countries, events will meander to a situation where, even if there is no conflict, there will be no settlement.

Talking to Pakistan Prime Minister

Solution of Kashmir Problem. "I know it will take time to find a solution to Kashmir," Prime Minister Nawaz Sharif said. "I am not expecting results tomorrow or the day after. Let it take years. But we must settle it. We should never become despondent, nor stop talking."

These words spoken to me at Islamabad last week reflect the mood of growing number of Pakistanis. They are keen to discuss Kashmir but do not expect quick results. In fact, they do not even dwell on Kashmir during discussions, as they did until a few months ago. Even the argument that Kashmir first and the rest later is heard less and less. Indeed, they appear anxious to have trade and contacts with the people in India and favour free movement between the two countries. They seem less deterred by the threats of fundamentalists and politicians. However, the atmosphere of fear has not disappeared completely.

Let all working groups meet simultaneously to discuss the seven "topics identified," said Nawaz Sharif. (The topics identified are: Kashmir, security, peace and confidence-building measures; drug and terrorism; tourism, trade and economic; Siachin glacier; Turlab dam and economic cooperation environments). Nawaz Sharif reportedly said at the Male meeting with Prime Minister Inder Gujral that it did not matter which group finished its task earlier. Whoever's recommendations were ready, they could be implemented straightaway. In other words, the journey towards normalcy can continue even when the core issue of Kashmir is under discussion.

Immaculately dressed in grey suit (*salwar kameez*) and sporting a brown jacket, the Pakistan Prime Minister talked to me at length in the library of his imposing official residence. He spoke mostly in English but used Urdu and Punjabi at times. He evaded no question. Nor did he fumble for an answer.

Gujral's Sincerity. He said he was determined to have good relations with India and it did not matter how long it would take. He wanted to strengthen the hands of Prime Minister Inder Gujral whom, he described as "a sincere and honest person." Nawaz Sharif said that he also conveyed to the US Under Secretary of State, Thomas Pickering, that Inder Gujral was sincere in his efforts to have good relations with Pakistan. "I know his domestic compulsions and he know mine," said Nawaz Sharif. "We should help each other in facing the situation." The Pakistan Prime Minister felt that it was the most opportune time to solve problems between Islamabad and New Delhi because "I am here and Gujral is there."

"I won election on the plank of friendship with India. I must redeem the promise Mushahid Hussain, Minister for Information, who was the only person present at the interview intervened to say that former Prime Minister Benazir Bhutto played an anti-India card and lost heavily.

No-War Pact. Once again Nawaz Sharif offered no-war pact. "Modalities can be worked out. But I want to put an end to hostilities between the two countries." The Prime Minister's reiteration, however runs counter to the Pakistan army chief's statement that Kashmir must be settled before a no-war pact is signed. This gives the impression that the army has its own agenda. Many journalists and academicians in Pakistan confirm this. (A few days ago when I was in Pakistan, newspapers front-paged a meeting of the trioka, President Farooq Ahmed Laghari, Prime Minister Nawaz Sharif and Chief of Army Staff Jehangir Karamat to "take stock of variety of matters, both internal and international.")

Sharif and Gujral. Nawaz Sharif said that he told Gujral at Male that he was willing to "go very far" to foster normal relations with India. Gujral's response, according to Sharif, was equally effusive and warm. "He really wants friendship," said Nawaz Sharif.

To emphasise that the two hit off well, the Pakistan Prime Minister volunteered some information. "Gujral," he said, "rang me up when there was firing on the border. I talked to my commanders and rang him back to set at rest his fears. The firing on both sides has stopped since."

Asked why he did not encourage people to people contact, the Pakistan Prime Minister said he was all for it. "Students from the two countries should also meet," interjected Mushahid Hussain. He said he had made the offer at Jawaharlal Nehru University when he was in Delhi two months ago. Nawaz Sharif welcomed the idea adding: "I want people from different professions to meet and pool ideas so as to help the two countries overcome the problems facing them." He said Pakistan had relaxed visa restrictions. "As many as 400 visas are being issued from New Delhi every day. We want to issue more," he said.

I pointed out that despite several efforts in the past, there was no exchange of newspapers and books. He said it should take place immediately. He turned to Mushahid Hussain and asked him to prepare a note for the implementation of the suggestion. I reminded the prime minister that such orders had been given in the past without any result. "The bureaucrats are primarily to blame," I said. The Pakistan prime minister agreed with me. "Yes, bureaucrats on both sides have sabotaged good efforts."

Sharif on Benazir. When it came to Benazir Bhutto corrupt practices, Nawaz Sharif talked about it with a relish. "She has herself said she kept the money out because it was not safe in Pakistan," Nawaz Sharif said. He inquired from me what procedure the Indian Parliament adopted in such cases. "The power to disqualify a member rested with the Election Commission in Pakistan," he said. But he did not know what it would do in Benazir's case. He wanted to know if India's Election Commission had any specific powers.

Talking about corruption of politicians he said there was no difference between India and Pakistan. All that came out in India was familiar. "We have similar things happening here," he said. Mushahid Hussain joined to emphasise how there was no difference between the two countries in such matters.

Land Reforms. "Why don't you think of land reforms," I asked him. (Pakistan has landholdings running into thousands of acres). "I have thought about it," Nawaz Sharif said. But it is still at the attention stage." He cited an anecdote to illustrate his observation. A person had an old heart disease. He did not let the family know. But when he fell ill, the family asked him why he had kept it a secret. He said it was not paining then.

Nawaz Sharif said that the question of land reforms was now getting his attention because "it is beginning to give pain."

Nawaz Sharif is good at narrating anecdotes to underline his points. He told another to describe the current confrontation between the government and the Chief Justice of Pakistan. A household went through a rough night because it had only one blanket to share. The following morning a neighbour, who sensed trouble, asked them about the predicament. They said that the problem of the blanket had been resolved because it had been stolen away, said Nawaz Sharif. 'I have no quarrel with anyone. It was the problem of the blanket." Although the press was full of the point of the return the two sides had reached yet he was calm and confident when he talked to me.

Sharif's Optimism. Nawaz Sharif was optimistic about Pakistan's economy. I interviewed him a day after World Bank president James Wolfenshon had met him in the wake of IMF's loan of $1.55 billion to Pakistan. He exuded confidence, although the Pakistan rupee had been devalued by 11 per cent one week earlier. This was the second devaluation in less than a year.

"Our crops are immensely good this time," said Nawaz Sharif. "Both cotton and sugarcane will have a surplus output. For agriculture we have allotted Rs. 3,500 crore against Rs. 500 crore last year. Now seeds and measures to protect the produce have been introduced vigorously."

Pervez Musharraf's Plan

President Pervez Musharraf can pat himself on the back because he has retrieved Kashmir from the backburner. He can also take credit for having refocused the international community's attention on the problem which, in his own words, is "simmering disconcertingly." In the process he has got the world prominence, which he would not have had as a military ruler. In his own country, he is getting recognition because democracy to most Pakistanis is only a means to an end. And the end is India's acceptance of Pakistan's prowess and viability.

This consideration may have probably weighed with President Musharraf when he changed his nation's agenda from what type of government it should have to how high it was status-wise, vis-a-vis India. Fifty years of distance and discord with India have made the Pakistanis accept anything but a lesser stature, definitely not New Delhi's impetuosity. Kashmir has come to epitomise Pakistan's stern attitude towards India, at least among the Punjabis who are in a majority in Pakistan.

When it is reported that the talks at the Agra summit have been "positive and constructive," it means that Prime Minister Atal Behari Vajpayee has been trying to find a way to assure Musharraf that Pakistan's sensitivity on Kashmir can be accommodated within a framework, which New Delhi will build to give the maximum autonomy to the state. President Musharraf on his part has been making sure that India's fears on cross-border terrorism will be set right. A mechanism of sorts for further dialogues and possible adjustments seems to be taking shape. This is confirmed by Vajpayee's acceptance of the invitation to visit Islamabad. So the dialogue continues and Kashmir and cross-border terrorism remain on the agenda.

His statement. It was not surprising to find Musharraf making his first statement on the soil of India on Kashmir during his meeting with the intellectuals in Delhi on the eve of the summit. He said that the line of control (LoC) was not acceptable and if any Pakistani leader agreed to it, it could not return to his country. One could visualise a favourable response to his statement in Pakistan, particularly from the fundamentalist groups that have been wedded to politics since the days of Zia-ul-Haq, another military ruler in the eighties. But Musharraf should have also realised that no government in India could stay in office if it agreed to change the LoC in any substantial way. Indeed, such solutions are harder to sell in a democracy than in the army-controlled country, which is not dependent on votes.

Had Jammu and Kashmir gone to Pakistan at the time of partition in August 1947, it would have evoked a bit of disappointment, nothing more. People would have been taken the state's integration with Pakistan in their stride. But after 54 years, how does India change its borders—and the constitution—without causing a great harm to its polity? This might reopen certain issues which India had more or less settled after a long period of blood and sacrifice.

The change in the LoC means an adjustment in the Jammu and Kashmir territory. The composition of the state is such that it has three regions: the Muslim-majority valley, the Hindu-majority Jammu and the Buddhist-majority Ladakh. Pakistan wants the valley and has all along blessed the All Party Hurriyat Conference that claims to represent it.

Policy of New Delhi. Were New Delhi to give Pakistan the valley or accept it as an independent state, it would do so on the basis of the population's complexion. It would be inferred that the Muslim majority area did not want to stay with India. The Hindutva forces would probably be praying for such a solution. It would help them polarise the country on the basis of religion: Hindus and Muslims. Such an eventuality may give these elements a majority in the Lok Sabha, otherwise an impossibility. Imagine the effect of such a solution on the Muslims who carry even today, after 54 years, the cross of partition. And what happens to the nation's secular ethos without which even democracy becomes a question mark?

The Insurgency. Out of 54 years of Kashmir's integration with India, the insurgency is only 12 years old. Even the Hurriyat leaders like Yasin Malik have said that they took arms in 1989 when they found that people could not get power through the ballot box. The crux of the problem is the popular rule, not the LoC. Islamabad trained and armed the Kashmiris who went across the border. Now the game plan is different because the Afghans, the Sudanese and other foreigners have joined them to change what was a liberation struggle into a *jihad*. Islamabad is offering them all assistance and has set up camps for them believing that one day Kashmir will fall in its lap. It is clear is that without Islamabad's sustenance, the uprising cannot go on.

I do not condone the atrocities and human rights violations that take place in the valley because of suppression. Some of us have written about them and Pakistan has extensively quoted from our reports at international forums to the embarrassment of India. The excesses have, indeed, drawn the world's attention to Kashmir and India will have to live down the battered image it has got in the process.

But the real question is that of governance, not borders. For this purpose, there should be fresh elections in J & K under the supervision of human rights activists from India, a suggestion made by Shabir Shah, a popular Kashmiri youth leader. The elected members to the assembly should form the government and New Delhi, in turn, should transfer to the states all subjects, except defence and foreign affairs. (New Delhi's 1951-52 agreement with Sheikh Abdullah gave India these two subjects and communications). Borders between Kashmir on both sides should be made soft, depending how soon militancy from across Pakistan ceases.

The new government at Srinagar can have its own flag, currency, seek foreign aid and receive tourists from abroad through the planes which can straightaway land at Srinagar. To help people of Kashmir on both sides to participate in matters of defence and foreign affairs, the elected Lok Sabha members from J&K should have the right to sit in Pakistan's National Assembly and those from Pak-occupied Kashmir in Lok Sabha. However, the sovereignty of this part of J&K will vest in India's while of the other part with Pakistan.

The right of self-determination, or any such demand, is aimed at transferring power to the people of J&K, not redrawing the boundaries. How will a change in the LoC make any difference if people are not given the real power? Musharraf should be considering these alternatives that meet the aspirations of the people and not the ones, which may tear apart India's fabric by religious or separatist forces.

While mentioning Kashmir, Musharraf talked of the symmetry. What he actually conveyed was that the progress in other fields would depend on the advance made on Kashmir. Both fields have to have the same pace. He cited the example of the late Pakistan's Commerce Minister Mahbub-ul-Haq, who entered into an agreement with India on trade and commerce. Since there was no progress on Kashmir, Musharraf said, the whole structure caved in.

The symmetry logic is strange. Suppose, if we can make progress on one subject, must we stop because Kashmir is not being solved? This amounts to giving veto to those who will be sorting out Kashmir. Whatever is agreed upon should be implemented first so that enough of goodwill is generated to solve Kashmir. Otherwise, we will get stuck unnecessarily.

Views of Advani and Hurriyat on Kashmir

Home Minister L.K. Advani has the reputation of not changing his decision. It has merit in the sense that there is finality about what he is thinking. But who is to blame if and when his inputs for reaching a decision are not correct? One such case is that of not allowing the Hurriyat leaders to go to

Pakistan.

Home Minister's plea—he has repeated it in the Rajya Sabha that the Hurriyat wants to act as a mediator between India and Pakistan and that his government would not allow them to play that role. If this is the Hurriyat's stand, it cannot be allowed to arrogate itself to the position, which is the State's prerogative. Very few would disagree with Advani if this were the position.

But the Hurriyat leaders, after a joint meeting at Srinagar a few days ago, said that they wanted to go to Pakistan to bring about "a multi-ceasefire." They explained that after the unilateral ceasefire by India, their task in Pakistan would be to meet the various groups of militants and persuade them to stop violence and militancy to create an atmosphere for talks. They specifically mentioned that their role was not that of a go-between.

Advani can argue that he has no faith in them. He can also say that the information he possesses indicates that the Hurriyat leaders would try to be mediators. But he has not taken that stand. All that he has said is that when New Delhi decides to hold talks with Islamabad, it would do so on its own.

There can be no exception to this approach because it is the government, which has to decide when and where to sit with Pakistan across the table. Again, it is the government, which has the authority to decide how far it wants to go in the matter relating to Kashmir. This problem is too serious to be left to the mediators. The government has always rejected the idea of a third party. How can it now accept the Hurriyat to act that way when even the offer by a country like America has been rejected out-rightly?

In the face of a categorical statement by the Hurriyat, it is clear that it wanted to talk to the militants in Pakistan to persuade them to reciprocate Prime Minister Atal Behari Vajpayee's unilateral ceasefire. Advani's refusal to allow them to visit Pakistan shows an attitude that is not based on facts. He looks like going against the general opinion in the country, which favours the Hurriyat's trip to Pakistan.

This does not, however, mean the nation supports the Hurriyat stand on Kashmir. Nor does it in any way reflect the government's weakness. All this means that New Delhi wants to explore every possible avenue to effect peace. Vajpayee's expectation is that the ceasefire will eventually act as pressure on Pakistan to respond positively.

All the Indian groups, which have gone to the other side in the last few weeks, have demanded in their statements that restrictions on the Hurriyat visit should be lifted. There was a delegation of former Indian diplomats, some of them are hand in glove with the BJP, who proposed the same thing on their return. Even some senior retired officers from the army and the navy came back with a similar feeling that the efforts towards conciliation would be strengthened if the Hurriyat leaders were to visit Pakistan. In fact, General Pervez Musharraf, the Pakistan's Chief Executive, complained to some members of the delegation that the Indian government had unnecessarily stalled the visit of the Hurriyat leaders. "We were prepared to talk to them and so were some militant groups," Musharraf has reportedly told the delegates.

Why Advani is adamant is not understandable. It shows he and Vajpayee have distanced themselves on matters relating to Kashmir. But where Advani has gone wrong is that the talks for peace do not in any way impinge on our stand. It also does not mean that any understanding beyond cessation of violence, which the Hurriyat may bring about will be binding on us. The visit is only to silence guns from the other side. The Hurriyat is conscious of its limited role and it has not made any statement or observation to the contrary.

Advani is quite right when he says that there are several points of view within the Hurriyat. Indeed, it is a divided house. One or two members are openly pro-Pakistan in their stance while some are pro-independent. A couple of them have India as their centre of attention. But their views or leanings are not the point at issue. Their visit has a limited purpose. If New Delhi were to allow them to go to the other side, it would help the country know how far the Hurriyat could influence the militants in Pakistan to respond to the ceasefire. This will come in handy in the days to come when the real negotiations would begin.

Hurriyat on Pakistan

There is a possibility that some Hurriyat leaders may say something in Pakistan that may not be to our liking. So what? They have said so many things, on so many occasions, which are not palatable to the country. The press has printed them all.

They may have been criticised for upholding certain views but none could punish them because the Constitution provides freedom of expression to all its nationals. What new would they say in Pakistan now? We have heard them all before. Their views are their own and are at variance with the country's stand. People and the government there already know from the press and TV networks their oft-repeated thinking. One more round will not put up Islamabad's back, nor will it weaken New Delhi's policy.

Maybe, Pakistan will also see chinks within the Hurriyat. They are under one umbrella, no doubt, but they differ on the concept of tomorrow's Kashmir—most of them believing in a secular state and a few supporting the Islamic order. It is possible that after their visit to Pakistan, some of them would return disillusioned. Even the hardcore among them might begin to realise that the Pakistan society was not fanatic enough to their liking.

By blocking the visit of the Hurriyat, New Delhi may also be hurting international opinion that supports our cause so far. Islamabad stands isolated because of the impression that it is training, arming and sending militants to Kashmir. Still the world wants hostilities to end. New Delhi's refusal may create the impression that India is not willing to compromise on even an innocuous step like the visit by Hurriyat to Pakistan.

Advani has done well to give an assurance in Parliament that the government will soon be talking to various groups in Kashmir. It shows that the ceasefire is not the end by itself but an opportunity to sort out things in the state. It also shows that for the first time all political elements will be invited for talks. Strange, Advani should mention the Hurriyat among the groups on the government list for talks but refuse permission to its leaders to go across the border.

Musharraf, LoC and Yasin Malik

As the summit is approaching, Pakistan Chief Executive Pervez Musharraf is making statements I wish he had made earlier. That would have improved the atmosphere for talks and deepened liberal thinking in Pakistan. Musharraf's statement that religion and politics cannot be mixed is an observation which would have taken the wind out of the sails of fundamentalists.

The legitimacy, which the forces of bigotry have got over the years, may well be the reason why their militants, although trained and sheltered by Islamabad, have challenged Musharraf's statement. They have used some mosques and shrines in Kashmir in the last few days to fight their parochial battle from there so as to prove that they do not differentiate between religion and politics.

That their organisations have their headquarters in Pakistan intact does not give credibility to Musharraf's statement. Without any doubt their purpose is to compel the security forces to damage the sacred places where militants hole up. New Delhi should keep this in mind while dealing with them. Maybe, storming in is not the best of tactics. The Sikh community has not yet got over the trauma of Operation Bluestar.

Of course, the Hurriyat is most to blame. It has tarnished the movement for the Kashmiri identity with the Islamic paint. Some of the Hurriyat leaders have openly aligned themselves with religious elements which have killed Hindus and Sikhs in cold blood. The Hurriyat, which claims to represent the valley, has asked militants to stop using mosques. It is a belated reaction, after much damage has been done to the Kashmiri society. In fact, it should have shown courage to condemn militants for demolishing Charar-e-Sharif, a shrine that the religious parties consider anti-Islamic.

During the Narasimha Rao regime, Yasin Malik, one of the Hurriyat leaders, had brokered an agreement which resulted in the withdrawal of the militants from Hazratbal. He had gone on fast unto death to make the two sides realise the gravity of the situation. Since he is abroad, some other leader should have come forward to persuade the militants. This would have given a proof of the Hurriyat's new policy not to call for hartals against "state terrorism" in view of the forthcoming summit.

But its leaders are sulking for having been left out. They should seriously consider revising their policy to mix religion with politics if they want to play any role in India or, for that matter, in India-Pakistan relations. Musharraf has realised the force behind the maxim.

If one were to look back, one would find that the founder of Pakistan, Qaide Azam Mohammad Ali Jinnah, wanted religion to be separated from politics. True, he played the Muslim card to muster support. But as soon as he found his dream of Pakistan coming true, he said that people in the subcontinent should cease to be Muslims and Hindus and consider themselves either Pakistanis or Indians. If Jinnah had lived a little longer, he would have established a secular state of Pakistan. This would have brought the two countries closer.

Not to mix religion with politics was the call Mahatma Gandhi gave during the independence movement. It remains the country's ethos, notwithstanding the noise which the fundamentalists on this side make in the name of *Hindu Rashtriya*. The basic belief in secularism is the main reason why India does not entertain the idea of dividing the state on religious grounds, separating the Muslim-majority valley from the rest of Jammu and Kashmir. New Delhi cannot be party to any settlement which can give a handle to religious forces because that will harm India's secular polity.

From that point of view, Musharraf has spoken against the religious organisations late. They have been holding Pakistan to ransom for a long time. And they, Lakshar-e-Tayyaba, Joishe-Mohammad and Hizbul Mujahideen, feel so entrenched and powerful that they are ready to bite the hand that feeds them. Maybe, they think that a regime, which supports the Taliban in Afghanistan, will not go far enough to take action against them. Since Islamabad has done little to stop cross-border militancy, they have reason to believe that they have the support of some in the Musharraf junta.

Musharraf's on Kashmiri Militants. Musharraf's interview with *The Herald*, a monthly of the Dawn group, does not help. He has said that the "time has not yet come" for him to ask the Kashmiri militants to scale down their activities. "The time will come when the talks are held and they make progress." How does this help the situation? One, it is an admission of what New Delhi has been all along saying that Islamabad's help goes beyond diplomatic and economic support. Two, it means that if the negotiations over Kashmir are protracted—they are bound to be—the Musharraf government would continue to hire, arms and send militants across the borders. Even if Musharraf is saying this to pacify religious groups, he is creating problems for Prime Minister Atal Behari Vajpayee, who had the courage and sense of history to invite him without waiting for Islamabad's interference to stop.

LOC. In fact, first announcement the two leaders should make after the meeting is that of a six-month ceasefire, meaning that no bullet would be fired, direct or indirect, open or hidden, at the LoC, the international border and within the valley. When I met Musharraf at Islamabad during a dinner at the South Asian Journalists Meet last year, I found him receptive to the idea.

It is true that Vajpayee took some time to reciprocate because of bad experience at Kargil after the Lahore Declaration. But when he gave his assent, Musharraf dragged his feet. The message sent through the Pakistan High Commissioner in Delhi was not acknowledged. Even a reminder and a letter to Musharraf elicited no reply. Although he ordered subsequently a ceasefire on the LoC and the international border, he did not stop militants from crossing into India.

As regards the solution, it would have to be worked out patiently and that too over a long period. Both countries would have go to away from the beaten path. What Jawaharlal Nehru told Zulfikar Ali Bhutto in November, 1961, in London is still true: "Zulfi, I know that we must find a solution for Kashmir. But we have got caught in a situation which we cannot get out of without causing damage to the system and structures of our respective societies."

The Vested Interest. What worries me is that even the announcement of summit has brought the hawks in the open in both countries with their long knives. Past experience indicates that they become active when the two sides decide to sit across the table. The hawks relish war, not peace.

Some journalists, academicians and experts among them have already dipped their pen—and hands—in poison. They peddle in hatred and they are the ones who will not allow normal, peaceful atmosphere to prevail. They have a vested interest in hostilities. They do not want the war lobbies they represent to go out of business. It will be a tragedy if Vajpayee and Musharraf listen to them.

9

Rajiv Gandhi and Benazir Bhutto: Hope for a New Phase at SAARC

Benazir Bhutto and Her Ideology

Talking to Miss Benazir Bhutto in Pakistan last week, I found her friendly to India, with a positive outlook, unlike her father, Z.A. Bhutto, who often talked in terms of thousand-year-war against India.

The acting chairperson of the Pakistan People's Party (PPP) said that Pakistan and India must bury the hatchet; "we have had enough of it. Let's start a new chapter".

Miss Bhutto said: "India has a new generation leadership. And I hope that Pakistan will also have a new generation leadership. I hope that these new generation leaderships will be able to settle problems, dealing with each other without any of the bitterness of the past and without any of the prejudices of the past".

At public meetings Miss Bhutto speaks in chaste Urdu, Pakistan's official language, which she was not fluent in even two years ago. She has worked hard to learn the language; she has also worked hard to gather facts and figures with which to condemn the military regime in Pakistan.

The interview she gave me was in English and she was very critical of the role of the military and General Zia-ul-Haq, the Pakistan President. But most of her observations were moderate and she gave the impression that she does not want to stir up the people's anger.

Miss Bhutto is many things to its people. She is their catharsis whereby purge their sense of guilt for not having protested against the execution of her father, now a legend in Pakistan. "Bhutto ham sharminda hain, tere katal zinda hain" (Bhutto, we are ashamed because killers are alive) is one of the slogans the people chant, while beating their chests, at the massive gatherings she is attracting even at wayside places.

The following are questions and answers referring to India:

You once mentioned that Pakistan should not play the Sikh card. Do you have firm evidence of Pakistan's complicity?

You see, there are times when I have information on certain matters, but I do believe in ever speaking about them because it is not fair to somebody. And I being a Pakistani, it is not fair for me to speak in a manner that could further embarrass my country whether I agree or do not agree with the regime. Let me say that as far as PPP is concerned we do not believe in creating tensions; we believe in reducing the tensions. It is a matter of pride for the party that during the period of PPP that democratic India and democratic Pakistan were able to arrive at the Simla Agreement which has provided the longest basis for good relations in the subcontinent . . .

Did you follow the Shah Bano case in India?

I did hear something about how it created a rumpus, I personally believe that there should be a personal law and civil law. And let the individual decide on the basis of personal law or on the basis of civil law. I do not believe that the government should interfere too much in the privacy of individual's life. But at the same time I do not believe in the cruel, barbaric punishments and laws which this regime (Zia's) has tried to bring about. We believe in equality of men and women and dignity of each and every individual . . .

Have you any plans to meet Prime Minister Rajiv Gandhi?

At present, as you can see, I am very involved with my aims and objectives for securing elections. But the Prime Minister of India has taken up many challenges and I wish him well in the task he is facing. No doubt, India is facing many problems but I am sure that he has the energy and capacity to deal with them because he has a good team to help him.

From Lahore airport itself one can see the signs of Benazir Bhutto hurricane that has passed by. New iron railings have come up: dismantled welcome gates are still there and so are the flags of the Pakistan People's Party.

In the main cities of Punjab, including Islamabad and Peshawar, the people still talk about the tumultuous reception she received everywhere. As I travelled through the interior of Pakistan's Punjab, I could see slogans like "Pakistani taqdir, Benazir, Benazir" (the future of Pakistan is Benazir, which in Urdu also means peerless) on the walls.

At Lahore the welcome was unexpected, wild and almost uncontrollable. With thousands of hands reaching out for her, Miss Bhutto stood for more than 15 hours to reach the place of meeting. Television cameras recorded the scenes and though the administration raided video shops to confiscate video tapes of her arrival in Lahore, many tapes are passing from house to house all over the country. (Pakistan television and radio did not carry anything about Miss Bhutto).

In the words of Mr Mushahid Hussain, editor of *Muslim*, in Islamabad: "Benazir Bhutto's populism has managed to zero in on a strategy that combines mass mobilisation with restrained militancy for peaceful political change."

Indeed, there is no need for a referendum to guage the people's true feelings after the response Miss Bhutto got. No leader in Pakistan comes near her anywhere, much less General Zia-ul Haq, who, is alleged to have rigged the referendum for his presidentship to convert a 10 per cent turnout into a 90 per cent vote.

And the members of the National Assembly (MNAs) are conspicuous by their silence. After spending Rs. 40 lakh to Rs. 50 lakh each to get elected, they have no intention to oblige Miss Bhutto by resigning and forcing a mid-term poll; they still have four years to go.

Many in Pakistan think that she has released the geni of people's power from the bottle and some fear even she may not be able to get it back into the bottle if and when she wants to. What they mean is that she has roused the masses, which may go out of hand. However, Mazhar Ali Khan, pro-Soviet liberal editor of *Viewpoint*, says: "The few, mostly the rich and powerful, watch the renewed mass upsurge in fear and trepidation; they hear a new ring in old slogans and, lacking confidence in the tone of moderation used, believe that those who shout 'inquilab zindabad' (long live revolution) have them as primary targets".

But that is perhaps an exaggeration. For industrialists and businessmen are reportedly financing Miss Bhutto's cavalcade. She has not talked of nationalisation, not even of those units which Bhutto, her father, had nationalised and General Zia had denationalised. She has talked of socialism but of a "Pakistan brand" and like "India's socialism," as she puts it. She has, in fact, admonished in private some who were Bhutto's minister for egging him on to nationalise certain industries, "for the sake of nationalisation".

The government has so far adopted an attitude of non-interference. But Gen. Zia has become suddenly active and addresses one or two meetings a day, even if they are thinly attended, to rule out mid-term polls—a demand put forward at every meeting by Miss Bhutto—and to warn "anti-state elements." There is also a spurt of statements, which newspapers dutifully publish, claiming that Gen. Zia has served the nation "well".

Undoubtedly the excitement and the sheer euphoria roused by Miss Bhutto's return have pushed Gen. Zia and other political leaders to the background. Not even dissensions in the PPP are of any consequence because she is the party, as Mrs Gandhi was the Congress (I). All that seems to matter with the people of Pakistan at present is the presence of Miss Bhutto in their midst. It is an event of immense significance for them. There is no doubt that it is. But how significant for the future one cannot say.

Miss Benazir Bhutto has said that General Zia-ul-Haq has "mishandled relations" with India and has "opened another front" when the Pakistan forces are already facing the Soviet Union in the north.

In an interview to me in Karachi a few days ago, she said it was Gen. Zia who had aggravated the situation to divert the people's attention from "the real problems" of Pakistan and that it was he who "seeks and builds" tension to sustain himself in power. He lost the Siachin glacier and one did not know what "humiliation" he would bring to Pakistan and in days to come, she said.

Asked if she would favour a no-war pact with India, Miss Bhutto said 'no'. Her argument was that the Simla Agreement, which her father, Zulfikar Ali Bhutto, signed with Mrs Indira Gandhi in 1972, was in essence a no-war pact; nothing more was required.

The interview was held at 70, Cliffton, a lonely bungalow, outside which hang a name plate with words 'Zulfikar Ali Bhutto, Bar-at-Law,' embossed in brass. Eight months ago when I met her at Okara, 80 kms from Lahore, I found her harried and edgy; she had then just taken over the Pakistan People's Party

(PPP) and faced the problem of its reorganisation. This time she was relaxed as if she had come to terms with herself, the party and the situation she faced. She still attracts crowds of thousands, the only leader in Pakistan to do so, but she gave me the impression of a person who has realised that it would be a long haul to power. She, however, said: "We will not wait till 1990," the year when the "elections" are due.

"I should have pushed things in autumn." Miss Bhutto recalled. Indeed, top politicians and journalists told me in Pakistan that had she asked Gen. Zia to negotiate with her when she received ovation from lakhs of people in Lahore and Rawalpindi after her arrival from abroad, she would have wrested power from his hands. "I did say in Lahore at that time if we wanted we could have captured power," was her comment. "We are against violence."

"At least 20,000 people courted arrest and many faced police brutalities on August 14, 1986, when I gave the call. Some were even butchered. Still the impression sought to be created is that the stir was a failure. Our problem is that we are struggling for a peaceful transfer of power," she said. She has no doubt that Gen. Zia would "go very soon". Asked about reasons of her optimism, she said: "I am a student of history. I have known dictators ultimately quitting. They get buried under their own weight; situations develop that way".

My repeated queries to her whether she would associate or seek the help of the armed forces to come to power elicited a Curt and categorical reply: "The armed forces have only their constitutional role to play and that is to defend the country". When I told her that I had the Turkish pattern in mind, she said she wanted "good relations with Turkey" but would accept no role of the armed forces in politics.

One thing I noticed about Miss Bhutt—and others confirmed it—was that she tended to separate Gen. Zia from the military. She would attribute Pakistan's troubles to him but not blame the armed forces or in any way criticise them.

A few days before I met her 20 bullets had been shot at her jeep in which she was to travel to Larkana but changed her mind at the last minute; three of her servants travelling in the jeep were kidnapped. She said that "Gen. Zia was wanting to kill her" and there had been some attempts on her life earlier also;

the kidnappers, she said, informed her servants that "they were Gen. Zia's men".

Miss Bhutto's perception about the creation of Bangladesh is quite novel. She said that Bangladesh was a result of India's peace and friendship treaty with the Soviet Union. When I asked her whether she really believed it, she said: "I know you will not agree with me but this is our understanding".

Commenting on Soviet peace offer in Afghanistan, Miss Bhutto said that the mere withdrawal of troops was not adequate; "conditions must be created which would give confidence to the three million refugees in Pakistan to return to their homes; until that happens the peace offer has no meaning". Afghanistan is the only subject on which I found little difference between her and Gen. Zia's government.

Hope for a New Phase at SAARC

Prime Minister Rajiv Gandhi has inclined his willingness to visit Islamabad for the South Asian Association of Regional Cooperation (SAARC) summit in December, it is learnt. This will be his first visit to the Pakistan capital since becoming Prime Minister.

The Pakistan government is said to have checked this with New Delhi before agreeing to hold the SAARC summit because Islamabad did not want to face the embarrassment of Mr. Rajiv Gandhi declining participation.

In fact, before fixing Islamabad as a venue, Mr. Gandhi was approached to find out if he had any objection to attending the meeting there. He is understood to have said that any date in December, except Christmas day, would suit him.

Mr. A.P. Venkateswaran had lost his foreign secretaryship because while in Islamabad, he had said at a press conference that Mr. Gandhi as chairman of SAARC, would be visiting Pakistan, as General Ershad, the Bangladesh president, the first chairman of SAARC had done.

Mr. Gandhi was annoyed that Mr. Venkateswaran had said that without clearing with him. But the fact is that Mr. Venkateswaram had only revealed what the Ministry of External Affairs had been told earlier that Mr. Gandhi was willing to visit all the SAARC countries, including Pakistan.

The SAARC summit was to be held in Colombo, but it declined it on the ground that the situation in Sri Lanka was 'not conducive' to holding the meeting there. The foreign ministers of the SAARC countries met in Kathmandu only this month and they accepted the offer of Mr. Sahebzada Yaqub Khan, the Pakistan foreign minister, to host the meeting.

Mr. P.V. Narasimha Rao, who was present at the meeting, consulted Mr. Gandhi before agreeing to Islamabad as the venue.

Mr. Gandhi has visited Pakistan only once after assumption of office. He flew to Peshawar for a few hours to pay homage to Khan Abdul Ghaffar Khan when he died some months ago. The Pakistan president, General Zia-ul-Haq, was keen that he should stop over at Islamabad while returning to New Delhi but Mr. Gandhi declined the invitation.

By the time Mr. Gandhi visits Islamabad, Pakistan would have held the 'non-party elections'. It is too early to predict which of the parties, behind the fiction of 'non-party' will emerge victorious or which among them will be allowed to form a government, even of the former prime minister Junejo type. But if leaders like Benazir, the chairperson of Pakistan People's Party (PPP) and Asghar Khan, chief of Isteqlal Tehrik, are kept out under one pretext or the other, the government emerging from the elections may not have any credibility in the eyes of Pakistan electorate.

Whether Mr. Gandhi would or should visit Pakistan if and when their rightful leaders are denied the positions in the government which they deserve is the question that New Delhi will have to ponder over seriously. There may be even protests from the people of Pakistan when Mr. Gandhi goes to Islamabad despite the rigged elections Gen. Zia proposed to hold.

New Delhi, Dec. 10, Mrs. Benazir Bhutto, the Pakistan Prime Minister, has requested Mr. Rajiv Gandhi, the Indian Prime Minister, to stay back for one day after the SAARC summit on Dec. 27 in Islamabad, it is learnt.

In a communication to Mr. Gandhi she has reportedly expressed her desire to have with him lengthier talk, which she believes, may not be possible on the opening day of SAARC. She has proposed even a few hours of delay in Mr. Gandhi's departure so that they get some time for talks.

Mrs. Benazir Bhutto reportedly feels that she would be so occupied with formalities of departure of heads of states till the afternoon of Dec. 27th that the talks with Mr. Gandhi would be hurried and sandwitched between engagements. She is said to be keen on having a 'serious dialogue.'

Mr. Gandhi is scheduled to leave for Islamabad to attend the SAARC summit on the 27th Dec. morning and return the same afternoon.

New Delhi has not sent any reply so far but Mr. Gandhi is likely to comply with the request of Mrs. Benazir Bhutto and prolong his stay in Islamabad, returning late at night.

The initiative by Mrs. Benazir Bhutto is seen in Delhi as 'a well-meaning' effort towards breaking the impasse between the two countries. The fact that after assuming power she has lost no time in inviting the Indian Prime Minister for talks is interpretted as the importance she gives to her relations with India.

At her first press conference as the Prime Minister of Pakistan, Mrs. Benazir Bhutto said she was confident that during the SAARC summit where 'the democratic leaders' of India and Pakistan were to meet measures would be 'found' to defuse tension between India and Pakistan.

That Mrs. Benazir Bhutto is anxious to have good relations with India is evident from what she told me in an interview in Karachi early 1987. She said: "Rajiv Gandhi and I belong to a new generation. We have some kinships; His mother was assassinated and so was my father; he has lost his brother and so have I. We both can start from a clean state."

Mrs. Benazir Bhutto was not at that time the Prime Minister of Pakistan. Nor had elections been announced then. But she was confident of her becoming the Prime Minister. And she was equally confident that India and Pakistan could bury the hatchet and begin a new chapter of amity and friendship.

Ten Days in Pakistan

I was given a visa to Pakistan after a lapse of two years. Former Prime Minister Benazir Bhutto had not liked some of my writings where I had found fault with her functioning. In fact, if one were to assess her role, her intolerance to criticism would stand out. What her husband, Asif Zardari, this time Mr. 100 per cent, did to the state only highlighted how corrupt was her governance.

She never outgrew her love of the dynasty, first the Bhuttos and then the Zardaris. And, over the years, she became so distant from the cadres of her Pakistan People's Party (PPP) that most of them did not stir out of their home, either to woo the electorate or to cast even their own vote. Hence a low turn out and her rout at the polls. She did not win a single seat in the National Assembly from Punjab and the North West Frontier Province, Pakistan's two-thirds.

Yet, a decade ago she led the party to victory when it was stuck in maelstrom of promises and engagements in the wake of her father, Zulfikar Ali Bhutto's execution. She was then the people's catharsis whereby they purged their sense of guilt for not having protested against his hanging. They made her Pakistan's prime minister twice. She failed them on both occasions, the second time more than the first. She was no liberal, no reformer, only a different face of feudalism and graft.

When I reached Karachi, which has returned to normalcy, the city was agog with rumours that Supreme Court would restore her government. She may now say that she knew it beforehand, casting aspersions on the court's credibility. But she took rumours so seriously that she asked her party's stalwarts to reach Islamabad. It turned out to be a mere wishful thinking. The verdict, 6 to 1, was a trenchant indictment of her administration: misuse of power, corruption, tapping of telephone and so on.

Maladministration or corruption leave unhappy traces behind. Still, the ground is recoverable. The ethnicity factor Benazir Bhutto has introduced to Pakistan's political scene may endanger the very integrity of the country. She has said repeatedly that she has 'suffered' at the hands of Punjabis (67 per cent) because she comes from a small province. In the process, she has let loose the demon of provincial chauvinism, which may be difficult to restrain even in the name of Islam, the religion of 95 per cent Pakistanis.

In one way, the sweep of Nawaz Sharif, a Punjabi, may turn out to be a good anti-dote for ethnic unrest. He can string together estranged Baluchistan, fractured Sindh, domineering Punjab and autonomous Frontier. The Punjabis could care less what other parts of Pakistan thought about them. But Nawaz Sharif may be able to arrest the trend, Confabulations at Lahore, my last stop over, suggest that the city will continue to be Pakistan's political capital. It should: Benazir Bhutto, who seems to be preferring the neutral territory of Islamabad, will be well advised to make Lahore as her headquarters. Punjab has to be taught, if it cannot learn on its own, how to play an all-Pakistan role. At present, it is too parochial, too power possessive.

The real problem is that of President Farooq Ahmed Khan Leghari, who is confined to Islamabad but who wants to project a political agenda from Lahore. He wants to be recognised as a Punjabi so that when the chips are down, he is not considered an outsider. The landslide victory by Nawaz Sharif has upset the applecart. Leghari would have been happy if Nawaz Sharif had been dependent on his men to have a clear majority in the National Assembly. But most of Leghari's men have lost, including his son. And the quirk of circumstances has made him dependent on Nawaz Sharif. As the latter has said, the National Assembly will consider whether to continue the 8th amendment, the 58 (2b) and the Council for Defence and National Security. In a way, he has thrown the guantlet to Leghari, who is in no position to pick it up.

The 8th amendment, appended to the constitution by the late Zia-ul-Haq, means that the President can dissolve a popularly elected government at the Centre and in the states at his will. Benazir Bhutto was dismissed first under the amendment. Nawaz Sharif was its second victim and Benazir Bhutto has been sent out again. Article 58 (2b) is still more dangerous. The Supreme Court has upheld the contention that the material against a government can be collected even after it has been axed. No government worth the name can live with posterior indictment. The armed forces, which have a say in the running of political apparatus in Pakistan, may not object to the end of dyarchy, the prime minister drawing his strength from people and the president from the constitution. An elected government has to be supreme.

Moves are already afoot to challenge the 8th amendment 58 (2b). Nawaz Sharif's party, Muslim League, expects that along with its allies, it will get two-thirds majority in the Senate (elections are in March) as it has done in the National Assembly. Then they can effect a change in the constitution.

A serious situation can, however, arise if and when Nawaz Sharif joins issue with the president on the Council for Defence and National Security. It will be a tough fight. All the three chiefs of services and the chief of general staff are the council members. Its authority extends to all defence, economic and law and other problems. Nawaz Sharif welcomed the council's formation before the polls. If he wants to challenge it now, he will have to do it quickly when people are still behind him.

Maybe, he should first strengthen popular support. And this is dependent on how he reduces prices, which went up abruptly in the last few months of Benazir Bhutto's regime. In fact, the price rise cost her deerly in elections. One straight way to cut prices may be to allow import of goods from across the border, India, so that the haulage charges are less. Nawaz Sharif has argued for economic ties with India during his pre and post-election speeches. But can he do so before settling the Kashmir problem, a one-point programme of Islamabad so far? Will the armed forces allow him?

It all depends on Nawaz Sharif, whether he wants to cut through the thicket of prejudice and bias against India. He would not only courage but also determination. He has also talked about curtailing defence expenditure. This entails building up the people's strength against those in the *Khaki*. It has not happened in Pakistan so far. Benazir Bhutto made up even with the executions of her father for the sake of prime ministership. Chalking out a line, which does not take into account the militancy, is desirable for democracy to take roots in Pakistan. Still, it is difficult to imagine Nawaz Sharif doing so.

Yet, Nawaz Sharif has no alternative to economic ties with India and cut in defence expenditure. He has the power to do so because the people have given him all the strength he wanted in the National Assembly. If he takes it easy and fails to make any difference in the living conditions of his people, the opinion can turn against him in six to eight months. His failure does not mean the return of Benazir Bhutto but probably the end of whatever democratic system prevails in Pakistan.

Even after 50 years of independence, people in Pakistan remain patient, credulous and hopeful. But then they are like people in India or elsewhere in the subcontinent. Every time they put faith in rulers, every time they are cheated. Politicians have exploited them for their personal ends. There is the same nexus between the bureaucracy, police, criminals and politicians in Pakistan as in India.

What they admire about us is the way the Supreme Court is exposing the corrupt in high places. And they have real respect for the democratic system which the country has been following. Indian bogey does not sell as much as before. People want to have emicable relationship with Indians. Many believe that their daily hardships will see the end if the two countries come closer. Kashmir has not receded into the background. But economic problems seem to be having precedence.

Liberals and Zardari in Pakistan

Liberals in Pakistan have a problem: They do not like Asif Ali Zardari, Benazir Bhutto's corrupt and uncouth husband. But they have no platform other than the relatively composite Pakistan People's Party (PPP), although they know that it is under his influence. The manner in which he is behaving these days, even though being a convict, shows that nothing has changed, neither his stock in the party nor his stay in politics. Even after being sentenced for possessing disproportionate wealth and for misusing power during Benazir's regime. Zardari is casting himself in the role of a hero who has been wronged. In fact, his six-year detention on various counts—some of the cases are still awaiting the court's disposal—seems to have given him a halo of "suffering" which goes down well in Pakistan. His wife is once again giving him all the support.

Zardari has only contempt for the liberals. He believes they have no base. He has found that they are as servile to his wife as are most leaders in the PPP to him. One evidence that emerged during Benazir's two stints of Prime Ministership, he was an extra-constitutional authority—like Sanjay Gandhi during the emergency. Not a single PPP leader even threatened to resign from the party in protest. Today, when Zardari is opening guiding the parliamentary wing of the party, he knows that he has Benazir behind him. The liberals, to their embarrassment, know that Benazir has sent word from abroad that they should "go to the hospital" where Zardari is confined and meet him.

To facilitate Zardari's activities, General Pervez Musharraf's government has provided him with a mobile phone. Not only that. It has relaxed restrictions on him so as to enable him to meet parties like the Muthahida Majlis-e-Amal (MMA), a conglomeration of six religious parties. The MMA has 45 seats and the Pakistan Muslim League-Qaid-e-Azam (PML-Q), cat's paw of the general and described as the King's Party, has the largest number—77 of the 272 contested seats.

However loud the denials of Musharraf and Benazir are, Zardari has become the communication channel between the two on the one hand and, on the other, between Benazir and the religious parties. Musharraf wants the PPP to support his PML-Q to lead the government. But Zardari wants first things first. He wants the cases against him and his wife withdrawn. He knows that it is necessary to get the green light from Musharraf. He also realises that his wife cannot return to Pakistan without the military's nod. The bargaining has moved ahead. The fact that Zardari's father has been allowed to go to America for medical treatment shows which way the wind is blowing.

The military does not like Benazir or Nawaz Sharif. But it prefers the former for two reasons. One, she is not as bothersome as Nawaz Sharif, who was ousted from the prime ministership. Two, she welcomed Musharraf's coup and even sent feelers that she would cooperate with his government. It is another matter that he was then riding a high horse.

Benazir's "pragmatic approach" to the military is well known. Although it executed his father, it found her quite cooperative when seeking to come to power. As prime minister, she had no compunction in going to the military headquarters to discuss state matters. When she was sworn in she had even agreed to the military's choice of people for heading ministries of foreign affairs and finance.

Zardari has more or less succeeded in stitching the torn connection between the military and Benazir again. Benazir has indicated her desire to do business with the military, particularly after her visit to Washington, where she found America supporting Musharraf to the hilt for his backing the US against the Al-Qaida.

Her only problem is ego. She does not want to play second fiddle to the religious parties or the PML-Q, which Musharraf himself guides. At one time she offered her party's support to the government. Musharraf chose from outside based on issues. But Zardari reportedly intervened to say that it was dependent on the withdrawal of cases against him and his wife and on rescinding the order of her arrest on charges of corruption.

Left to Musharraf, he would have his PML-Q in a saddle: He might still have it with the PPP support if the "deal" is struck. But having the religious parties in the wilderness does not sound good when the Al-Qaida is far from eliminated. On the other hand, the religious parties want him to wind up the US bases in Pakistan and adopt an anti-Washington posture, which, according to them, will go down well with the people of Pakistan. How can he afford to be seen on the side of Jamait-e-Ulema Islam chief Fazlur Rehman, who has won on the plank of a Taliban-style government at Islamabad? Incidentally, Rehma is son of Maulana Mufti Mahmood who, as the member of Jamiat-e-Ulema Islam. Hind, participated in the Quit India movement in 1942 under the leadership of Mahatma Gandhi.

"Keep out beards," is the message Musharraf has received from Washington. He tried to do so even during the elections which the European Union described as "seriously flawed." Musharraf concentrated on defeating first Nawaz Sharif's men in Punjab and then Benazir's nominees in Sind. He succeeded to a large extent, allowing the religious parties to quietly walk in. But his calculations still went wrong. He wanted his PML-Q to fill the space from which the PPP and PML (N) were ousted.

Still the problem facing him is not that difficult. He knows how to use the religious parties as he has been doing to maintain pressure on America. Washington is too naive or too helpless to get out of his clutches because they need him in the fight against the Al-Qaida. The real problem is that of the liberals who will be forced to go alongwith the PPP, knowing well that Musharraf can push them in the direction he wants through Zardari.

10

Pakistan's Terrorism and Militants' Role: A Serious Concern of India

A No-win Situation

At times certain situations between the countries develop in a way which they will have pernicious results. Yet they to be helpless to avoid them. Both India and Pakistan know the consequences of hostilities. Still, as in a Greek tragedy, they are restlessly moving towards a disaster.

The rulers on both sides should step back and think what they will gain from the war, which is likely to go nuclear. Rhetoric is all right for the purpose of playing to the gallery. Even the military build-up is understandable because of pressure. What is not understandable is why there is no serious effort by both New Delhi and Islamabad to find an honourable way out.

One foreign journalist phoned me from Pakistan a few days ago to suggest that India should have a dialogue with Pakistan to defuse the situation. I wish it could be as simple as that New Delhi has reached the point of no-talks because there has been no end of cross-border terrorism which Islamabad has promised to stop many a time. India says that it will not respond to any talks until Pakistan's proxy war in terms of terrorism stops.

Islamabad's interference is that terrorism is the only way to keep the Kashmir issue alive. In its absence, New Delhi puts it on the back burner. This is not entirely correct because from the Tashkent agreement in 1966 to the Lahore Declaration three years ago, India discussed Kashmir several times. It has repeatedly given an undertaking for "a final settlement of Jammu and Kashmir."

Why the meetings between the two countries have ended

in a deadlock is because the priorities of the two have been different. India has been wanting some outstanding problems between the two countries to be sorted out first so as to create an atmosphere of amity in which the knotty problems of Kashmir could be taken up. Pakistan, on the other hand, has been saying that "other problems" are peripheral and the core problem between the two is Kashmir.

The priorities have not been changed over the years. Even today when the world's attention is focussed on the region, India wants cross-border terrorism to stop before it sits with Pakistan across the table. Prime Minister Atal Behari Vajpayee has said: "We will respond if there are results on the ground." In other words, if cross-border terrorism were to stop, India would be willing to resume talks.

But Pakistan wants to hold dialogue on Kashmir straightaway. It has come to believe that the only pressure which works on New Delhi is the killing and destruction which the terrorists effect. Were they to stop, India would be let off the hook.

This is a no-win situation. The loss of confidence between the two is understandable because they have had to no contacts except the one at Agra. But countries like America can play a role. This should not be that of a mediator or an arbitrator but of a communicator. Washington can convey New Delhi's assurance to Islamabad that the talks will be held when there is concrete evidence on the ground that Pakistan is no longer sending terrorists across the border. America, with all its intelligence agencies and satellites functioning in the region, can easily assess the veracity of General Pervez Musharraf's claim that the cross-border terrorism has already stopped.

New Delhi believes that while Musharraf is cooperating with America in action against Al-Qaida and the Taliban, he is conniving at the activities of the jehadis waging an undeclared war against India. New Delhi has very little confidence in him. Can America disabuse India's mind? Probably, Musharraf is under pressure within his own country. A person who had a hand in building up the Taliban and the Al-Qaida had to disown and fight them. He may be playing the Indian card to placate them and other religious leaders.

What about Kashmir? I believe there is a change in the

perception of people in India. Increasingly they realise that they have to get out of the mess New Delhi has made. It has denied the state free and fair elections and has imposed a chief minister on Kashmir at will. The people's mood is that the real representatives should emerge from the coming state elections.

Even the supervision of polling by human rights activists and eminent people from India may be acceptable. People in India do not want any rigging which forced many youths after the 1987 elections to prefer bullet to ballot. They went to Pakistan for training and weapons. Pakistan had tried to woo them earlier but had failed. The disappointment by youths over "rigged" elections became grist to the mill of terrorism.

The problem is with the Hurriyat, which does not favour election. It would once again threaten or force voters not to participate in the polls. More and more Kashmiris are disappointed with the Hurriyat. A recent independent survey confirms this. Still the Hurriyat, through violene of threat—Islamabad may be a party to it—will try to bring the proposed new political process to naught. The more people participate in elections, the more irrelevant the Hurriyat becomes.

As for a dialogue if the integration of the Muslim-majority valley with Pakistan is its objective, New Delhi may have little to talk about. Over the last five decades, Jammu and Kashmir, however wanting in good administration and clean politics, has come to be considered part and parcel of the country. The trouble in the valley is attributed to Pakistan's "machinations and interferences." The Indian people may be prepared for more autonomy to the state but they will not brook any part seceding from the country. How to reconcile the two irreconcilables is the problem.

And the question that still remains unanswered is how far New Delhi is willing to go and whether that 'far' would satisfy the Pakistani establishment. It is not clear that the West does not understand the problem. It has come to realise that the assumption that the passage of time will solve the problem is like waiting for the cows to come home.

It is worried that any small skirmish between India and Pakistan may lead to a bigger conflagration and divert attention from the Al-Qaida. The type of rhetoric in which leaders of India and Pakistan indulge were not used even by the US and the then Soviet Union throughout the cold war. As for nuclear war, America and the Soviet Union had a long physical distance between them. Information is now available how America rectified its mistake within a few months of sending nuclear weapons to the then Soviet Union. But then situation as they are, they had time to retrace.

In the case of India and Pakistan, there is no time available. New Delhi is only one and a half minutes away in terms of Islamabad's missile range and Mumbai two and a half minutes. The West considers this a real threat. That is why the Western countries have asked all their nationals and non-diplomatic staff to leave India and Pakistan. In fact, the international community would not have shown so much interest in standoff between India and Pakistan if they were not nuclear powers.

Still the priority of America is to eliminate the Al-Qaida and the Taliban who have slipped into Pakistan. Focused on their extermination, America does not want to annoy or go away from Musharraf who has helped it in Afghanistan and who, Washington believes, is its best bet in finishing the remnants of the Al-Qaida. It cannot go beyond a point in putting pressure on Musharraf since the road to the Al-Qaida goes through Islamabad.

India has made available to Pakistan the concrete evidence it has of Islamabad's complicity in terrorist activities in Punjab and is awaiting a reply before taking further steps.

The exact sites where terrorists have been trained and the routes through which they have been sent back have been given to Islamabad. Since the training camps, provided for 10 to 12 people at a time, are changed over and over again, the information might be a bit "dated", it has been mentioned to Pakistan.

Individual cases of murder and sabotage are bad enough, but what has perturbed New Delhi most is the stories of recent concessions which indicate that extremists have been asked to concentrate on Sikh soldiers to spread dissatisfaction among them.

India has taken such serious note of this that it might adversely affect future meetings between New Delhi and Islamabad. No oral protest or written communication has made any difference so far.

"One reason why we are not making such progress in our talks with Pakistan is its continued support to extremists," said one top External Affairs Ministry official. "This was the main reason why India had discontinued further meetings in May 1984, but Pakistan has not changed its attitude," he added.

The government also contemplates circulating the evidence among the leading nations of the world, including the US, Britain, and France, to let them see how far Islamabad has gone to interfere in India's domestic affairs. Not long ago, these and some other countries were told how Pakistan supplied at Lahore a pistol to the hijackers of an Indian Airlines plane and how the Intelligence Department of Pakistan had imported the pistol from West Germany.

America, Britain and West Europe are already aware from Indian sources of the proximity of Pakistan's missions to organisations like Babbar Khalsa and protagonists of Khalistan like Gurdial Singh Dhillon in Washington and Jagjit Singh Chauhan in London. It is significant that the Sikh News weekly, published by the World Sikh Organisation in Washington, carried an advertisement relating to a Pakistan ordnance factory.

Gen. Zia-ul Haq, Pakistan's President, makes no secret of his meetings with Mr. Chauhan and Mr. Dhillon. The two and many others have visited Pakistan many times and despite the fact that New Delhi has given a list of 12 people with the request that Islamabad should not allow them to visit Pakistan, the Zia government has not taken notice of it except in the case of Mr. Chauhan, who was not allowed in a few months ago.

When Shahbzada Yakub Khan, Pakistan's Foreign Minister, was in New Delhi two months ago, India complained about Pakistan's involvement with terrorists. Missions on both sides have gone over the exercise many times, New Delhi making allegations and Islamabad saying that the charges are "baseless".

The Pakistan government's hand in training, arming and giving shelter to Sikh terrorists is admitted by senior members in the main opposition parties.

I had talked to a few leaders and many responsible members at various levels Pakistan People's Party (PPP), Tehrik-e-Istiqlal and National Awami Party (NAP) and found them no secret of their administration's complicity what has been happening in Punjab. They are unhappy about it but express their helplessness.

Two leaders, who do not want their names to be disclosed,

specifically mentioned jail in Faisalabad (formerly Layalpur) as one of training centres. Some have alleged that General Zia-ul-Haq makes it a point to meet practically every Sikh visiting Pakistan, and Mr. Ganga Singh Dhillon and Dr. Jagjit Singh Chauhan, both Khalistan protagonists, are said to be personal friends of President Zia.

The general reaction is that of exasperation; the people by and large do not like the government's involvement, some out of fear that the proposed Khalistan will embrace certain parts of Pakistan like Nankana Sahib, the birth place of Guru Nanak and some out of memories of the 1947 holocaust in which they allege they suffered most at the hands of Sikhs. But most people do not want to "provoke" India because the defeat in the Bangladesh war is still fresh in their mind.

The government circles vehemently deny any involvement whatsoever. One top official has told me that after Prime Minister Rajiv Gandhi has mentioned to General Zia that the people in India suspected Pakistan's hand, "We are not taking any chances". The official mentioned how one Sikh, said to be a suspect, was forcibly put in a plane and sent out.

The Pakistan foreign office is unhappy over the Indian embassy's "over reaction" on the "scuffle" between the Canadian Sikhs and the embassy's two officials. The foreign office feels that they did what they could but the incident was blown up beyond proportions.

However, both official and non-official circles are conscious of the fact that most Indians suspect the Pakistan government's hand in Sikh terrorism. But they believe that the suspicion has declined to a large extent.

Nine out of 10 Pakistanis you meet will ask about Punjab. And the majority has come to believe that the accord reached between Prime Minister Rajiv Gandhi and Sant Longowal has nearly solved the problem. One top expert told me that he really thought that the Akalis would never make up with New Delhi.

In any case, Pakistan wants to put its best foot forward because it is holding several meetings with India in the next three, four weeks. Finance Ministers of the two countries are meeting at Islamabad from January 8 for three days, followed by a meeting of the Defence Secretaries to discuss the unending war over the Siachin glacier on January 16, Foreign Secretary

Romesh Bhandari will meet his counterpart, Mr. Naiz Naik, at Islamabad. In the third and fourth week of January, the sub-commission on specific subjects will resume their discussions both in Islamabad and in New Delhi. The visit of Prime Minister Rajiv Gandhi, keenly awaited in Pakistan, is expected some time in April or May.

The Religious Virus

Any untoward happening in Pakistan gives India some kind of fiendish satisfaction. The reaction to the victory of religius parties in that country has been no different. As if it had to happen to a country which was founded on the two-nation theory.

But Pakistan did not have so much religion when it was created. True, religion was the basis on which it was constituted. However, its founder Qaid-e-Azam Mohammad Ali Jinnah, had second thoughts on the two-nation thesis. He told his people that the two nations did not represent Hindus and Muslims but Indians and Pakistanis.

This took the wind out of the sails of religious parties. What they did in the united India to create divisions was no more relevant. They could not harness support on the slogan that Islam was in danger. The preponderance of Muslims in Pakistan had made such a cry futile. Religious parties realised this to their dismay when they failed at one poll after another.

It was general Zia-ul-Haq's drive for the Islamisation, even in the armed forces, which contributed to revivalism. The absence of democracy only strengthened the self-proclaimed fanatics. The field became open.

Political parties, on the other hand, were too complacent and too confident. They dismissed religious outfits as a nuisance. But the mullahs and the maulvis never gave up and made their nefarious activities felt from the sinecure of mosques and madrasas. Today's Pakistan is a product of those efforts operaing over decades.

I can see the beginning of what happened in Pakistan in my own country. The one-nation ideal, which animated our national struggle, is still there. But, without spelling out the two-nation theory, some political combinations are foisting it on the country under a different terminology: The Hindus are one nation and the minorities another.

The phenomenon is more visible in the fields of information and education. In the name of tradition and heritage, India's multi-cultural society is sought to be pawned to the demagogues of one culture. Information Minister Sushma Swaraj and Human Resource Minister Murli Manohar Joshi are the worst culprits. The first is peddling a particular point of view, the majority community's religious beliefs and superstitions to the detriment of pluralism and clear thinking. The second is introducing new textbooks in schools and appointing the Sangh parivar men in government or government-aided institutions to disseminate prejudice and distortion in the name of history. Both defend themselves that their purpose is to ensure that our "national values" stay intact. The Sangh parivar-inclined intellectuals, journalists, historians and others are being broken into saffronisation and organised.

Both Sushma and Joshi stop at nothing. I was horrified to see on Doordarshan the other day MF Hussain, Shabana Azmi and Tezu saying individually: "I am an Indian." If after so many years they, who represent the best in our secular ethos, are forced to make such statements, there is something definitely wrong with our rulers. The history books that Joshi's men have rewritten omit the assassination of Gandhi because the killer represented the Hindutva forces.

Like Pakistan, political parties in India avowing secularism indulge in the same kind of complacency. They argue that religious parties can never succeed in a country which is traditionally rooted in pluralism. They may be absolutely wrong. But this is their point of view. However, the reality is that the Bhartiya Janata Party (BJP) and the Shiv Sena have already occupied a large space by playing the religious card. The two are in a more advantageous position than the religious parties in Pakistan. For example, the Jamaat-e-Islami and the Jamaat Ulema-Islam were never in the corridors of power at Islamabad.

Unfortunately, both the BJP and the Sena are partners in the governance at the centre. This gives them a cover and also immunity. While they are there, the Vishwa Hindu Parishad (VHP) and the Bajrang Dal can never be banned although their record is worse than that of the SIMI. Pro-BJP state governments cannot be dismissed, whatever their acts of omission and commission. The BJP has been able to cobble together, with the help of pseudo-secularists; a coalition which gives it clout.

If this had not been the case, Chief Minister Narendra Modi would have been dismissed soon after the carnage in the state. Bal Thackerey of the Sena would have been tried after the Srikrishna Commission report implicated him in the Mumbai riots and, more recently, arrested when he threatened the Muslims. And Ashok Singhal of the VHP would have been behind bars after his announcement that there can be more Gujarats.

Today's Modi, Thackerey and Singhal will be tomorrow's Qazi Hussain Ahmed, Moulana Shah Ahmed and Fazalur Rehman of Pakistan. This is what we have to guard against. The three Muslim leaders are important figures. They have emerged from the mosques and the madrasas, in elections under the banner of Muttahida Majlis-e-Amal (United Forum for Action). They have gained substantial strength in Pakistan's National Assembly and in the legislatures in the North Western Frontier Province and Baluchistan.

These religious parties were of no consequence till now. They never won more than three or four seats in the National Assembly. India too was a haven of secularism before 1977. Till then the Jana Sangh, the predecessor of the BJP, did not have even a two-digit figure in the Lok Sabha. Now they have 181 in the 545-member house.

What saved India soon after independence was not the irrelevance of religious parties. The Hindu Mahasabha and others came into the field in August 1947 itself to incite Hindus that the *Bharatmata* had been cut into pieces. Anger had begun building up against the Muslims who had supported the demand for Pakistan.

It was Mahatma Gandhi's assassination by an extremist Hindu that came to strengthen our secular ethos. The RSS was banned and religious leaders went into hiding. People would literally beat up those who even vaguely mentioned Hindutva. They associated them with the Mahatma's murderer.

The question that Pakistan is facing today may be more acute than India's Pakistan is a country where religion has played an important role. India's saving grace is that it is a secular democratic society that has never been threatened by any military coup. People believe in the constitution and have respect for democratic traditions.

India's strength also lies in the fact that certain institutions act independently, whatever the colour of the government. For example, the Election Commission withstood all pressures and threats on the Gujarat election. But the Hindutva elements are dismantling our secular edifice, brick by brick. Institutions are under pressure. Saffronisation is being pushed in all fields. The middle class appears more contaminate than the rest because it is beginning to find in Hindutva its long-lost identity. What most of them do not seem to realise that no one identity represents India. It is the combination of different identities that makes India.

The saffronised elite must also keep in mind that militant organisations like the VHP and Bajrang Dal are going to replace the BJP one day. This is how fascism rose in Germany and took over. Secular forces are too complacent to fight against the danger. I remember Atal Behari Vajpayee, long before he became the Prime Minister, telling me that they might be able to stop the storm that was brewing in the country. He did not elucidate what he meant. Probably, he had in mind the storm of fundamentalism. I wonder whether he can stall it if L.K. Advani goes on building up persons like Modi and does not utter a word against a new contraption called Parveen Togadia.

Not long ago, whenever a discussion on the increasing strength of the BJP members in the Lok Sabha took place in Lahore, Islamabad or Karachi, I would be told that the phenomenon in Pakistan, although an Islamic state, was different. *Deeni* (religious) parties seldom crossed the figure of five in the National Assembly because people did not take them seriously.

Indeed, this was true. Religious parties had a poor showing in the polls held in Pakistan from its very birth. The Muslim League, which founded the country on the two-nation theory, did not get a majority in the first general election held in Pakistan. Even then, there were extremist people like Qazi Hussain Ahmed, leader of the Jamaat-e-Islami, who has been on the scene for a long time. They would collect crowds, not votes. Their tally in the state assemblies would be poor and still poorer in the National Assembly.

But elections held this month, even though described as flawed by every observer, foreign or Pakistani, would indicate that the trend has changed. There is now an upsurge of religious bias. The Muthahida Majlis-e-Amal (MMA), a conglomerate of six religious parties, is No. 2 in a 272-member National Assembly. The No. 1 is naturally the General Pervez Musharraf inspired set-up, Pakistan Muslim League (Qaide Azam), general known as the King's Party. The MMA is also the largest party in legislatures in the North Western Frontier Province (NWFP) and Baluchistan. The two states had Congress governments in power before partition. In fact, till the advent of General Musharraf, both had liberal Muslim parties in tow.

To infer that religious fervour is sweeping the areas bordering Afghanistan is not wrong. The MMA has harnessed the people's resentment against the demolition of the apparatus of fundamentalism, which the Taliban and Al-Qaida had built next door. The MMA's victory is also a strong denunciation of General Musharraf's policy, whatever that is, to contain theocracy and revivalism. But above all the verdict is against the Americans for ousting the Taliban government. No wonder the first demand by the MMA is to close down the US bases in Pakistan and oust American soldiers.

There is no doubt that the ISI has played a major role. Since the Soviet invasion on Afghanistan in December 1979, the agency has dug itself deep in the area. Islamabad knows how jittery Washington is over even a semblance of evidence of Islamic revivalism. But it is apparent that the MMA has been allow to go thus far and not further so that President Bush is convinced that there is no alternative to General Musharraf. Washington's reaction after the polls confirms this. The State Department spokesman, Richard Boucher, said that the election itself was "an important milestone in Pakistan's on going transition to democracy."

Whatever America's certificate, it will be hard for democracy to return to Pakistan. Election itself is a boon given by the Supreme Court, which fixed October 2002 as the time limit by which General Musharraf should hold the polls. Still the military junta did everything possible not to have a fair election. Both the European team and the Commonwealth team have pointed out dishonest practices. The low participation of voters, around 31 per cent, itself shows that people were disgusted over the pre-poll rigging. Except for a few pockets, there was no enthusiasm. And there was no issue, not even the whipping boy, India.

It was known before the polls that the PML (Q), the King's Party, would be No. 1. All government efforts were directed at getting it a clear majority. If it has not happened, the fault is not that of Pakistan's intelligence agencies, politicised to the fingertip, but of the PML (Q) candidates whose reputation deterred voters.

The ascendancy of bigots is not surprising. It happens in Pakistan when the military takes over. The maulvis and the mullahs came back in a big way during the 12-long-year of General Zia-ul-Haq's rule. He, in fact, started the system of paying them from the government treasury. General Musharraf pandered to religious elements to keep the liberals down so that military coup would have some support. He had also to reckon with the fundamentalist groups within the armed forces. After he switched over to the American side, abandoning the Taliban regime he had built, General Musharraf tried to put a squeeze on fundamentalists. But by then they had turned into Frankenstein's monsters.

Still he could use them against India because he gave the name of jehad to cross-border terrorism. If Washington ever expressed concern over the instances of terrorism in India, he would lessen the infiltration. America felt satisfied that its "pressure" worked. What America did not see was that General Musharraf could tap or untap terrorism at will. So long as he played the game with America, he was all right. President Bush was happy. Prime Minister Atal Behari Vajpayee is quite right when he says that the West has double standards on terrorism.

New Delhi has faced similar situation in the past. But its reaction to General Musharraf's doings has been panicky. There was no need to position the armed forces right up to the border when it was an open secret that there would be no war. Partial or substantial unilateral withdrawal of troops, although belated, is a welcome step. But New Delhi's moves were directed towards Islamabad, knowing well that the government there is not kindly disposed towards it. Why not do something to placate the people?

What I have in mind is the resumption of air and bus services between India and Pakistan. Contacts on popular level had begun to pay dividends, however limited. It is quite possible that Islamabad may not reciprocate India's gestures as it has done in the case of allowing Pakistan aircraft to fly over the Indian airspace. But the pressure on Pakistan and the international opinion will be strong that Islamabad cannot but reciprocate. The only way to fight fundamentalism is to be more liberal.

Movement for Restoration of Democracy

The Movement for Restoration of Democracy in Pakistan has now moved from the attack on government buildings to the blocking of railways and railway tracks connecting Sind with Punjab; this is what a leading member of the Alliance in Punjab said that the next as step in the government of General Zia-ul-Haq would be direct action against communication to the landlocked province from strife-torn Sind.

The prosperous Punjab, whose communities of traders, businessmen and small landowners have shown to inclination to take the streets against President Zia's rule, depend to a large extent on the import of goods, particularly oil, from the port of Karachi in the south.

According to Mr. Zalqarmain Rana, president of the National Liberation Front in Punjab, these supplies will be disrupted by the ambushing of trains, the burning of road tankers, and the blowing up of numerous canal bridge in Sind.

Several trains have been fired already, railway stations have been burnt and lines blocked by rioting crowds in the northern rural areas. Petrol tankers have also been set alight.

"Within two weeks," Mr. Rana said, "If these supplies can be successfully restricted, the reserve oil stocks will be at an end and petrol pumps will run dry. When the traders have nothing in their shops to sell, then they will join us."

The continuing turmoil in Sind is testimony to what, however, much the general blames it on a few agitators and virtually all intellectuals, with the exception of a few right-wing Islamic scholars, most of the professions, particularly the lawyers, and many trade unionists are implacably hostile. After six years of being threatened with jail, physical punishment and suspansion of normal human rights they are anxious for it to end.

This is what Dawn, though strangled by press censorship, has written for the people to read between the lines. Simple facts that reflect the movement of life rather than the inertia of things have overtaken the idle talk of the ideologues. Winds of change have disturbed the dust of centuries enveloping the plains of Sind... The MRD movement has completed one month and entered another. More people who remain nameless and faceless have marched into prisons. More judgments have been pronounced in the Summary Military Courts. More headlines have assured us that there is really no political unrest in the country—or in Sind.

This was the week that the President "helicopted" to some towns in Sind, including Dadu and Badin. He found that except for a few pockets here and there, "the situation is quite satisfactory and pretty will under control". This he said in a news conference recently in Hyderabad immediately after his visit to Dadu. Then he was in India.

Later, as the official handout said, five persons died when "law enforcing agencies" opened fire upon agitators in "self-defence" in Khairpur Mathan Shah, a town about 25 miles from Dadu. A goods train was fired at near Mawabahan and the engine driver was seriously hurt.

More recently, the Moro incident had prompted mystification. Eight policemen had died in that encounter. Last week, Khairpur Mathan Shah demands understanding. What did really happen? What are the facts? Why has the interior of Sind become as distant for Karachi which, come of think of it, is an integral part of the province?

When I was in Sind early this year, I found C.M. Kye Sayed, who wants an independent Sind, the most popular man in that state, the young, particularly have been attracted to this movement. In Karachi the Sindhis made no secret of the fact that they would not have anything to do with Pakistan if the Punjabis (who constitute 80 per cent in the armed in the armed forces) were to be the arbiters of their destiny.

The domination of the Punjabis in Pakistan—and the execution of their "own" Zulfikar Ali Bhutto—has further pushed the Sindhis to assert their entity which is Sindhi and not Islamic in its concept. Gen. Zia's refusal to open the Sind-Rajasthan border through Khokrapar—has infuriated them and they plan to submit a petition with lakh of signatures to press this demand.

There is no doubt that most people are yet reluctant to come out in the streets, the Punjabis are mute and confused. But there are some people who defied the military might in 1977 when Bhutto used it to curb the stir against the rigged polls. What has happened is that the brutalities the military has committed has created fear in the mind of the public. Detentions without trial have crossed the figure of 60,000 since Gen. Zia's takeover; even now 30,000 people including 150 women, are in jail. Instances of whipping are more than 25,000, according to a human rights' supporter who has kept a faithful record for every district.

Now there is not a home, club or restaurant where abuses are not heaped on Gen. Zia. For the first time since his takeover, Gen. Zia is under pressure from all sides. The MRD, which has kept the flag fly of the people's rule flying, is undaunted. The Pakistan People's Party of Bhutto, the National Democratic Party of Wali Khan and Tohrik Istqlal of Air Marshal Asghar Khan, which are the MRD members, are also pressing for civil rights; so is the Jamiat Islami, fairly strong and till recently Gen. Zia's ardent supporter. It looks as if it is difficult for him to escape some kind of concessions and he may be forced to quit making way for another General for the time being.

Policy of Pakistan

One top Indian foreign ministry official asked me the other day: "What has people-to-people contact achieved so far?" It is difficult to quantify its achievement but it has sustained hope that the two countries will one day normalise their relations because people on both sides want to live in peace. This is despite the negative attitude of their governments.

People-to-people contact means contact between ordinary men and women on both sides, the freedom to come and go, without police surveillance and without a visa only an identity card should be required for entry. Obviously, this will take time because the mistrust has to go first. But in the meanwhile, the so-called "elite" groups have surfaced again. They are the same old people, who during their tenure, as military or civil servants, did their worst to spoil any attempt at conciliation. Blessed by the foreign office they went over the same exercise for years. They will repeat the same observations when they meet again. Even their faces have become a cliché.

What I have in mind is a soft border which Prime Minister Atal Behari Vajpayee advocated when he was foreign minister (1977-79). Then Prime Minister Morarji Desai shot down the proposal on the plea that it would be an open invitation to spies to come in hordes. He did not know that spies do not use the checkpoints to enter each other's territory. They have their own "checkpoints."

True, borders cannot be soft until cross-border terrorism stops. Islamabad has to be convinced about its futility. Certain quarters there believe a proxy war is the only way to make India bleed. The situation has to be normal to have normal relations. Guns, open or secret, do not make for peace.

However, we should hasten the process to restore the status quo, the state of relationship prevailing before the attack on the Indian parliament. After having done so, New Delhi should take stock of cross-border terrorism which from all accounts is less than before.

The Pakistan parliamentarians came to India a bit too soon. The government distanced itself from them, not because it was unwilling, but because it was unprepared. It wanted to let the fallout from Vajpaye's initiative settle down.

Indeed, a request was made to defer the visit by a few days. But some among the organisers on both sides did not agree to it. Their contention was that they wanted to utilise the presence of Indian parliamentarians in Delhi before the adjournment of the two houses on May 9. The Pakistani parliamentarians reached on the 8th night.

However, when the visit was mooted three months ago, the purpose was to create some movement in the otherwise static situation. Indian parliamentarians were to go to Pakistan first but this did not materalise. MPs from both countries can cross over from any checkpoint without permission and without a visa under the SAARC rules.

None knew then that Vajpayee would say at Srinagar that he wanted to have a dialogue with Pakistan. His observation provided the much-needed momentum. By the time the parliamentarians arrived the PM had initiated the thaw. The general impression is that the parliamentarians came as a follow-up to Vajpayee's initiative. This is not factually correct. Theirs was an independent visit, planned much earlier. Nonetheless, it has further helped soften the rigid position the two sides had taken.

The response to the parliamentarians in Delhi, Mumbai

and Kolkata was electrifying. They were hard-pressed for time to attend the functions which people wanted to arrange in their honour. They themselves were touched by the love and affection shown. What it really means is that the natural reaction of the Indian people towards the people of Pakistan is that of closeness. They are sick and tired of the distance which has been growing for the last 55 years. People's attitude in Pakistan, which I visited three months ago, is no different.

When just a speech by Vajpayee and a telephone call from Pakistan Prime Minister Jamali can change the entire climate, it is obvious that the hostility is a forcibly contrived thing. People on both sides want to be friends. Their desire for proximity will force their governments to sit across the table soon.

Unfortunately, the BJP's spokesman has thrown cold water on all the optimism that Vajpayee has generated. The spokesman runs down those who arranged the visit of parliamentarians. He used the sneering phrase "pseudo secularists" about the organisers. It indicates that the party is far from happy over their visit.

In fact, a battle is raging within the party on making up with Pakistan. Both the "pseudo-secularists" and the PM are on one side furthering the cause of building relations with Pakistan. The criticism may well be the party's polite tick-off which the Prime Minister must have noted.

The BJP is the ruling party. It should not be seen taking conflicting postures in public. It cannot commend the PM's initiative on the one hand and criticise those who involved the parliamentarians on the other. The effort is to strengthen the initiative. If the BJP's criticism is serious, the talks are doomed. How far is it willing to give up its anti-Pakistan stance which the party believes adds to its votes? Hindutva as a poll plank may sound the death-knell of rapprochement. Can the party afford to give up its fundamentalist stand before elections are over in four sates this year and the general elections in 2004? That is the question.

Pakistan's problem is different: How far is the *fauj* (armed forces) prepared to give up the territory it has occupied in the political field? Real power lies with General Pervez Musharraf. For more than four decades, the armed forces have been an arbiter in Pakistan. Are they willing to vacate that position? The military face another problem: if there is a settlement there will be demands for a drastic cut on defence spending. Is the *fauj* prepared for it?

Will the National Security Council which has the three service chiefs as its members be adequate for the military to safeguard its interests? It is difficult to imagine it at this point of time. Still this is the scenario which will take shape one day. The armed forces will have to go back to the barracks. The pressure of public opinion will make it happen.

India, too, is under pressure. There is increasing realisation that the majority of its problems stem from its relations with Pakistan. The enthusiasm with which the parliamentarians were received shows how anxious the people are to bury the hatchet. In fact, people in both countries seem to be ahead of their governments.

Maybe, wide and frequent contact will throw up a solution of Kashmir as well. The first requirement is to open borders to all those who want to visit each other's country. How to facilitate and sustain the contact is the core of the problem.

Since everyone is talking about roadmap these days, let the line of control (LoC) be the "line of peace," as Zulfikar Ali Bhutto suggested to me in an interview before the Shimla conference. The onus of maintaining it will be on Islamabad because the terrorists are using its territory to cross into India.

People-to-people contact has to reckon with the reverses. But it is heartening to see a few who ask for the impossible and strive for it.

11

India's Attitude After the Kargil War and Army Coup

The Kargil Fallout
No war, however limited, is without a fallout. The Kargil fighting was confined to one part of the Line of Control (LoC). Yet, its repercussions will be far-reaching. Both India and Pakistan will feel tremors for a long time to come. The biggest fallout will be in the political field.

Take India first, the main advantage of Kargil looks like going to the Bhartiya Janata Party (BJP). Prime Minister Atal Behari Vajpayee has become taller in stature and he is generally seen as the person who led the nation to victory. The BJP will gain because of his image.

His warning that Kargil should not be politicised has been of no avail. Kushabhau Thakre, the BJP chief, and his other colleagues, are going all over the country, receiving kudos for the job which the armed forces have done. As the election campaign picks up pace, the BJP and its allies will be more strident in their slogans of victory.

Were they to stop at that, it would be less disconcerting. What is dreadful is the mood of jingoism which is sought to be developed in the country. It is nationalism in name but sheer communalism in reality. It has manifesed itself in different forms. One was the demonstration outside the residence of Dilip Kumar to ask him to return the Nishan-e-Pakistan award which late Prime Minister Morarji Desai also received.

Another was the thoughtless order by Information and Broadcasting Minister Pramod Mahajan to ban the Pak TV channel, which has now been lifted. Yet another was the closure of web sites of two Pakistani newspapers, *The Nation* and *The Dawn*. The Pakistani press has justifiably picked holes in India's liberalism. One of them has written: "Denying people access to the sources of information of their own choice characteristics totalitarian regimes and thus runs counter to India's claim of being a democracy."

Patriotism does not mean dittoing what a particular political party says to reap dividends at the polls. Some people, who are in the government, do not understand that India is a different type of society—open, democratic and liberal. You may not agree with what a person says. Still you defend his right to say it. Whatever the situation, the nation cannot demolish its values of tolerance and dissent, which are necessary to stay pluralistic and democratic.

The country solidly rallied behind the armed forces, not the party which is trying to hog the limelight. It is true that the nation was initially in a state of shock. But once the armed forces put their act together, it overcome the jolt. In the name of defence, nothing spurious should be sold to it.

In fact, it goes to the credit of the country that the anger against Pakistan never took the shape of anti-Muslim feelings. During wars in 1965 and 1971, the RSS and its parivar were able to foul the atmosphere. This time even they did not dare to do so. On the other hand, the Muslims, who generally stayed indoors during wars, were as much on the streets as the Hindus to ventilate their disgust over the Pakistan aggression. Some Muslims in the army have died on the front trying to oust the intruders.

In contrast to the BJP's bellowing, other political parties have been quiet. It has been difficult for them to do the balancing act: criticising the government while supporting the war efforts. Now that the hostilities are almost over, it may be free for all. The negligence part will come to the fore. The Congress should put its act together. It looks angry with neither coherent nor rational. The bus diplomacy was not wrong; Islamabad's perfidy was. The waves the party was making once seem to have subsided.

In Pakistan, a joke that is doing the rounds is that Nawaz Sharif intruded in Kargil to help his friend, Vajpayee, to win the elections. Sharif's political opponents are not going to leave him alone. They may start an agitation which may ultimately prepare the ground for the Pakistan People's Party chairperson, Benazir Bhutto, to return. Sharif has lost in stature and even though his two-thirds majority is intact in the National Assembly, Pakistan's

Lower House, dissidents within the party are growing in number. The Ayub Gohar group is restive. Gohar has neither forgotten nor forgiven Sharif for taking him away from the Foreign Affairs portfolio.

The humiliation of Pakistani forces can lead to two things: one, the army will be cut to size as it happened in the wake of defeat in the Bangladesh war. Two, the army can lick its wounds till such time as it gets an opportunity to have its revenge on the rulers. One interesting side sidelight which is being projected abroad is that Sharif went alongwith the intrusion so as to deal with the much-lionised army effectively once it got bruised.

The mujahideen are not such a problem as is being presented. Most of them belong to the armed forces and the rest are Sharif's own creatures, depending on his generosity. Even those from Afghanistan or Sudan are hired by the ISI. That they are not under Islamabad's control or that they are fighting for their independence are mere arguments to frighten the West or to convey that Sharif is doing his best to tackle an impossible situation—for example, what the terrorists have done in Bandipur, near Srinagar, against the BSF.

The economy of both countries has been hit the most. India is in a bit better position because of its size. But the fact remains that both sides are spending crores and will be spending much more, farnishing the fields of education, health and employment.

My experience is that the situation like the weather in the subcontinent does not change materially: It is hot, hotter or the hottest. Sometimes, I fear that Kargil may well be the Rann of Kutch type operation, which was followed by the 1965 war within a year. Lal Bahadur Shastri, then India's Prime Minister, had warned Pakistan that if it ever repeated the Rann of Kutch, India would fight it at the place of its choosing. This happened in 1965 when he ordered the forces to march towards Lahore to relieve pressure on Kashmir.

That Pakistan is an intransigent neighbour or that the fundamentalists and the anti-India elements there have more influence than their number is not a revelation. India knows this to its cost. Talks between India and Pakistan may create an atmosphere where the beleaguered liberals, the harassed journalists and others come to the side of peace and defeat those who still talk in terms of *jehad* and who want the two countries to end up in a nuclear war. What Sharif should realise is that trust is not something which can be switched on or off at will. Vajpayee feels let down and he cannot sit across the table on his asking.

Even otherwise, the talks will have to wait till the elections in India are over and the new government is in the saddle. That means sometime in November. Even if the foreign secretary-level talks were to resume immediately, they would be only perfunctory. A care-taker government cannot take a decision which is the prerogative of an elected government.

It is difficult to assess the impact on their future relations, their limited contacts and still more limited efforts towards normalcy. One thing is sure: the atmosphere created in the wake of the meeting between Vajpayee and Sharif at Lahore in February will not return for a long time to come.

Who Failed Where?

Victory is announced with the beat of drum, but reverses are suppressed with all the subterfuge. Both India and Pakistan have indulged in a cover-up job during the recent hostilities. Briefing on both sides was boastful. Why? Probably to keep the morale high. Does it help? The truth can be devastating when it comes out. The public realises that it has been fed on lies and kept ignorant.

How the intruders came or occupied the territory on the Indian side of Line of Control (LoC) is pretty well known. The newsy part is that Pakistan had been preparing for the intrusion for the last three winters. How much of it was known to Prime Minister Nawaz Sharif is still a matter of conjecture. But he had a general idea of what was being planned.

By the time the Indian soldiers saw men from the other side, India had lost part of its territory. The infiltrators, who included Pakistan forces, had occupied pockets along the 120 kilometres of the LoC, which is 776 km. long. The deepest intrusion was that of 11 kilometres each, in Batalik, Drass and Mushkoh.

The thrust in Kakashar was to the extent of four kilometres. There was an effort to advance in Turtok but it was repulsed effectively because the Pakistan push was aimed at cutting off the Siachen glacier from the rest of the area. Nonetheless, the Pakistan intruders made the traffic on the Srinagar-Leh road called, IA national highway, come to stop. They overlooked the highway and shelled it from the positions they were occupying.

It took us much too long to gear up to it. The plan on the offensive by our army was not ready till America had mooted a proposal for the withdrawal of the intruders. Although at a disadvantage, the Indian forces showed grit and fought bravely. The air force coordinated well. India had cleared two-thirds of the occupied territory when Pakistan asked the intruders to return home. There are miscalculation on the part of Pakistan's top brass that it could demarcate another LoC to its advantage. However, they are still dragging their feet in Mushkoh.

Just as New Delhi never gave out how much territory it lost, Islamabad too did not tell about its reverses. The Tiger Hill had been re-captured by India when Pakistan briefed the media that the mujahideen control on the Tiger Hill was intact. Had the Pakistanis been kept informed on the reverses, their feeling of humiliation would not have been so deep as it is today.

Such observations have been made as: No matter what sort of a face one might try to put on the mujahideen disengagement from the commanding heights of Kargil "it has an element of abruptness hard to swallow"; whether it is just an intermission or the end of "a climatic real life play remains to be seen."

Of course, people like General Mirza Aslam Beg, Pakistan's former chief of army staff, and Lt. Gen. Hamid Gul, former ISI chief, are fuming with rage and putting all the blame on the Sharif government. Beg writes in an article: "... The end result of all diplomatic, political manoeuvres and military measures has been that it is the Pakistan army whose image is being tarnished. The US media, Israel and India have collaborated in the vilification campaign and Pakistan's bastion of strength—its armed forces stand scapegoated for the Kargil fiasco, and the civil government is being projected as if it was the only responsible entity which saved the country from a catastrophic war."

Addressing the Lahore High Court Bar Association, Gul has said: "The mujahideen had won the battle while India was in trouble when our immature leadership tried to turn this victory into a debacle. American leaning towards India is obvious as it is engaged against China." In his opinion, the Shimla Accord was not a treaty or an agreement having legal value to turn the ceasefire line into the LoC.

Both Beg and Gul are considered hawks in Pakistan itself. But practically every retired military officer or ex-bureaucrat is against close, much less friendly, relations with India. Sharif's own camp has many such persons. All of them are behind the fundamentalists indulging in the cold-blooded murders in Kashmir. How can the process to span the distance between the two countries begin? And even if it does, how far will it reach when there is so much hatred? Pakistan's attitude is attributed to books, schools, the teaching at *madrasas* and New Delhi's big brother posture. The list of reasons why there is bad blood between the two is long. Maybe, this is a case for an in-depth study by some objective outsiders.

In India, there is a case for another type of study, more so an inquiry into ill-preparedness and negligence on the part of the government and the armed forces. One did not want to apportion blame in the thick of war. But we should now find out who failed where. There was a long list of weapons and other supplies pending with the Defence Ministry when the Pakistani forces crossed into Kargil. Some are still pending. There are so many aspects of defence which have remained neglected. Political leaders have a lot to explain. So have the armed forces, although they have done a tremendous job in pushing out the infiltrators.

There are no two opinions that the intelligence agencies failed miserably. RAW, IB, the army's own intelligence branch and others are blaming one another. But all of them were found wanting. Lt. Gen. Harbaksh Singh, hero of the 1965 war, has demanded in an interview that some heads must roll. There is no such likelihood because the government feels on the top of the world.

However, one positive thing is that the government is in favour of appointing a commission of inquiry to pinpoint the responsibility for three things: one, unpeparedness, two, negligence and three, intelligence failure. The probe is important, not only to punish the guilty but also to plug the loopholes. The job should be entrusted to a top, respected person. But he or she should not belong to a political party, the bureaucracy or the armed forces. An objective assessment is required.

The government should also give an assurance to publish

the inquiry report. The Henderson Brookes inquiry report on the 1962 debacle at the hands of the Chinese is still a top secret document. Some of the guilty have died by now. I demanded the publication of the report through a question in Parliament. The reply given by the Defence Minister was that it was "a state secret" which could not be disclosed in the "public interest". Where does public interest come in? Even after 37 years, such a plea makes a mockery of the right to know. By this time the report should have been placed in the archives of India for scholars and experts to analyse.

Incidentally, the Jawaharlal Nehru papers of those days are also not in the archives. The Nehru Library has them. But they are the property of the Nehru *parivar,* headed by Sonia Gandhi. None can have access to them until she gives permission. The papers are part of India's history. They should be for consultation by historians, scholars and others. Why should they be under the custody of one family is not understandable. Strange as it may sound, the papers were made available for more than two years to an American scholar who is writing a book.

Meaning of the Coup for India

Army coups by nature are sudden and secretive, but not in Pakistan. You can see the clouds gathering, then threatening to burst and ultimately coming down in torrents. When the first Martial Law Administrator, General Ayub Khan, took over power on Oct. 8, 1958, he had already discussed "malaise in the political and administrative life" with the then President Sikandar Mirza for nearly two years before discarding the *khaki* uniform of the commander-in-chief.

The coup by General Parvez Musharaff, Chief of the Army Staff, was open, in broad day light. You could see the whole thing building up. On Sept. 24, he held a meeting of army commanders and other senior officers, ostensibly to discuss Kargil. The scene was so ominous that even the US administration issued a warning that it would oppose any attempt to overthrow the constitutionally elected government.

Still the rumours were so persistent that Mushahid Hussain, Information Minister of the ousted government, contradicted a reporter's question about an impending army coup with the words: 'Not at all, not at all'. He went on to add that the

US statement was a response to those opposition politicians who had been seeking American support to undermine the democratic system in Pakistan.

But it was clear that Musharaff was smarting under the oft-repeated accusation that the army had failed at Kargil. In fact, he began saying that "everyone was on board", meaning that Nawaz Sharif was part and parcel of the operation. As far his own future, Musharaff would say". I am going to complete my tenure".

Still, the army could not rub off the stigma of having staged the Kargil intrusion on its own and involving Nawaz Sharif unnecessarily. Musharaff was embarrassed over the observation by Pakistan former Foreign Secretary Niaz Naik, who travelled between Islamabad and New Delhi to broker a solution on Kashmir. He said that Nawaz Sharif got to know about Kargil on April 26, more or less at the time when New Delhi became aware of it. In fact, Defence Minister George Fernandes had insinuated in the beginning of the Kargil operation that the Pakistan army had launched it without either consulting the Prime Minister or the ISI.

That the ISI, which is generally an initiator of such operations, did not know anything about it is clear from the appointment of Lt. Gen. Khwaja Ziauddin, the ISI Chief, as successor to Musharaff when he was dismissed a few hours before his return from Sri Lanka. The whereabouts of the Lt. General are not known at present. He was reportedly sitting with Nawaz Sharif when the Prime Minister's house was surrounded by troops.

It was clear that the gap between Nawaz Sharif and Musharaff did not fill over the period. Both seemed to be planning their strategy. Nawaz Sharif tried to lull Musharaff into complacency by giving him one year's extension. Apparently, it did not work. Musharaff had done his home work properly. Whether Nawaz Sharif consulted corps commanders before dismissing Musharraf or not is not known. Obviously, he did not because Musharaff has been supported by the commanders. They are the ones who ultimately decide things in Pakistan, democracy or no democracy.

One report was that five corps commanders, including the one at Rawalpindi, were on the side of Nawaz Sharif and four on

Musharaff's. This was not true. When the chips were down. Musharaff was the winner. "History," as Winston Churchill has said, judges a man, not by his victories or defeats but by their results. Nawaz Sharif lost. True, the Rawalpindi corps commander did not send his troops to surround the Prime Minister's House. They belonged to the III brigade. But that might have been a sham. Ultimately, everyone fell in line, including the Naval Chief whose appointment had led to the resignation of the incumbent, Admiral Faish Bokhar.

The surprising part is the smoothness with which the coup took place. The Pakistan armed forces do the exercise well because of their past experience. There were some gunshots in Lahore and Islamabad. But they were by the loyal policemen, not the troops. America, as usual, did not anticipate the events. Its ambassador to Pakistan, William B. Milan, issued a statement a few days ago to allay the fears about an army coup being round the corner.

That the Americans preferred the democratically elected Nawaz Sharif government to the army rule is clear. Their post-coup statement is stern and expects early restoration of democracy. General Zia-ul-Haq promised 90 days for election and stayed on for nine years.

Probably, Musharraf would be forced to hold election within 90 days as provided in the Pakistan constitution. But the biggest casualty is conciliation with India which Nawaz Sharif was trying to bring about. His ousting itself may well be because of the vested interest of the armed forces in confrontation against India.

It is an open secret that the Pakistan army was trying to escalate the operation at Kargil to internationalise the Kashmir issue. It did not happen. The withdrawal was considered a humiliation. Perhaps Nawaz Sharif realised—when he involved President Clinton—that the Kargil operation might end up in a war between India and Pakistan, with the possibilities of a nuclear holocaust. This reconfirms the impression that the Lahore process was destroyed by the top brass, who find rapprochement with India an anti thesis of enmity which they believe provides the ethos to Pakistan.

This may pose problems to New Delhi. In an effort to stoke the fires of hatred, the armed forces in Pakistan may pursue a policy of confrontation with more venom. They may find the diparate elements that constitute Pakistan uncontrollable, unless the common enemy, India, was projected in a big way. The armed forces might be tempted to externalise their problems. In any case, the chances of reconciliation between New Delhi and Islamabad have further receded. And it is a tragedy that a compromise, which would have had the stamp of the BJP representing Hindus in India and the Muslim League in Pakistan, may not be possible now.

It is sad to see the democratic forces supporting the coup. No doubt, Nawaz Sharif had alienated the opposition. In fact, he had opened too many fronts. Apart from political parties, the fundamentalists were also pushed on the opposite side. But this should have been a matter between them and Nawaz Sharif. If they believe that the army is the only force to deal with him, they are injuring whatever is left of democracy in Pakistan.

The right to pull down a government elected by the people belongs to the people. If commanders are to decide who the rulers should be, it can be any other system, not democratic. True, the armed forces have been wanting to acquire a role in the administration. The late Gen. Zia-ul-Haq, Martial Law Administrator, told me in an interview that the army should have the constitutional right to walk in whenever it felt that things were going wrong in Pakistan. General Jehangir Karmat, who resigned one year before his term to pave the way for Musharaff's succession, also favoured more say of the armed forces in the running of Pakistan.

What the leaders of the Pakistani armed forces do not realise is that in a democracy the people elect their rulers. However wanting in performance, they represent them. To strengthen democracy, there should be more democracy, not less.

Fallout from the Sharif Trial

It is a strange coincidence that President K.R. Narayanan gave awards for bravery at Kargil on the day and the time when former Pakistan Prime Minister Sharif was sentenced to 25 years. The latter too, said in a statement before the court that he was being 'punished' for Kargil.

Nawaz Sharif meant that he was being tried for the withdrawals at Kargil. He may well be speaking the truth. But the judgment is the worst form of nemesis. It is a retribution of sorts since it is well established by now that Sharif was in the know about the Kargil operation.

The probe that India conducted confirms this. So does the statement by Pakistan Chief Executive Pervez Musharraf that "everyone was on board." The unkindest cut is that Sharif knew about the operation when he welcomed Prime Minister Atal Behari Vajpayee at the Amritsar-Wagah border last year.

Still, as far as the judgment is concerned, it is brutal and bewildering. Brutal because a sentence for 25 years is nearly double the period of life imprisonment—14 years—the maximum given to a culprit in the subcontinent. Bewildering because the judge's claim that the conspiracy has been proved hangs in the air. All the co-conspirators have been left off. Only Nawaz Sharif has been punished. How could he have hatched the conspiracy single-handed?

The Anti-Terrorist Court Judge Rehmatullah Jaffari, who gave the verdict, was the second judge to try Nawaz Sharif. The first judge who took the case complained that he was unable to perform his duties with plain-clothes security personnel attending the proceedings. He referred the case to another court. The sentence is, however, ominous for the prospects of the democracy in Pakistan. The judgement has buried it still deeper. In the past 25 years, two elected Prime Ministers have been disgraced in public and their families harassed. One was hanged and the other has been sentenced to imprisonment for two and a half decades. The fact remains that people voted them in.

Normally, the armed forces should defend the constitution, which guarantees institutions like parliament, not thwart it. But then that is the course which Pakistan has followed for the last 40 years. The experience tells us that the armed forces in the third world seldom give up their hold even when they return to the barracks after intervention.

None can predict how events will unfold themselves in Pakistan in the next few years. It can stay authoritarian for a long time. Still one can say with certainty that Sharif will not serve the full term of 25 years. Sooner or later, Pakistan will return to a democratic set-up. Political institutions will then revive. Whichever party or combination comes to power, it will release Sharif. He may be a lesser person by then.

But that too depends on the outcome of cases of corruption against him. The jail sentence in the subcontinent often gives a halo of suffering to the politicians. The example of Laloo Yadav, former chief minister of Bihar, is there. But if the corruption cases against Nawaz Sharif are proved beyond doubt, his image will indeed be shattered.

As days go by, the judgment against Sharif will have its fallout. The Muslim League, which has endorsed his leadership, may split. Dissidents are unlikely to sit idle till the outcome of the appeal which will take time, first in the High Court and then in the Supreme Court. On the other hand, there was very little protest. Only a handful of people stood outside the Anti-Terrorist Court to express their solidarity with Sharif, although the betting on his conviction was heavy. A bookie in Karachi reportedly made lakhs of rupees because he was not hanged. (Of course, people gave credit to President Clinton for that).

Another fallout from the sentence is the restoration of some institutions. International pressure on Islamabad, particularly that of America, is relentless. Whichever country Musharraf visits, he is told to hold elections and restore the National Assembly. If Pakistan does not want to stay isolated, as was the warning administered by President Clinton, it will have to resurrect democracy. The economic assistance by the World Bank and the International Monetary Fund is dependent upon Musharraf's response. And he was very little staying power. At one time the thinking of the military was reflected in the suggestion made by Musharraf, then the Chief of the Army Staff, before accompanying Sharif to Washington. Musharraf conveyed that Shahbaz Sharif, then the Punjab Chief Minister, should come to the centre to 'strengthen' the hands of the brother, Nawaz Sharif. Shahbaz was visibly unhappy over the Lahore process and Musharraf knew about it. It was Aba Ji (father of Nawaz and Shahbaz) who turned down the proposal. Otherwise, Nawaz Sharif might have been replaced by Shahbaz.

Can Musharraf pick up the thread from where he left off? Aba Ji is a chastened person now. Even Nawaz may not stand in the way, knowing well that the alternative is to cool his heels in the jail. But the rearrest of Shahbaz on charges of corruption gives another message unless this too is an exercise which is being gone over to clear the ground.

Shahbaz, as was clear from the trial, was in no way a target. It came as no surprise when he said in his statement before the judge that he did not know anything because he was sleeping when the coup was taking place. Significantly, during the trial he was removed from the jail and put in "a hospital" where he was given royal treatment.

The question is what will happen to Musharraf or, for that matter, to the military? Pakistan has itself provided the answer in the past. The armed forces have gone back to the barracks but have overlooked the shoulders of civilian rulers. People and politicians have accepted the situation in the past. Why will they behave differently this time? In fact, when asked by an Indian journalist how the world could reconcile itself to the military rule, Musharraf's blunt reply was: "For the past many years, the armed forces ruled Pakistan indirectly. Why should any country be so sensitive now?"

However, it looks as if the military would like their role to be institutionalised. They have cited the example of Turkey where there is a top governance body, the National Security Council. The Council, with the three service chiefs, has a great say in deciding when to step in to "put democracy back on the rails."

General Ayub Khan and General Zia-ul-Haq wanted to constitute a similar body. But it never came to that. They did not need it when they were in power. The democratic regimes which succeeded them did not find it necessary because they always felt the presence of the third man, the GHQ.

Nawaz Sharif was the first one to try to clip the wings of the armed forces. At his request, Jehangir Karamat, Musharraf's predecessor put in his resignation. This time, Musharraf had the promise of most corps commanders that they would stand by him if he was asked to quit. Almost all of them did so when Nawaz Sharif dismissed him. The rest is history.*EOM*

Musharraf Sitting Pretty

Dictators, almost by definition, are afraid to allow free play of press opinion. It is, however, strange that General Pervez Musharraf, who took over Pakistan in military coup, has not muzzled the press. Even a short visit to the country shows that newspapers and journals are savage in their criticism of the regime.

"We are not pressurised even through advertisements which the earlier rulers used as a reward or punishment," said an editor of a leading daily of Lahore. "The import duty on the newsprint has been reduced, although the government is suffering economic hardship."

One reason for the press freedom can be that it serves as a catharsis for the pent-up emotions of the people. There is no other medium of expression like a public meeting. The opinion ventilated by the press is not followed up. Political parties are there. But they have no room to activise their workers to take up an issue.

A political commentator at Islamabad has another explanation: "The army has realised that we are only paper tigers. It matters little what we say so long as we are not inciting people to come on the streets." He is probably right but relentless criticism can begin to build up an atmosphere of defiance.

There is, however, no such evidence even after nine months of Musharrafs rule. Officials support cite the reports by the monitoring units established throughout Pakistan at the city and district levels. They have reported that the press criticism has not fomented discontentment. "They can shout to their heart's content. It will not make any difference," says a Pakistani insider.

How long this claim will hold good is difficult to say. But there is no doubt that the Musharraf regime does not face any challenge, either from within the army or from politicians. The top brass which rules the country is a well-knit unit, conscious of the fact that another coup would only spread the impression that they were hungry for power, not determined to "clean up the government," as was the declaration art the time of takeover.

As for politicians, Musharraf has himself started talking to them to find "a consensus on reforms to effect better governance. But there is no compulsion for him to do so. Leaders of the National Assembly and the Senate, comprising Pakistan's parliament, readily admit it.

Musharraf's advantage is that the faces of politicians are so smeared with corruption and nonperformance that the public has come to feel that the armed forces are their only saviours. And, as one finds after talking to people from different walks of life, the public generally wants to give them ample time to clean up "the mess created by the politicians."

The resentment against the politicians must be deep because the non-performance by the Musharraf government is what stares you in the face. I was in Pakistan four months ago. Even at that time the promise to improve the lot of the people was as loud as I found a few days ago. But when you come to concretise the achievements. There are hardly any. Compared to India, the price of essential commodities is high. Wheat is selling at Rs. 12 a kilo, rice at Rs. 28 and bananas at Rs. 30 a dozen.

More burdens have been heaped on the common Pakistani. There are fresh imposts on the land. Holdings up to 10 acres were free of any revenue but the dragnet has been spread to include anything above five now. The happy news in the countryside is that there has been a bumper crop of wheat, rice and cotton. So, hardships on the other counts may get lessened. But the new imposts are creating murmurs.

The most articulate critics of Musharraf interpret whatever little murmur there is in the country as the beginning of protest. But even they have to concede: "The regime will go on and there is nothing to dislodge it." It appears to be true. Even if one were to take into account of the Supreme Court's pronouncement of the three-year limit for fresh elections. Musharraf has still a little more than two years to go.

"I shall definitely quit then (by 2003) and not seek any post," he said at the last session of a South-Asia media conference. But he added that he might not be finish doing all that had in mind. His Information Minister Javid Jaffar confirms the deadline, although he says that they may cross it by a few more weeks.

People in Pakistan seem to have generally accepted the time limit. They probably realise that what Musharraf's critics call "the nightmare" may not be over before that. Politicians too are reconciled to that. But some industrialists and businessmen say that "things cannot go on like this because the economic crisis is gradually building up."

Their warning may have some weight. But the country does not look like caving in. Stores are as crowded as before. The US dollar has not appreciated after the army take-over, the exchange rate is still around Rs. 55 to the dollar. Inflation is more or less the same, less than five per cent.

There seems to be a belief in every quarter that America will not allow Pakistan to go down. "We shall be kept on a drip," says a Pakistan economist, "but we would not be allowed to die." The international Monetary Fund is expected to give money after its meeting with Islamabad later in the month.

"If there could be trade with New Delhi..." is one remark which you hear at every party or discussion. There is also an element of envy that India has gone ahead so well. But there is also realisation that the access to Indian markets is a long cry.

But from wherever you begin a discussion, it ends with Kashmir. Over the years, even those who were sitting on the sideline have been sucked in. It is an obsession but it is there, something which cannot be diluted or washed away. No solution is being offered except at times a suggestion that it should be left to the people of Kashmir. And even the third option, independence, is not ruled out.

Musharraf was asked pointblank by an Indian journalist whether he would support the demand for independence. He said he had left the choice to the people of Kashmir. He did not reject the concept of independence, as Benazir Bhutto and Nawaz Sharif, the two former Prime Ministers of Pakistan, had done.

But, even while sticking to his position on Kashmir, he sounded like a person who very much wanted to have talks with India. He seemed keen to reach New Delhi through Indian journalists. Musharraf comes out as a blunt person who wears heart on his sleeves. For a head of state, he is too forthcoming. Discretion or cautions use of words would make him more acceptable. But, as he puts it, that the confidential reports during his army career have one thing in common: too articulate.

Musharraf too refers to Kashmir whenever he addresses any meeting. He is willing to discuss other peripheral issues, he says. But Kashmir is a must. It is as if he is trying to convey that Kashmir is giving Pakistan its ethos. His single-minded focus on Kashmir may also be one reason why he has no challenge. When it comes to Kashmir, the Pakistan have no ranks, no differences, no separate voices.

Cease-fire: Delhi Caught Napping

It is not yet clear why Prime Minister Atal Behari Vajpayee did not entertain feelers from Chief Executive Pervez Musharraf for an overall cease-fire, embracing the Line of Control (LoC) as well. Vajpayee understandably feels betrayed over the Kargil operation after he had led a bus to Lahore to sign the peace declaration with the deposed Prime Minister Nawaz Sharif. But the architect of Kargil was probably trying to rectify his mistake.

The unilateral cease-fire by the Hizbul Mujahideen could not have been without Musharraf's nod because Pakistan trains, arms and finances the organisation. He probably wanted to convey to Vajpayee that he was serious about the feelers he had sent to him.

Even now it is not late. An overall cease-fire should be worked out to create a peaceful atmosphere for a dialogue. That New Delhi has taken the Phelgam killings in its stride appears to be on the understanding that all militants are not amenable to Islamabad's discipline. Home Minister L.K. Advani's reaction to honour the cease-fire is a step in the right direction.

If feelers are pursued, army commanders from both sides can discuss the modalities to ensure that no gun boomed, directly or indirectly, secretly or openly. The activities of ISI and RAW should also be covered. To begin with, the cease-fire should be at least for six months. Hizbul's offer of three months is too short a period.

Even otherwise, the cease-fire is a messy affair. When partial, it is shoddier and hard to maintain as killings in the last few days have proved. It gives the impression of half-heartedness. One gets the feeling as if the two exercises war and peace are being carried out at the same time.

In this case, New Delhi will be at a disadvantage. It may have to spell out what it means by the maximum extent within the framework of the Constitution, not knowing how far Islamabad is willing to go. One side may have to put all its cards on the table while the other may keep them close to its chest.

As the events have unfolded, the cease-fire has taken New Delhi by surprise. It has gone along without any preparation or strategy. Parliamentary Affairs Minister Pramod Mahajan confirmed the worst fears when he said that the picture would be clear in three-four days, while appealing to MPs for deferring the discussion on Kashmir autonomy.

He may have spoken out of turn but he has told the truth: the cease-fire offer has been accepted without New Delhi knowing the details. This suggests that no ground work was done through formal or informal sources. Mature governments do not work on hunches or half-baked information. And, as usual, the opposition was not consulted. It will not be a surprise if most constituents of the ruling National Democratic Alliance (NDA) were as ignorant as the public is. There should have been prior discussions among political parties to have a consensus on the goings-on in Kashmir.

The tragedy is that the BJP and other political parties react to the developments on Kashmir, not to the people's long-standing demands or grievances. No party has any policy beyond Article 370, which gives a special status to Jammu and Kashmir. The BJP is for scrapping it and others for retaining it. Chief Minister Farooq Abdullah was informed about the cease-fire but not consulted. His demand through an assembly resolution to go back to the 1953 status may have hastened the process of the cease-fire. Many Kashmiris consider the 1953 status a fulfillment of their desire to have their own entity.

While formulating the strategy, New Delhi should analyse why the unilateral cease-fire has been offered. It does not take long to figure it out. They were at the end of the road. A decade of militancy—and the Kargil operation—made it clear to the Hizbul and its supporters across the border that New Delhi, whatever the cost, would defend its side of Kashmir.

People in the valley, although alienated from India, were sick of terrorism. Both the state and the militants tormented them equally. Islamabad too could not see a breakthrough in the deadlock despite Musharraf's repeated offers for a talk at any level, at any place and at any time. The West, which is influenced by America on Kashmir, was not willing to step in until India, like Pakistan, sought its good offices. Islamabad felt besieged.

Still, New Delhi should not fritter away the opportunity, however limited it is. It can pave the way for talks with Islamabad. The cease-fire does largely fulfill India's condition to stop cross-border terrorism. It is a matter of time before the rest of the guns fell silent because Islamabad is keen on a dialogue. Otherwise, the entire sequence of events does not make much sense.

Some straws in the wind indicate to the possibility of an agreement. Islamabad has said that whatever is acceptable to